Gavin Esler
How Britain Ends

English Nationalism and the Rebirth of Four Nations

HEAD
ZEUS

An Apollo Book

First published in the UK in 2021 by Head of Zeus Ltd
This paperback edition first published in 2021 by Head of Zeus Ltd
An Apollo book

9 7 5 3 1 2 4 6 8

A catalogue record for this book is available from
the British Library.

ISBN (PB): 9781800241060
ISBN (E): 9781800241077

Typeset by Adrian McLaughlin

Printed and bound in Great Britain by
CPI Group (UK) Ltd, Croydon CR0 4YY

Head of Zeus Ltd
5–8 Hardwick Street
London EC1R 4RG

WWW.HEADOFZEUS.COM

How Britain Ends *was written for the generation which will have to pick up the pieces of what was once a United Kingdom, in particular Lucy, Amelia, James and Charlotte. It's also dedicated to the memory of a great Englishman and European, and a great friend, Toby Eady.*

'Scotland has sent a very clear message – we don't want a
Boris Johnson government, we don't want to leave the EU.
Boris Johnson has a mandate to take England out of
the EU but he must accept that I have a mandate to
give Scotland a choice for an alternative future.'

*Scotland's First Minister Nicola Sturgeon after the General
Election of December 2019. Her Scottish National Party won 48
out of 59 seats in Scotland. Boris Johnson's Conservatives
won the UK General Election with a majority of 80*

'We in this One Nation Conservative government will
never ignore your good and positive feelings of warmth
and sympathy towards the other nations of Europe.'

Boris Johnson Election Victory Speech, December 2019

'When Boris Johnson speaks of being a "One Nation"
Conservative, by "One Nation" he means England.'

*Disgruntled Scotsman of my acquaintance
who wishes to remain anonymous*

'Research by Lord Ashcroft, the Conservative donor,
found that 76 per cent of English Conservatives who voted
Leave in 2016 would prioritise Brexit even if it meant
Scotland gained independence. Of the same demographic,
74 per cent would choose leaving the EU over Northern
Ireland remaining part of the UK.'

Kieran Andrews, The Times, 22 October 2019

Contents

PART ONE

Nations and Irritations

I

The English Question

'Who do you think you are kidding, Mister Hitler,
If you think old England's done?'

Bud Flanagan, Who do you think you're kidding Mr Hitler
(Dad's Army *theme song*)

It is a familiar scene, televised round the world, a symbol of Britishness. The date is May 2016. The location, central London. A sunny day, and the ceremonial State Opening of what the British regard as the Mother of Parliaments. Inside, a sea of ermine, as members of the House of Lords, hereditary peers, political party grandees, a sprinkling of business, academic and other high achievers and senior clergy from the Church of England, move through the Palace of Westminster. They are joined by leading politicians from the House of Commons, the prime minister and leader of the opposition, bringing with them MPs from England, Scotland, Northern Ireland and Wales. Beefeaters from the Tower of London assemble in their distinctive red, gold and black uniforms. Soldiers from the Household Division form a guard of honour awaiting the arrival of the head of state, Queen Elizabeth II. The seven regiments of the Household Division are famous for their uniforms, especially the cavalry – white riding breeches, shiny helmets with horse-hair plumes, swords and gleaming breastplates known as cuirassiers – the uniform of British empire victories of 200 or more years ago. At ninety years old the Queen is immensely popular, a remarkable unifying figure for a diverse United Kingdom. Her life of public service stretches from that of a young princess who endured the Blitz with the common people of London in the Second World War, through the difficult years of retreat from empire, to the new Britain and Commonwealth of the twenty-first century.

The State Opening of Parliament manages to be a celebration of a modern democracy, but with the trappings of hundreds of years of practice. Like all traditions, what happens next is a glorious invention. The Queen and her husband, the Duke of Edinburgh, travel from Buckingham Palace in the horse-drawn Diamond Jubilee state coach. The coach carries ancient symbols of royal power – the Sword of State, the Cap of Maintenance and the Imperial State Crown. The Queen could of course arrive in a modern limousine, flanked by a military parade of soldiers in the uniforms of the twenty-first century, but the gold-encrusted coach, the clip-clop of hooves and the gleaming breastplates are a deliberate, nostalgic, choice. The coach is of a 200-year-old design, yet it is just two years old, commissioned in 2012, completed in 2014, and by 2016 still newer than most cars on British roads. Nevertheless, symbols of Britishness are important at an event in which the monarch, Lords and Commons come together to celebrate a new chapter in an ancient democracy, a public display of a United Kingdom. But behind the pomp, all is not well. Real unity is hard to find. In live TV broadcasts of the occasion politicians argue about the Brexit referendum scheduled to take place the following month. The Brexit debate has been caused by an upsurge in a rarely discussed phenomenon – English nationalism and its clash with the other competing nationalisms on these islands. Despite the unifying presence of a much-loved monarch and a parliament which is supposed to represent the people's voice in British democracy, despite all the gold, ermine and faux-antique trappings, this ancient British democracy is in trouble. Without reinvention or reformation the United Kingdom, as we think we know it, may soon cease to exist.

Our country is a most peculiar union. It consists of four nations in one. As our children learn at school, the United Kingdom of Great Britain and Northern Ireland – to give it the title as it appears on British passports – is made up of England, Scotland, Northern Ireland and Wales. England is, and always has been, bigger, more populous, richer and more economically powerful than the other three nations put together. Despite surviving and generally thriving for 400 years, now in the twenty-first century this lopsided union may finally be coming to an end. There have been doom-filled prophecies of the end times before. The United Kingdom survived the attentions of Napoleon, Hitler, Stalin and his successors – although perhaps it is more accurate to say that it survived *because* of the attentions of Napoleon, Hitler and the others. Historians, most notably Linda Colley, point out that for centuries the glue that held the United Kingdom together was a mixture of three powerful elements – Protestantism, empire and war. In the twenty-first century these traditional elements of 'Britishness' seem less relevant, or completely irrelevant, to many of the people of these islands. For centuries Britain has also weathered domestic rebellions, most seriously that organized by Irish republican terrorists but also by Welsh and Scottish nationalists, and a kind of reactive ultra-Britishness from Ulster unionists. Further nationalist storms are now upon us, but one type of neglected and under-analysed nationalism could by itself result in the end of Britain.

The central argument of this book is that while the United Kingdom can survive Irish, Scottish and Welsh nationalisms it cannot survive English nationalism. For many English people, 'nationalism' is an affliction visited upon others. The English anthropologist Kate Fox claims that 'the English are not usually given to patriotic boasting'. In itself this is a very English way of boasting, a humble-brag about English exceptionalism.[1] The economist Sir Dennis Robertson noted that 'the Englishman has long been used to living in a certain haze as to what his country is – whether England or England-and-Wales or Great Britain or the United Kingdom of Great Britain and Northern Ireland or the United Kingdom plus its dependent territories or that larger unit which he used to call the British Empire'[2]. The historian David Edgerton noted that 'nationalism in British parlance was the doctrine which encapsulated the dubious claims of natives, whether Indian, African, Irish, Scottish, Welsh'. Edgerton places Irish, Scottish and Welsh people in that list of 'natives', but not the English, who are presumed exceptional in not being burdened with such 'dubious claims'.[3] As we will see, the facts suggest otherwise.

For increasing numbers of English people the haze about nation or country appears to be lifting, the idea of English exceptionalism is increasingly difficult to sustain, and Edgerton's 'dubious claims' of nationalism turn out to be a highly significant and growing political force in England in the twenty-first century. English nationalism was the principal cause of Britain's decision to leave the European Union. Brexit is both a symptom and also now a cause of the widening cracks in the union of the United Kingdom. The majority of people in England appear to want for their future an outcome that a majority of Scots and Northern Irish people plus many in Wales clearly oppose. The Scottish writer and broadcaster Ludovic Kennedy once described Scotland's relationship with England as being 'in bed with an elephant'. Over the past twenty years the pachyderm has grown increasingly restless. Many British national institutions are clearly dysfunctional, especially Westminster, as is the relationship between various parts of government, parliament, the monarchy and the courts. Some of those sharing the bed of union worry that they may need to make their escape or be crushed. The decision of England to leave that other union, the European Union, while Scotland and Northern Ireland voted to stay, is part of that crushing process. As a post-Brexit joke puts it: 'An Englishman, Scotsman and Irishman walk into a bar. The Englishman wants to go home – so everyone else has to leave.'

The English Question

For the United Kingdom to continue to survive, it is necessary to recognize the existence of an English Question, and then begin to answer it. What does England want? That question can be stated in various ways, but at its heart it is this: is there something about the United Kingdom of Great Britain and Northern Ireland, our once precious union, which is so valuable in the twenty-first century to the English and three other diverse nations of almost 70 million inhabitants that it is worth preserving? Do our competing nationalisms still add up to a common idea of 'Britishness', or is it time for Britain as currently constructed to come to an end? To reverse the argument about Scottish independence, should the most powerful part of the union – England itself – be an independent country, perhaps with Wales tagging along? Is that what 'the English' want? Whether English people want it or not, an 'independent' England may very well happen anyway, by accident or carelessness, if Scotland finds a way of leaving the United Kingdom, and people in Northern Ireland consider whether a different union, that with the Irish Republic, may also now be at hand.

Scots talk sometimes glibly of 'independence' from the UK. English people talk of 'independence' from Brussels, but it is not clear what any of this means in practical terms in an increasingly interdependent world. The biggest problems we face – disease and pandemics, economic meltdown, trade disruption, climate change, international crime and terrorism – are all global in scale. National solutions are useless without international cooperation. Whatever the future holds, cooperation between the constituent parts of the United Kingdom will be necessary no matter how we order or reform our political and constitutional arrangements. But change is coming. Discontent with the status quo and distrust of politics and politicians are common to all parts of the United Kingdom. In pursuing their own versions of Edgerton's 'dubious claims' of nationalism, Scots, Welsh and Ulster folk have considered such questions and their different levels of identity for years. English people have not often bothered. Why would they? The English make up 84 per cent of the population of the United Kingdom. Naturally, therefore, they speak of being British when they mean that they are English. But what does it mean to be British in the twenty-first century? What are the ties that bind the supposedly United Kingdom, given the erosion of the glue which has held us together for centuries, the end of empire, the decline of Protestantism, the unlikely threat of a continental enemy and the fact that a major international war for the foreseeable future seems unlikely?

Say 'British', But Mean 'English'

Matthew Goodwin, a well-known politics professor and an expert on populism, recently issued an appeal on social media for some book recommendations: 'Twitter, what's the best book you've read on British identity?' The replies about 'Britishness' were revelatory. None of them really answered the question. Among the most popular suggestions were George Orwell's 1941 essay 'England Your England' and Linda Colley's history of Britishness, *Britons*. Orwell wrote his essay while

London was under attack from the Luftwaffe in 1941 and, as the title suggests, it is about England, not Britain, although the two are often elided or confused. Colley's excellent history is indeed about Britain and British identity. It was written in 1992, before formal devolution to Scotland and Wales, and it covers the rise of Britishness from 1707 until the accession of Queen Victoria in 1837. Informative though both works are, they are not in any sense a guide to British identity in the twenty-first century.

The Scottish writer and independence supporter Gerry Hassan mischievously suggested Tom Nairn's *The Break-up of Britain* from 1977. Other replies included *Asterix in Britain*, the *Beano* and *Viz*. What was striking is that no truly up-to-date significant work of scholarship on British identity came to mind for the Twitterati, and most respondents answered by recommending essays, poems or novels that somehow crystallized English identity. Among the suggestions were Roger Scruton's *England: An Elegy*, Jeremy Paxman's *The English*, Kate Fox's *Watching the English*, the American-born T. S. Eliot's wartime sequence *Four Quartets*, Orwell's *The Road to Wigan Pier*, A. A. Milne's *Winnie the Pooh*, the Scottish writer Kenneth Grahame's *The Wind in the Willows*, Tolkien's *The Hobbit*, *Notes from a Small Island* by another naturalized American Bill Bryson, *Heroic Failure* by Fintan O'Toole, *The Making of the English Working Class* by E. P. Thompson, the screenplay of *Withnail and I*, the radio programme *Sorry, I Haven't a Clue*, *The English Gentleman* – Simon Raven's irreverent elegy for that class, *Harry Potter*, Patrick O'Brian's Master and Commander series, *The Secret Diary of Adrian Mole*, Shakespeare's *Henry V*, *The Goon Show*, anything by P. G. Wodehouse, the Hungarian émigré George Mikes's *How to be an Alien*, *The Story of England* by Michael Wood, E. M. Forster's *Howards End* and *Three Men in a Boat*. The list elides Englishness and Britishness and has a strong element of English exceptionalism and nostalgia for an England which either never existed or is long gone. None of the respondents could think of any up-to-date consideration of Britishness in the twenty-first century, other than the Irish writer Fintan O'Toole's polemic on Brexit, nor could any offer ideas for a coherent cheerleader for the concept of what being

British means. It is also striking how many of the recommended texts are written by foreigners.

What is not surprising is that many English people, living in the overwhelmingly dominant part of a union, believe they *are* the union and that Englishness therefore defines 'Britishness'. But paying little or no attention to the desires of partners in any union is not the recipe for a happy modern marriage. Scots, Welsh and Ulster people rarely confuse their own national identities with being British. They know the difference. They are able to separate the layers of identity which make them who they are, but a fresh consideration of who 'we' are, and who 'they' are, is long overdue. Scots, Welsh and Ulster people also know that whatever way they vote, English voters will largely determine their future. It cannot be otherwise. There are 650 parliamentary seats at Westminster, and of those 533 are in England compared with 59 MPs from Scotland, 40 from Wales and 18 from Northern Ireland.

In the 2016 Brexit referendum English voters determined to leave the European Union, Wales voted narrowly in favour of Leave, while Scotland and Northern Ireland voters chose to remain. The decision to leave was confirmed again by the Conservative election landslide in the UK General Election of December 2019, based once more on the strong Tory vote in England. Yet Scotland pulled in the opposite direction with an even more impressive landslide for the Scottish National Party. The first minister of Scotland, Nicola Sturgeon, felt she had to make clear that many Scots believed there was a profound democratic deficit for their nation; that their views on Brexit (and other matters) did not count, and that if Scots wanted to leave any union it was the union known as the United Kingdom. As she put it: 'Scotland has sent a very clear message – we don't want a Boris Johnson government, we don't want to leave the EU. Boris Johnson has a mandate to take England out of the EU but he must accept that I have a mandate to give Scotland a choice for an alternative future.' By that Ms Sturgeon meant a second Scottish independence referendum. Boris Johnson refused to accept this demand, but the demand will be renewed again and again, and the more it is opposed by English government ministers in London, the more Scots will feel they are victims of precisely the kind of 'democratic deficit' the SNP and others complain about. It's a curiosity of these odd times that by opting to leave the European Union in the name of 'independence' English voters and the political party formally known as the Conservative and Unionist Party may inadvertently have set in motion a train of events leading to the end of the United Kingdom and 'independence' of some kind for Scotland.

Federalism by Stealth

Beyond Westminster, other British institutions, usually headquartered in London, also often confuse Englishness and Britishness. Some appear to claim to speak for all the people of these islands when their focus is not merely relentlessly English, but centred on the English 'Home Counties' and London. This is apparent even when funding for national British institutions is spread across the entire state and their powers are often in whole or in part devolved to Scotland, Wales and Northern Ireland. Some British institutions are British in name only. There is no 'British education system' or 'British justice system'. Even 'the British NHS' and 'British democracy' are convenient fictions. There is no one system of 'British democracy'. There are four. The voting systems for devolved administrations in Scotland, Wales and Northern Ireland and their responsibilities are all different from each other and very different from the antiquated system by which we elect the Westminster government. Boris Johnson's 2019 landslide – and his eighty-seat majority in the House of Commons – was not won with a majority of votes but with a plurality of 43 per cent. The majority of voters – 57 per cent – rejected Mr Johnson as prime minister. Such an obviously unfair system looks increasingly dubious compared to the different versions of democracy that now operate in the other nations of the United Kingdom – excepting, of course, in England.

Scotland has always maintained its own laws, justice system, school system and universities, as well as its own church. Education is a devolved matter for Wales and Northern Ireland. Even the pound notes in your pocket, though worth the same and guaranteed by the Bank of England (there is no Bank of Britain), look very different in Scotland and Northern Ireland. The same is true of that most proudly British invention, the National Health Service. Throughout the coronavirus pandemic it was clear that the NHS has a common purpose and ethos. But it was also clear that, even faced with a common virological crisis, NHS functions, organization and day-to-day management are devolved. The Scottish government decides how healthcare money is spent in Scotland. Northern Ireland has its own system linking (wisely) health with social care. There is not one single chief medical officer in Britain, there are four – one each for England, Scotland, Northern Ireland and Wales, with the CMO in England reporting to the UK government – there being no devolved administration for England. While every part of the UK shared the same aims – saving lives, reviving the economy, finding a cure for coronavirus – the first ministers of Scotland, Wales and Northern Ireland all made it clear they were prepared to move at a different pace and take different measures from those of the United Kingdom government in London.

Properly coordinated, these differences in approach could be a source of strength rather than weakness. There is no reason why people in Aberdeen should expect or want precisely the same services as those in Aberystwyth or Ashford. Part of the argument of what follows is that the United Kingdom has for years been creeping by stealth towards an undeclared federal system. Unfortunately, we have neither fully recognized this federalization nor discussed it in a way which would lead us towards resolving the conflicts and resentments that inevitably result. These conflicts – exacerbated by Brexit – are especially sharp over the role of London and, in particular, the government at Westminster, including the division of wealth for public spending known as the Barnett Formula. That's the extremely complex method by which since 1978 the UK Treasury adjusts the amounts of public expenditure allocated to Northern Ireland, Scotland and Wales to reflect changes in spending levels set by the government in London. Every *truly* federal system, like Germany or the USA, has a written constitution to separate powers and explain how conflicts between states and the central government may be resolved. Britain has never felt the need to have a written constitution, despite the fact that British experts have written or helped write such documents for at least seventy former colonies and dominions, and also postwar Germany, twenty-first century Iraq and the nineteenth-century Ottoman empire.

Apologists for the United Kingdom system famously claim it benefits from the supposed glories of an unwritten constitution. Lord Macaulay, the Victorian Whig historian, thought written constitutions were like paper money, a trashy substitute for pure gold. In the twenty-first century of Bitcoin, cardless touch-and-go payments and online banking, an unwritten constitution is by now only appropriate in those countries in which people have to pay for things in gold, if any such countries exist. More accurately, Britain does have a written but uncodified constitution. It's a jigsaw, a series of laws, judgements, traditions and precedents which are excessively complicated and open to broadly different interpretations. In the end, the government in Westminster holds the whip hand, and yet it is subject to review from the courts, and exercises authority through what is called 'the Crown in Parliament'. As the parliament website puts it: 'Along with the House of Commons and the House of Lords, the Crown is an integral part of the institution of Parliament.' This, as a concept, is about as easy for most people to comprehend as the Holy Trinity of Father, Son and Holy Spirit, three persons in one God, and one in three, clinging to several different identities yet insisting they are united. In what follows the creakiness of this British system, or rather systems, will be increasingly obvious. So will the complacency with which a system of government unfit for the twenty-first century is often defended. If the UK is to remain a United Kingdom its system of governance needs to be reformed. If the system of governance is not reformed, the imagined community we call Britain is coming to an end. Scotland is not the only part of the UK believing it suffers from a 'democratic deficit'. Many English people feel so too.

Muddle England

In recent years I have travelled all over the UK, both as a writer and also as a speaker at public meetings, political gatherings and literary and other festivals. I've gone from the coast near Dover in Kent to the north of England, from Shetland and Northern Ireland to the West Country and from Cornwall to the big cities of the English Midlands. Ask people in Chester, Liverpool, Leeds, Manchester, Scunthorpe, Warrington, Cleethorpes or small southern towns like Faversham, Totnes and Canterbury if they feel that those who make decisions in London are familiar with the lives most English people lead, and the answer will generally be negative. That's one of the reasons 'Take Back Control' was such a powerful slogan in the Brexit debate. It captured the idea that England's own 'democratic deficit' and perceived loss of 'control' could be cured by leaving the European Union. The slogan also expressed nostalgia for some previous Golden Age when England somehow did have 'control' and that can now be returned. Unfortunately, as we will explore, whatever Brexit may achieve, returning 'control' from Brussels to Westminster is unlikely to solve the English Question or heal the divisions in our lopsided union. That's because most nations only have a limited amount of control in a globalized world anyway, and very little of that control was ceded to the European Union. Ultimate 'control' of the lives of most British people on most issues they care about remains rooted in Westminster and a parliament run by politicians who are among the least trusted people in the nation they claim to serve.

The challenge is urgent. If the union we call our United Kingdom is still important, we need to reinvent it for a new century. That involves not 'taking back control' but *giving back* control – to English regions, large cities outside London, local councils, plus the devolved assemblies and parliaments in Edinburgh, Belfast and Cardiff, and ultimately to the people of the UK. If, however, the people of these islands decide that the ancient union called the United Kingdom is not important enough, we need to think through how to make separate arrangements that work in future for all the people of these islands.

Scottish, Welsh and Irish people have thought about these matters for years. English people need to think about them now.

You, Me and Us

Like most Scots of my generation I have several identities. Born in Scotland, I live in England. I have family roots in Northern Ireland, lived for a time in South Wales and I'm a Londoner by choice. I place more emphasis on one or other of these identities depending on circumstances. On the London Tube I am definitely a Londoner, the greatest city in the world. I get impatient when visitors stand on the left on escalators in rush hour despite all the signs urging them to stand on the right. I dislike people saying London is 'unfriendly'. It isn't. It's brusque and fast and businesslike, which is why I love it, but it's also warm, tolerant, diverse and welcoming to strangers, including me. Watching rugby or football I am definitely Scottish. At the Olympics, I am definitely British. And when I walk the streets of European cities, in Lübeck or Berlin, Salzburg or Rome, Athens or Edinburgh, I feel undeniably part of European culture. But an old Scottish friend of mine, who has similarly complicated loyalties and identities, expressed the frustration many Scots now feel. We met at the Edinburgh Festival during the impassioned Brexit debate in the summer of 2019. My friend said: 'Like you, I am Scottish and British and European. But now these bastards in London are telling me I have to drop one of my identities. Well, I am not going to stop being European. And I cannot stop being Scottish.' There followed a pause. My friend is from a pro-unionist background. In 2014 he and most of his family voted 'No' to independence in the Scottish referendum. 'Are you saying you would now vote Yes for independence?' I asked him. He nodded. 'And so would most of my friends and family.' I was surprised.

'So what changed?'

'What changed,' he replied, 'is that in 2014 we were told that voting No to independence meant Scotland would stay in the European Union. Well, that's not true, is it? F*** them.'

My friend worked for many years in England and has many English friends. He has never been remotely 'anti-English'. He is rather the epitome of a liberal unionist Scot with an internationalist spirit, uneasy about anything that could be called 'nationalism'. But he was clearly aggrieved. He saw a resurgent English nationalism directly affecting how he thought about himself, his country and Europe. I argued that Scotland is not a radical place. It is a small-c conservative country in which change comes slowly. Because Scottish independence is a radical change it has been a hard sell, especially in Edinburgh where the 'New Town' where we met is 200 years old.

'The conservative thing to do in 2014 was to vote No to independence,' I said. 'For those who do not like sudden change.'

'True,' he agreed. 'But voting *for* Scottish independence next time will also be the conservative thing to do. Keeping us in the EU. It's the wreckers in England who are the revolutionaries taking the leap in the dark. The English Conservative Party is not a conservative party any more. They are wrecking the union.'

That conversation in the Scottish capital is one of the inspirations for this book. Big changes lie ahead, either as a result of the increasing and unstoppable demands for Scottish independence or a rethink about what is necessary to keep the United Kingdom together, or the fact that English nationalists may soon recognize that leaving the European Union is the wrong answer to the right question: does Britishness mean anything any more? British institutions – such as they are – have lost trust and respect, feel threatened and under siege. This is true not just in the disaffected Celtic fringes or English regions that feel ignored, but even in London itself. From the Westminster parliament to the financial sector, banks to the civil service and the BBC, local government to the relationship between the Supreme Court and the executive, the twenty-first century has raised many questions about how the United Kingdom works, or fails to work, and how united it really can be. Reinvigorating this union will not be easy. It may not be possible. For some, especially in Scotland and Northern Ireland, it may not even be desirable. But above all it is English people who need to look in the mirror and ask themselves, when they speak of being British, do they just mean English? Who are 'we' in the twenty-first century? Who are 'they', the other members of our peculiar union? And what does 'our' union in the United Kingdom mean to 'us' when some of our citizens feel they are treated as 'them?'

Clearly the union means a lot less than it used to. To take one striking example, a 2019 poll, organized by the Conservative activist and funder Lord Ashcroft, of English Conservative voters who wished to leave the European Union revealed that more than three-quarters of them prioritized Brexit over the unity of the United Kingdom. In other words, they wanted to leave the EU so desperately – an arrangement which at that point had lasted forty-six years – that they were prepared to countenance breaking up another union, the United Kingdom, an arrangement which had lasted four centuries. Just short of three-quarters of these same voters chose leaving the EU even if it meant that Northern Ireland would become part of a united Ireland. A section of the English electorate that had remained resolute in the face of more than thirty years of IRA terrorism and the attempted assassination of their heroine Margaret Thatcher could not tolerate the fact that Scotland and Northern Ireland wish by their democratic votes to remain in the EU while England does not. If Conservatives and supposed unionists in England are so enthusiastic about the radical change called Brexit that they have become at best lukewarm about the union, then the end of Britain is only a matter of time.

For their part, Scottish and Welsh voters clearly and consistently see their Scottish and Welsh identities as paramount in their lives, far more important to them than any sense of Britishness. In Northern Ireland, again according to an Ashcroft poll, a shade more than half, 51 per cent of voters, were by 2019 ready to countenance a united Ireland. Among younger Northern Ireland voters the majority for reunification was even higher, and the only age group in favour of the union was that of the over-sixty-fives. This is in a region where up to two-thirds of the population have historically identified as unionist and consistently voted for parties that defend the union. Polls change, of course. Opinions change. But taken together, these polls, at the very least, ring alarm bells about the end of the United Kingdom.

The English Question, however, could be rephrased in a more positive way. Is there something about Britain and Britishness which is so compelling beyond sentiment, nostalgia for the Battle of Britain and other past glories that it can ensure the United Kingdom should continue to exist? The historian Jeremy Black points out that 'British-ness is a time-limited, essentially political, concept and of value within a state shaped by very different historical legacies and with individuals and communities holding multiple identities.'[4] Since so many of the things that affect our daily lives – schools, hospitals, universities, the law – are already devolved, should we explore and legislate for some kind of federal solution, ensuring that English voters and their representatives have a clearer voice on purely English issues, perhaps through a devolved English assembly? Should there be Home Rule for England? This has been suggested before. After decades of agita-tion for Home Rule in Ireland, in 1886 the Liberal Unionist Joseph Chamberlain proposed the idea of 'Home Rule All Round', a 'proto-federalist' solution for Scotland, England and Wales. The idea was revived again at the end of the First World War but it was blocked by conservative forces whose attitude was summed up in a smug phrase by the lord chancellor Lord Birkenhead that 'we had muddled along tolerably well for ten centuries'. By 'we' Lord Birkenhead here could only have been referring to England. We will explore in detail whether 'muddling along' is a useful strategy for England and the other parts of the United Kingdom in the twenty-first century, but the idea of 'Home Rule All Round' was resurrected once more in 2014. In the independence referendum Scotland voted to stay in the United Kingdom following the promise of more powers for the devolved parliament. Wales's first minister, Carwyn Jones, told the Labour Party conference in Manchester on 22 September 2014, 'The future we promised to Scotland must be delivered – an equal share of resources, a seat at the table, a powerful parliament – that must be offered to Wales and Northern Ireland too. Not just home rule for Scotland, but home rule all round.' But David Cameron's Conservative government offered very little in terms of new powers. Instead of 'Home Rule All Round', he focused on appeasing the forces of English nationalism by offering a referendum on leaving the European Union, widening the cracks between the competing nationalisms within the United Kingdom by carelessly reinvigorating rather than neutralizing Scottish nationalism.

As a Scot I have often been impressed by the fact that the people of England have generally tolerated with equanimity (if not always enthusiasm) being ruled by foreign monarchs from 1603 until Queen Victoria came to the throne in 1837. Queen Victoria's first language was German. Her consort was Prince Albert of Saxe-Coburg and Gotha. Today's royal family changed their name during the First World War by royal proclamation on 17 July 1917 from Saxe-Coburg-Gotha to the more suitably English designation of Windsor. That long list of Scottish Stuarts, the Dutch William of Orange and various Hanoverians managed to engender a strong attachment to an idea of Britain, even a mythical sense of 'Albion', while in our own time the unity of Britain has become much shakier despite that admired and indefatigable Windsor, HM Queen Elizabeth II. So what has gone wrong? Has the presence of devolved assemblies or parliaments with very limited powers in Edinburgh, Belfast and Cardiff helped ignite a degree of English nationalism unknown in the past? Between 1880 and 1935 five of the ten prime ministers of the United Kingdom were Scottish, and their Scottishness was never a significant political issue; nor was the fact that David Lloyd George was a Welsh speaker. All were 'British'. So what is it about fairly sober-minded politicians in Holyrood, Stormont and Cardiff Bay that has encouraged English nationalism to thrive in our own times?

There is an even wider question for the future. It was first asked almost sixty years ago by an American statesman and it has never properly been answered by any subsequent British government. In 1962 the former US secretary of state Dean Acheson, speaking to an audience at the US Military Academy at West Point, observed that

Britain had lost an empire but had not yet found a role. It was a shrewd and much-quoted comment, yet the reasoning behind Acheson's observation is often overlooked. He went on to explain:

> Britain's attempt to play a separate power role – that is, a role apart from Europe, a role based on a 'special relationship' with the United States, a role based on being the head of a Commonwealth which has no political structure or unity or strength and enjoys a fragile and precarious economic relationship – this role is about played out.

Acheson was proved wrong but only because throughout the 1960s Britain had begun to seek a new 'power role' by actively engaging with the idea of joining European institutions. French President Charles de Gaulle famously replied 'non' – but when the opposition from Paris was finally overcome, this new role was achieved. The United Kingdom joined the Common Market (along with the Irish Republic) in 1973. The decision to join was reaffirmed overwhelmingly with 67 per cent support for membership in the first all-UK political referendum in 1975. Now as the UK separates from Europe's main political structure by leaving the European Union, that new role has gone, 'played out' at last. Acheson's question has a new potency and a new urgency. It is at the heart of the crisis we need to face, a crisis even greater than Brexit. What role does Britain see in the world, 'apart from Europe', enjoying no realistic 'special' relationship with a post-Trump USA and acting as merely the titular head of a Commonwealth which six decades after Dean Acheson pointed it out, still has no significant political structure, unity or economic strength?

Some, including the historian David Edgerton, see reasons to be cheerful about the break-up of the United Kingdom, especially for England:

> Freed from the grip of the decayed British nation and British state, England could finally be done with its delusions of grandeur. Fanciful beliefs about British importance in the world would

crumble. England would be only around the eighth-largest economy in the world. And it would probably have to give up its nuclear weapons – the United Kingdom's nuclear submarine base is in Scotland. England need not be, as many fear, a rump United Kingdom, parochial, perhaps even irredentist. Less cock-sure and more understanding of its real place in the world, it may soon rethink its hostility to the European Union.[5]

Edgerton is right to be optimistic for England provided English nationalism can shake off its nostalgic pessimism and think more about the future rather than the past. Given the character of some of the leading English nationalists, that may not be easy. But Edgerton is also correct to suggest that the end of Britain may soon be with us and that there could be significant advantages for all four nations cooperating together in a revived notion of 'Home Rule All Round'. But there will have to be big changes. An independent Scotland will not accept being home to the UK's nuclear submarine base in Faslane. England, out of the EU, freed of the UK and no longer a significant nuclear power, would face other hard choices. How would a land border with Scotland – seeking to remain in the EU, while England has left – be managed? Could England alone or England-and-Wales retain the UK's current Permanent Five membership (P5) of the United Nations Security Council? This seems unlikely. It also seems unlikely that England alone or England-and-Wales could play as significant a role in the world as the United Kingdom did in the past. The people of England, inventive and rich in talent, may have cause to echo the laconic comment of Scotland's Earl of Seafield when in 1707 he signed the act which dissolved the Scottish parliament by subsuming it within that of England. 'There's ane end to ane auld sang,' he quipped – an end to an old song. Britain's old song may be entering its final chorus.

My personal interest is that of a British citizen who has lived in the capital cities of each of our four nations – Edinburgh, Belfast, Cardiff and London – plus Glasgow, Yorkshire and Kent. I have worked for a great British institution, the BBC, for many years while reporting on other institutions including those of various governments and devolved assemblies. Perhaps more importantly, I am from a Scottish and Ulster unionist family stretching back to the seventeenth century. My forebears arrived in Scotland as Protestant refugees from Germany during the Thirty Years War. In 1912 a dozen of my relatives signed the Ulster Covenant in the hope of remaining British rather than breaking away and becoming Irish. Six of those relatives who signed the Ulster Covenant did so with a cross, suggesting they were illiterate. I have a strong unionist background and inclination, yet I have come to believe that Britain may indeed be coming to its end. It is not alarm bells I hear. It's a death knell. Here's why.

2

British or English?

'Nationalism is a feeling as much as a principle.'

Jeremy Black, English Nationalism

'Unable to exit Britain, the English did the next best thing and told the EU to fuck off.'

Anthony Barnett, The Lure of Greatness

'The Tories, Labour and the Lib Dems? They're just three different colours of the same shite.'

Glasgow voter during the 2015
General Election campaign

In August 2017, a year after the Brexit vote, the cabinet minister and leading Brexit campaigner Jacob Rees-Mogg was described in the German newspaper *Die Zeit* as an Über-Conservative member of the British elite and possibly a future British prime minister. This acknowledgement of his talents was somewhat undermined when they also called him '*ein lebendes Fossil*', a living fossil.[1] The clear implication was that Mr Rees-Mogg represented a paleo-Conservative vision of England, irredeemably stuck in the past, politically powerful in the present and potentially even more powerful in the future. The accompanying photograph showed Mr Rees-Mogg in what the caption said was an expensive 'nostalgic toy store'. The picture shows the MP standing in his double-breasted suit in front of what looks like a Victorian cabinet stuffed with vintage cuddly toys. The article suggested that he stood to attention for 'God Save the Queen' even when in the bath. Making fun of the man sometimes called the Honourable Member for the eighteenth century is not confined to Germany. British politics in recent years has inspired comedians from Ireland and France to Australia and North America, as well as plenty of domestic comedy. By 2016, the year of the Brexit vote, the satirical magazine *Private Eye* reported the highest sales figures in its fifty-five-year history. It also showed Rees-Mogg on a cover announcing that after Brexit 'We must trade freely again... with Persia, Mesopotamia and Cathay.'[2] And yet for some British people he appeared to strike an appropriately patriotic note when he addressed the Conservative Party conference in October 2017. 'We need to be reiterating the benefits of Brexit,' he said. 'Oh, this is so important in the history of our country... It's Waterloo! It's Crécy! It's Agincourt! We win all these things!'

These historical references chimed well with the Brexit slogans about 'taking our country back', or 'taking back control', and other common rhetorical flourishes about Britain as an island nation separate and distinct from our close neighbours over the sea, a land called 'Europe'. The idea of leaving the European Union as if it were victory in a military campaign against foreign foes exposed various fault lines. The most obvious was that between Britain and the countries of the European Union, but the more significant fault line is a division within the United Kingdom itself. In 'taking back control', who is doing the taking? You? Me? Which country is being taken back by Brexit? Is it Britain, or England? And what did Mr Rees-Mogg really mean by the 'history of *our* country'? The Battle of Waterloo, of course, was a British-led victory over Napoleon in 1815, but the other two battles were strictly English affairs. Crécy took place in 1346 and Agincourt in 1415, victories over the French two centuries or more before Britain even existed. As every Scottish, Ulster or Irish schoolboy or girl learns, in those battles and many others for centuries past, Scotland and Ireland were not on the side of England. 'We' were 'them'. In Scotland people occasionally still talk of the 'Auld Alliance' with France against the 'Auld Enemy', England. Moreover, Waterloo was won thanks to the genius of the Dublin-born Arthur Wellesley, later the Duke of Wellington. He called the battle the 'nearest-run thing you have ever seen in your life'. But Wellington also accepted it was not an English-only or British-only affair. It was won thanks to the arrival of Blücher's Prussian forces before the sun went down. 'Give me night or give me Blücher,' was one of Wellington's best-known phrases.

A vital alliance with the Germans at Waterloo was perhaps not central to Mr Rees-Mogg's nostalgia that 'we' win 'all these things' in Europe. The fossilization of English twenty-first-century political rhetoric in constantly invoking past victories, and even defeats like Dunkirk, has often been remarked upon. Neil McGregor, the former director of the British Museum, spoke of Germans' 'deep admira-tion' for Britain but they are 'very dismayed that when they come to Britain, they're greeted with Nazi salutes! Bewildered that Britain doesn't want to appear to know about Germany now, but wants to freeze the relationship as it was 70 years ago.'[3] A friend of mine, the former Liberal Democrat MEP for London Irina von Wiese, was born in Cologne but has lived in London for decades. On 31 January 2020, the day Britain formally left the European Union, she was interviewed in London's Parliament Square by a reporter for the international German TV station Deutsche Welle. During the interview, conducted as usual for Deutsche Welle in English, Brexit supporters gathering in Parliament Square interrupted her with Hitler salutes and shouts referencing the Nazis. The Brexit Party's MEP Ann Widdecombe was among those who suggested in May 2019 that Britain survived the Blitz and so Brexit wouldn't be so bad. Brexit, she said, 'is as nothing compared to the sacrifice that we asked a previous generation to make in order to ensure Britain's freedom… my granny was bombed out in Plymouth… People lost sons and husbands and fathers, and they did this because they wanted freedom.' Drawing a comparison between a narrow Brexit victory in what we were told was an 'advisory' democratic referendum and the Blitz, in which 60,000 British people died violently, is both absurd and in poor taste. My own grandmother was bombed out of her house during an attack on the shipyards of Clydebank and would have been scathing about the way these analogies were employed. But invocations of the 'Blitz spirit' persist. The same language was used at the start of the coronavirus pandemic, jarring sharply with images of panic-buying shoppers scuttling from supermarkets pushing trolleys filled with toilet rolls.

War rhetoric has other consequences too. On social media and in some newspapers, British politicians and others who continued to oppose Brexit were described in words and phrases familiar from the 1940s. They were traitors, Quislings, saboteurs, enemies of the people and appeasers, told to 'man up' and 'grow a pair' and adopt the stoicism of the British at Dunkirk. An additional perspective on the pleasures of suffering was offered by Ant Middleton, a former special forces soldier and star of Channel 4's programme *SAS: Who Dares Wins*. In 2018 he Tweeted: 'A "no deal" for our country would actually be a blessing in disguise. It would force us into hardship and suffering which would unite & bring us together, bringing back *British values* of loyalty and a sense of community! Extreme change is needed!' (My italics.)

What is striking in these comments is that a democratic vote to change the UK's future relationship with European democracies was being interpreted as if it resembled long-gone wars or a survivalist challenge, rather than a difference of opinion between reasonable people on how to conduct trade and other matters. More significant for the future relationship between the constituent parts of the United Kingdom is the way in which the rhetoric of these public discussions frequently used the words 'we' and 'us' and 'them'. The philosopher Bertrand Russell called such words 'egocentric particulars', meaning they have a relationship to the person speaking and can differentiate or separate that person from others. 'We' didn't win all these battles, if by 'we' Mr Rees-Mogg means Britain. But it is obvious that he did not mean Britain. He meant England. This is a recurring theme. That's why he talked of Crécy and Agincourt. It used to be said of Charles de Gaulle that when he spoke of Europe he really meant France. One theme in what follows is the tendency of many powerful figures in British public life to speak of Britain but to mean only England. When the prime minister Boris Johnson speaks of being a 'One Nation Conservative', by his actions, his words, his mannerisms and his Eton-and-Oxford demeanour, many on these islands will conclude that the 'one nation' of which he speaks is not Britain but England. Egocentric particulars are inclusive for those who feel themselves part of the 'in' group, but to other nations or regions of the United Kingdom they are symptoms of exclusivity. The Palestinian-American academic and writer Edward Said had a word for this behaviour. He called it 'othering'. He meant that people, often unthinkingly, use words to create differences between a group we call 'us' and 'others' who are not really part of 'us'. And within the four nations of the United Kingdom, this matters.

Listening to Mr Rees-Mogg, to many debates in the Westminster parliament, and even to reports on TV and radio from the London-based media, many people in Scotland, Wales, Northern Ireland and even in parts of England feel they have been repeatedly 'othered', not just by Brexit but also by the wider political and cultural discourse across the UK. Sometimes they respond by blaming what they see as a London-centred 'metropolitan elite'. At other times they focus on the narrowness of class and background among our leaders, a different sense of 'us' and 'them'. It's worth noting that since Winston Churchill every British prime minister who went to university attended the same English institution, the University of Oxford, except Gordon Brown, who went to Edinburgh. Of fifty-five British prime ministers since Horace Walpole, more than a third, twenty, were products of the same English school, Eton. Jacob Rees-Mogg was also a product of Eton and Oxford. The narrowness of the English political elite is nothing new. But this class of predominantly white, male leaders we see on television directing the course of political life is increasingly out of step with, and ultimately destructive of, the diverse Britain of four nations and almost 70 million citizens we see around us.

Whatever the precise reasons for a sense of 'othering', there are profound political consequences as we drift towards what for the United Kingdom is an existential crisis. We need to think seriously about our separate nationalisms to consider different ideas about who 'we' are if 'we' are not to break up into 'us' and 'them'. We need to contemplate the idea of the end of Britain, at least as it is currently configured, even if it is not inevitable, and may be turned from a threat to an opportunity. The best place to begin thinking about our differences is in the most important part of our existing union, and the most confused about its own national identity, England.

The Rise of English Nationalism

Like many London residents, I thought the 2012 Olympic Games might be a bit of an annoyance. Those of us who live in Europe's largest (and, to me, undeniably greatest) city were told that there would be traffic disruption, special lanes on our crowded roads for vehicles going to Olympic events, the possibility of even more cramped Tube trains, increased security and the potential threat of terrorism. But then even the grumpiest of us sat down to watch the Olympic opening ceremony on 27 July, and it was as if the sun had driven away the gloom. The ceremony was called 'Isles of Wonder'. It began at 9 p.m. and lasted four hours, and millions of us – almost a billion round the world – stayed with it. The master choreographer was Danny Boyle, a Lancashire-born Englishman with Irish parents from Galway, a man who went to university in Wales and who became famous for directing *Trainspotting*, a film based on the novel by a Scotsman, Irvine Welsh. The celebration, like its creator, was the most magnificent account of Britain and Britishness, in all its diversity, history and humour. We had the Industrial Revolution, the National Health Service and James Bond filmed as if jumping out of a plane with the Queen on a parachute. It came after another celebration of Britishness, the wedding of Prince William to Kate Middleton – the man and woman who are destined to become king and queen of the United Kingdom. But even as we celebrated these great national – that is, British – events, the tectonic plates of other nationalisms in our 'Isles of Wonder' were moving apart.

Immediately before the 2016 Brexit referendum, the Institute of Public Policy Research (IPPR) produced two papers about the rise of nationalistic feeling in England. As they put it:

In January 2012, IPPR published *The Dog That Finally Barked: England as an Emerging Political Community*. In it we argued that an emerging English political identity may over time come to challenge the institutions and practices of the UK more profoundly than anything happening in the so-called Celtic fringe, even Scottish independence.

In their follow-up report, *England and Its Two Unions*, the IPPR examined the relationship between feelings of Englishness and sentiment towards the United Kingdom and the European Union. This came after those highly popular British events that might have been designed to improve a sense of British national cohesion – the Olympics and a royal wedding. The IPPR concluded:

This new survey, conducted in November 2012, confirms that more people in England continue to identify more strongly as English than British: there was no discernible 'British bounce' following the public flag-waving events of 2012. Those who do identify more strongly as English also hold stronger feelings of discontentment with England's unions. That is, they are dissatisfied with the constitutional status quo within the UK, which is seen to favour Scotland and under-represent England's interests, and with England's place in Europe: English people – much more than any other regional population in Europe – see the European parliament as being highly influential. By this analysis, Euroscepticism appears more strongly to be an English concern than a British concern… According to people's political preferences, there is a strong relationship between identifying as English, feeling discontentment with the constitutional status quo and supporting UKIP – by this evidence, UKIP is much less the UK independence party than it is an English nationalist party. Although it has been reluctant to play the 'English card', doing so could strengthen its appeal to voters in England, with potentially far-reaching political implications.

The IPPR's 2012 research was controversial at the time, perhaps because English people often seem to regard nationalism as an affliction suffered by other people, not themselves – 'I am patriotic. You are nationalistic. He is a chauvinist.' But the IPPR report also proved prophetic. A census has been taken in the UK every ten years since 1801. The most recent census, in 2011, showed the great strength of English national – as opposed to British national – sentiment. Some 60 per cent of the English population identified themselves as English rather than the option of declaring themselves British. Only 29 per cent chose the British option. The apparent rise of English nationalism since 2011 was remarked upon by few English political commentators. But the most prominent commentators are based in London, where identification with English identity was least obvious. In the capital, only about a third of respondents (37 per cent) identified themselves as exclusively English, whereas the proportion was much higher in the north-east (70 per cent), the north-west, East Midlands and Yorkshire (66 per cent). This geographical division within England over the rising strength of an English, and the declining strength of a British, identity was to have political consequences, most obviously by mirroring results in the Brexit vote five years later. In 2016 London voted overwhelmingly Remain, while much of the rest of England, especially smaller towns and rural areas in the north and midlands, voted Leave. The rise in a sense of Englishness in those areas appeared at least in part to be a reaction against the creation of a Welsh assembly and more significantly an increasingly assertive Scottish parliament. The IPPR report certainly points in that direction.

Back in 1999, when the Scottish parliament was founded but before it could make an impact, a clear majority of English people – 62 per cent – told the IPPR that they agreed with the status quo, namely that 'England should be governed *as it is now* with laws made by the UK parliament' (my italics). But by 2008 all that had changed. Support for the status quo in England had dropped to about half, 51 per cent. By 2012, as the Scottish parliament really began to assert itself, and preparations were being made for the 2014 Scottish independence referendum, support in England for the status quo dropped even further, down to just 21 per cent. To state this extraordinary change more clearly, these results show that by 2014 *as few as one in five English voters* believed that the way they were being governed was acceptable to them. This is a demonstration of what has been called 'a democratic deficit'. Loss of confidence in the British system of government affected Scotland too, but there was a major difference. English nationalist sentiment blamed Brussels for imposing laws and rules against 'our' will, while Scottish nationalist sentiment blamed London and Westminster. The English Question became entangled with the Scottish Question, but the people affected by each were demanding very different solutions.

'The Vow'

I'm guessing that unless you are Scottish, if I mention 'The Vow', you'll have no idea what I mean. If you are Scottish, you will know exactly where this is going and you will have an opinion, probably a very forthright one. In Scotland, just two days before the September

2014 independence referendum vote, the popular Scottish tabloid newspaper *The Daily Record* published a front-page report with 'The Vow' as the headline. It was one of the most dramatic interventions in the independence campaign. 'The Vow' was a written promise signed by three Englishmen, leaders of three British unionist parties, David Cameron, Ed Miliband and Nick Clegg, on behalf of the Conservatives, Labour and Liberal Democrats respectively. They promised more powers for Scotland in the event of a No vote taking independence off the table. Scots talked excitedly of 'Devo Max' or 'Home Rule' – that is, maximum devolution to Scotland while still remaining in the UK. Two days later Scotland did indeed vote to reject independence: the No vote was 55 per cent and Yes was 45 per cent. 'The Vow' helped the unionist cause, at least for a time. But that was short-lived.

Once independence was rejected by Scottish voters, Mr Cameron offered Scotland something which – disappointingly for those nationalists who felt betrayed once more by Westminster – looked very different from the Devo Max they had hoped for. It began with that age-old bureaucratic device of delay and distraction, in the form of a committee to produce a report. Cameron set up a commission of inquiry under Lord Smith of Kelvin. He was asked to consider new powers for Scotland. The Smith Commission acted and reported in good faith, but Cameron had already moved on to other problems. He had ahead of him the 2015 General Election, which opinion polls suggested he would lose because of the surge on the right to the English nationalists of UKIP. Granting more powers to Scotland potentially would make the English nationalist problem even worse. Cameron was confronted with a cat-fight on the right wing of his own party over Europe, with Tory MPs fearful they would lose their seats to UKIP and Nigel Farage. Besides, the 2014 Scottish referendum was old news. Alex Salmond resigned as SNP leader and his successor as first minister, Nicola Sturgeon, accepted that the independence question had been settled for a generation, although with an important caveat: 'Something material would have to change in terms of the circumstances or public opinion before I think it would be appropriate to have a proposal for a referendum.' Something material was about to change, but not in the way anyone could have predicted. Two competing nationalisms were on the rise, one in England, the other in Scotland. In Scotland's case many voters, not just SNP supporters, were angry that David Cameron in the end offered only relatively minor changes to existing devolved powers. Nicola Sturgeon summed up the sense of disappointment: 'I want to have the power in our hands to create a better system to lift people out of poverty, to get our economy growing. That's the kind of powerhouse parliament I want. Sadly it's not the one that's going to be delivered.' Scottish nationalists believed that 'The Vow' had been broken. Their anger was reflected in the results of the 2015 British General Election, in which an overwhelming SNP victory represented the collapse of unionism in Scotland. Yet even that was nothing compared to what was happening within English nationalism, especially in the shires and small towns across vast swathes of England-outside-London.

The Disenfranchisement of English Nationalists

The 2015 General Election produced a series of astonishing results. The most obvious was that David Cameron won with a slim but workable majority of twelve. Most observers were surprised. Ed Miliband's team were shocked and despondent. Cameron's victory came about because the rise of English nationalism and UKIP in England proved less of a problem for the Conservative Party than the problems created for Labour by the upsurge of Scottish nationalism north of the border. In Scotland all three of 'The Vow' parties, the Conservatives, Labour and Liberal Democrats, were almost wiped out. Labour went into the election defending forty-one out of Scotland's fifty-nine seats and had by far the most to lose. And they lost almost all of it. As I travelled up and down Scotland in the spring of 2015, the Labour wipe-out was utterly predictable. I attended a dinner in Edinburgh a few days before the vote where the former Conservative Party chairman, donor and pollster Lord Ashcroft told the assembled business leaders about focus groups he had been running in Scotland. Ashcroft's team asked Scottish voters why they were turning away from the three unionist parties and switching to the SNP. The researchers received a pithy Glaswegian answer. One voter replied: 'The Tories, Labour and the Lib Dems? They're just three different colours of the same shite.'

The SNP won fifty-six out of fifty-nine seats with around a million and a half votes. The 'three different colours of the same shite' parties of 'The Vow', the Conservatives, Labour and the Liberal Democrats, held on to just one seat each, the worst performance in Scotland for unionist parties in history. Scots joked that there were more giant pandas in Edinburgh Zoo (two) than Scottish Tories (one) at Westminster. The Scottish Conservative leader at the time, Ruth Davidson, wryly told me that for her 'it was easier coming out as a lesbian than as a f---ing Tory'. But it was Labour which was destroyed in Scotland and therefore excluded from power in Downing Street. If Labour had held a score or more of its Scottish constituencies in 2015, Ed Miliband would have been prime minister of the United Kingdom, David Cameron would have resigned, and the Brexit referendum would never have happened. Perhaps a Miliband administration would even have delivered Devo Max, Home Rule for Scotland or something like it. Instead, after his surprising victory David Cameron felt he could legitimately ignore Scottish nationalism. He had bigger problems on home turf, with that enormous boost for English nationalism and UKIP. But UKIP also had a problem. Despite the strongest showing for an English nationalist party in modern British politics, they emerged with next to nothing – and then nothing.

The Conservative Party took 11 million votes and secured 306 seats. UKIP took almost four million votes (3,881,099), and yet their voters were rewarded with only one seat – that of a Conservative defector called Douglas Carswell. Carswell was later to quit UKIP and sit as an independent. The result demonstrated the staggering unfairness of the British electoral system, in this case punishing English nationalists who had demonstrably strong support spread across England, but who were penalized by FPTP, First Past The Post, the traditional

British way of 'democracy'. In a reasonably fair proportional representation system, as employed in elections across Europe, UKIP, with 12.6 per cent of the total votes cast, could have expected around eighty seats in the 650-member House of Commons. The party would then have been forced to come up with policies other than merely rehearsing perceived grievances about the supposedly 'undemocratic' European Union. Instead, UKIP voters were confronted with an egregious example of England's own democratic deficit. This is defined by political theorists as an insufficient level of democracy in the operation of political institutions and procedures in comparison with a theoretical ideal of a democratic government. UKIP voters I talked to in the months after that election were quietly outraged. Some pointed out that Scotland had its own parliament and its own SNP-led government, and the SNP also now had a huge group of MPs at Westminster who could vote on English laws, making decisions about a country these Scots wanted to 'separate' from. How could this be fair? The people of England, on the other hand, had no exclusively English parliament, while English taxpayers – as UKIP voters sometimes put it – 'subsidized' Scotland, Wales and Northern Ireland.

The 2015 General Election was a watershed for competing nationalisms in the UK. The results confirmed the SNP's dominance in Scotland. The election also confirmed that English nationalists were right in assuming that the political establishment ignored or even derided their concerns. UKIP voters recalled that David Cameron in 2006 had dismissed their party as 'fruitcakes, loonies and closet racists, mostly', and that they were ignored and laughed at by 'the London establishment', the 'Oxbridge public-school elite' and the 'mainstream media'. Their smouldering anger reflected G. K. Chesterton's famous 1907 poem 'The Secret People':

> Smile at us, pay us, pass us; but do not quite forget;
> For we are the people of England, that never have spoken yet.

David Cameron at least recognized that English nationalists had begun to find their voice, even if they could not find representation through UKIP at Westminster. By late 2015 Cameron had switched his focus away from Scottish nationalism, which now could be ignored, to English nationalism, which could not. Nigel Farage and other English nationalists meanwhile intensified their rhetoric. They claimed again and again – with justification – that 'the system' was 'rigged' by the 'establishment elite'. This kind of angry rhetoric was by now ubiquitous. Insurgent politicians of the right and left and not just in the UK, were delivering the same kinds of messages. In the United States Donald Trump, Elizabeth Warren and Bernie Sanders all used similar words and phrases along with Matteo Salvini and the Five Star Movement in Italy, Marine Le Pen in France, Podemos in Spain, Rodrigo Duterte in the Philippines and others. By 2015 almost 4 million of Cameron's supposed fruitcakes, loonies and closet racists were impossible to ignore. Tory MPs feared Nigel Farage was a strong communicator who had divided their political base and who could eventually split the party, eclipsing the Conservatives as the natural party for right-of-centre voters in England. It was even possible that more of Cameron's own MPs on the right of the Conservative Party might follow the example of Douglas Carswell and defect to Farage's party. If just half a dozen Conservatives did quit, Cameron would lose his parliamentary majority. Nigel Farage meanwhile was becoming a constant presence on TV and radio talk shows. In interviews he was articulate, amusing and engaging, someone who spoke for those in England who 'never have spoken yet'. As the Labour Party embarked on its own internal civil war, Cameron decided he needed to neutralize what the IPPR report had called 'the English nationalist party', UKIP. He had a cunning plan.

Don't Get Mad – Get EVEL

Even before the 2014 Scotland vote, David Cameron had tried to address the surge in English nationalism by promising a referendum on leaving the EU. The SNP in Scotland and Plaid Cymru in Wales pointed out that this could become a highly divisive issue between the nations of the UK unless Cameron promised that a majority in each of England, Scotland, Wales and Northern Ireland had to vote to leave, otherwise the United Kingdom should remain within the EU. Cameron, concerned that English nationalist voters would feel outraged at the idea of a veto from one of the other UK nations, rejected the idea. Besides, he was supremely confident about winning. Europe was a niche issue, with strong resonance for a minority of voters, but not of great concern to most people. This view was shared widely in British political circles and elsewhere in Europe. The *French Journal of British Studies* explained why mainstream UK parties tended not to raise the issue:

> When asked about their main concerns, voters hardly ever mention Europe, but rather domestic issues such as the economy, the NHS and immigration. 2015 was no exception to this rule, with only 6% of voters mentioning the European Union (EU) as the most important issue for them, in spite of the apparent rise of Euroscepticism in the country. Politicians know that they have little to gain therefore from tackling the issue, as William Hague learnt the hard way when he tried to campaign to '*Keep the Pound*' against New Labour in 2001, and made no electoral gain out of it.[4]

Nevertheless, an issue of little salience to voters as a whole was of great significance within the Conservative Party. Cameron began to address the English Question with a not-quite-devolution offer nicknamed 'EVEL' – English Votes for English Laws. The acronym was catchy, but the plan was dull: a parliamentary procedure unlikely to set English nationalist hearts beating. The 2015 Conservative Party manifesto described it in terms that only a jargon-loving bureaucrat would love. It promised that England-only legislation would require approval from a Legislative Grand Committee prior to its Third Reading in the House of Commons. In effect English constituency MPs would be the ones to decide on English-only laws, and the fifty-six SNP MPs would not be allowed to take part. It is difficult to imagine many English voters feeling any significant or productive change to their lives as a result of these Grand Committee proceedings. There were no street parties in celebration. Instead, the English Question continued to evolve, and English national identity became a more potent force than ever before in modern British politics.

At the same time, the Scottish Question had not gone away. Instead of independence being sidelined for a generation, David Cameron's misjudgements and failure to live up to the expectations created by 'The Vow', the rise of English nationalism, the success of UKIP and the looming Brexit referendum taken together meant Scots began talking of what social media called '#indyref2', another independence referendum. Scotland in 2014 had chosen to stay in the United Kingdom in large part because the Cameron government had threatened that voting Yes meant an independent Scotland would be ejected from the European Union. Voting No to independence was supposed to guarantee staying in the EU. The Scottish political writer Iain Macwhirter didn't buy this argument, even at the time. He forecast that 'there was and is far greater risk of Scotland finding itself outside the European Union by remaining in the UK given the rising tide of anti-Europeanism, UKIP and David Cameron's promise of an in/out referendum'.[5] Macwhirter's forecast was proved correct by the Brexit referendum two years later. Scotland was being forced out of the European Union against its will by English voters; England was seeing a surge of English nationalist sentiment. Two increasingly assertive nationalisms were pulling in different directions.

By June 2018 a BBC survey of 20,000 people found that 'eight out of 10 people in England identify strongly as English', with 34 per cent, or just over a third of the total, seeing themselves as more English than British. Summing up the shift in mood in England and the possibilities of further constitutional change, the Irish writer Fintan O'Toole wrote that the English were practising 'a form of silent secession' from the idea of a United Kingdom.[6] English nationalism was beginning to pull the United Kingdom apart. It had grown steadily since the creation of the Scottish parliament on 12 May 1999. Its potency was confirmed by the large UKIP vote of 2015 and turned into an even more powerful and embittered political force by the unfairness of the election results that year ultimately denying UKIP a voice. Despite being one of the biggest political stories of the last twenty years, this extraordinary phenomenon of English national-ism continued to attract little serious consideration in much of the British – or English – media. But the English Question was explored in other areas of British culture. Jez Butterworth's extraordinary play *Jerusalem* is a particularly striking example.

The play premiered at the Royal Court theatre in 2009, starring Mark Rylance as the central character, Johnny 'Rooster' Byron. The action of *Jerusalem* begins on St George's Day, and as the lights come on the audience sees a curtain showing 'a faded Cross of St George'. A fifteen-year-old girl dressed as a fairy appears and sings William Blake's words for 'Jerusalem':

And did those feet in ancient time
Walk upon England's mountains green:
And was the holy Lamb of God,
On England's pleasant pastures seen.
And did the countenance divine
Shine forth upon those clouded hills
And was Jerusalem builded here
Among those dark satanic—

The authorities, or the 'Establishment', in the shape of two Kennet and Avon Council jobsworths appear. They try to hold Byron to account for various misdemeanours. He is a kind of free spirit of English independence – at first glance a 'fruitcake and loony', who ends up cursing all those in authority with an anger that has passion but no positive direction:

I Rooster Johnny Byron hereby place a curse
Upon the Kennet and Avon Council
May they wander the land forever...

And all their newborn babies
Be born mangled with the same marks
The same wounds as their fathers.
Any uniform which brushes a single leaf of this wood
Is cursed and he who wears it this St George's Day
May he not see the next.

The spirit of Johnny Byron found devastatingly powerful political expression beyond the defence of ancient woodland. It was voiced in the English Brexit vote of 2016. In the summer of 2016 one of my friends, a self-employed English builder in 'Farage country', on the Kent coast, told me he did not vote in General Elections because 'they never listen'. He meant not Kennet and Avon Council but politicians in Westminster. The builder mentioned the unfairness of the 2015 General Election where UKIP was concerned. My friend decided to vote for Brexit, because, he told me, he wanted to stick up two fingers to those in authority. His vote was not some well-thought-out plan to renegotiate trade deals with Brussels or a commentary on future GDP figures. Instead, my friend's vote was best described by the writer, campaigner and founder of openDemocracy Anthony Barnett. Invoking the spirit of Johnny Byron, Barnett wrote: 'Unable to exit Britain, the English did the next best thing and told the EU to fuck off.'[7]

Scots, meanwhile, did precisely the opposite. In the 2016 Brexit referendum an overwhelming 62 per cent of Scots chose to reject Brexit. Every one of Scotland's thirty-two electoral districts voted to stay in the European Union. Northern Ireland also voted Remain, as did London (the part of England where surveys have shown the least identification with being English-only). A majority of voters in most big English cities also chose to stay in the EU. A humorous redesign of the London Tube map appeared on Twitter. It showed the Northern Line linking those areas of the country which chose Remain, running north from Camden Town to Kentish Town and Tufnell Park and then a dotted line all the way up to Scotland. The rest of England was a blur of nothingness for voting Leave. But this time English nationalism was too big and too powerful to be rubbed out of the picture. And there was a twist.

By the General Election of December 2019, Boris Johnson did something quite remarkable. He destroyed the influence of the Brexit Party, Nigel Farage's latest political vehicle, the successor to UKIP. The Brexit Party took no seats because Boris Johnson had turned his Conservative Party into the party of choice for English nationalist voters. English nationalists had once been the fruitcakes, loonies and closet racists, the barbarians at the gate. Now they were inside the castle, and in government, with Mr Johnson demanding that all members of his cabinet be willing not merely to leave the EU but to agree to leave it without a deal, if necessary. What then followed from Prime Minister Johnson was the impossible promise to reunite the United Kingdom, bringing Leave and Remain together. But rather than symbolizing a coming together, the Johnson majority of eighty seats merely confirmed how far apart we had by now become.

In Scotland the Conservative Party was no longer credibly the Conservative and *Unionist* Party. It was not even small-c conservative any more. It had become a radical voice and vehicle for English nationalism, taking the majority of Scots out of the EU against their will. Scots were appalled. The vote against independence in 2014 had been lost in part because they were promised that the only way to stay in the EU was to stay in the UK. Now, tied to the UK, they were being forced out of the EU by English voters. 'The Vow' and the word of the three unionist parties and their leaders counted for nothing.

Did Your Marks and Spencer Close?

In analysing the December 2019 General Election results the former YouGov pollster Peter Kellner emphasized the degree to which the Conservatives had become the vehicle for English nationalism. He pointed out that the divisions over Brexit coincided more or less exactly with those between Conservative and non-Conservative voting areas. The differences were most obvious between big urban populations and those people, like Butterworth's Johnny Byron, who lived in or on the edge of smaller towns or in the countryside. Kellner chose a striking parallel. He looked at the pattern of closures affecting another British institution, Marks and Spencer:

> If you live in Darlington, Keighley, Barrow, Stockton, Walsall or Warrington, you probably know that your once-Labour town voted Leave in 2016 and now has a Conservative MP. You are even more likely to know something else. Your town has lost its Marks and Spencer. For some residents, the loss of their M&S is of little importance; for others it matters more than politics.[8]

If, following Kellner, we think of closures of an iconic British institution not just as a series of unfortunate local events or merely a reflection of the falling sales of underpants, we can illuminate one of the great forces that have reshaped British politics. M&S has closed forty-two clothing stores since November 2016. With few exceptions the closures were in towns that voted Leave in the Brexit referendum. And these were towns, not cities. As Kellner puts it:

> Outside London, M&S has closed none of its big-city stores. The parallel with the Brexit referendum and recent elections is stark. Three weeks ago [the December 2019 election], the Tories gained one seat in Birmingham. They gained no seats in any other major British city. Manchester, Liverpool, Leeds and Newcastle all remain Tory-free cities, as do Bristol, Cardiff, Glasgow and Edinburgh; and all eight rejected Brexit.[9]

The United Kingdom, in Kellner's analysis, remains utterly divided. England itself is also divided between big cities on one hand and small towns and the country shires. Brexit is not the cause of such divisions. It is one of the results. And the consequences of Brexit are still to be played out. So are the consequences of O'Toole's 'silent secession', the idea of nationalism in England pushing destructively inside the United Kingdom while Scotland pulls away from it in a renewed quest for independence. The unresolved English Question is at the core of all these political dramas. At one level it is the directionless rage of Johnny Byron. Social media since the Brexit vote has been full of snide comments from Remain voters about the incoherence of Brexit voters in their 'vox pops' in television interviews or on public access shows such as the BBC's *Question Time*. Remain supporters on Twitter and elsewhere recycle TV clips ridiculing the Brexit-voting man and woman in the English street for being unable to explain anything about what they voted for beyond vague recycled soundbites and quotes from *Daily Mail* headlines. This is counter-productive as well as condescending.

At the Edinburgh Book Festival in August 2019 I appeared on a panel with the politics professor Anand Menon. Anand tells the story of being in Newcastle just before the 2016 referendum for a debate about the impact of Brexit on the UK. He spoke of the predicted drop in the UK's GDP. A woman in the audience yelled back: 'That's *your* bloody GDP. Not ours.' Anand tells the story not to ridicule that woman but quite the opposite – to point out the disconnection between the world of academia, facts and figures, expert predictions, the 'Establishment' – and one might add the mythical Kennet and Avon Council authorities – and those like my friend the seaside builder, the shoppers who see their local M&S has closed or Johnny Byron, who feels that the English Jerusalem is somehow being lost.

There are now two likely outcomes. One is that in the simmering rage of English nationalism we are witnessing the first whispers of how Britain ends. The second possibility is that this discontent will prove to be the catalyst for a reinvention of the UK as some yet unclear but nevertheless newly Re-United Kingdom. A third option is maintaining the status quo, but following Brexit that is no longer possible. However, before we begin to think about reinventing ourselves, we need to be clear who 'we' are, who we are not, and why some of 'us' are treated like 'them'.

3

Us and Them

'Britishness, as an identity, is in crisis. It is still linked in the imaginations of people of all races to the concept of whiteness. A 2017 poll found that more than half of the British population felt the presence of people from ethnic minorities threatened their culture. Not surprisingly, there is widespread distrust in the language of integration. It's the only answer political leaders currently have to offer and represents the unspoken hope that eventually these visible 'others' will have their otherness neutralised by British culture. They will eventually disappear, leaving nothing more than a trace of curly hair, a splash of extra freckles, a liberal, harmless version of a foreign faith, or the memory of a funny-sounding name, their culture blending seamlessly into the mainstream British experience.'

Afua Hirsch, National Geographic, *19 April 2018*

'It has still never occurred to one single Englishman that not everybody would regard it as a step up, as a promotion, to become English… And if Britannia does not rule the waves, very well, that is only and exclusively because the waves of the world do not deserve it any more.'

George Mikes, How to Be a Brit

I ranian revolutionary mobs know they hate us but they seem unclear about who 'we' are. This is from the front page of *The Times*: 'Iranian protesters burnt the Union Jack outside the British embassy in Tehran last night as the diplomatic crisis over the arrest of the UK ambassador grew. A crowd of hardline religion students and regime supporters chanted "Death to England".'[1] One must surely feel sympathy, if not for the protesters' cause, at least for their confusion. In the space of two sentences *The Times* suggests that 'we' citizens of these islands and targets for foreign demonstrators have a 'British embassy' but a 'UK ambassador' and are offended by chants of 'Death to England'. In the old song 'New York, New York', the city was 'so good they named it twice'. British people are even more blessed to live in a country so wonderful we named it three times or more. We call ourselves Britain, Great Britain, the United Kingdom and sometimes even attempt to include the Irish Republic, a foreign country, in what some (but not Irish people) call 'the British Isles'. Some of us are British but not English. Others, such as people in Northern Ireland, live in the United Kingdom, but do not live in Britain, even though they have British passports. Ulster unionists insist on the fact that they are indeed British. (Technically they are not, nor do they represent all of 'Ulster', but we will leave that booby-trap until later.)

It's not just the Iranian mob who are confused. One of the most obvious confusions is the elision of English with British. This at times irritates Scots and others but it is mostly benign and understandable. England clearly is – and always has been – the biggest part of the union, truly the elephant in the bed. At Westminster the English elephant has roughly five times the political representation of Scotland, Wales and Northern Ireland put together, and even that is an underestimation of the economic and cultural significance of England, especially the Greater London area, compared to the rest of the UK. For at least 200 years the English elephant has been growing faster in relative size to the rest of the UK, and since 1945 London has been growing fastest of all. This matters in terms of England's population, economic vitality, political power and the increasing sense of English national identity.

But it also matters in terms of various resentments, within England directed towards the London 'city-state', and within the rest of the United Kingdom directed towards England. An expanding nation – England – with a glorious history was locked into a union with three other tiny nations, and this was bound to be difficult to manage. When the elephant sees the mice seeking and obtaining more power and a greater share of the benefits of union than their size apparently merits, resentments within England are inevitable. And so is change. To understand the complexity of this awkward union and who 'we' are, we need to begin with a brief historical reminder about who we were and why we got together in the first place.

History Matters – For the Future

The United Kingdom began in 1603 with the Union of the Scottish and English crowns. Wales by that time was already united with England, but Wales is not a 'kingdom'. It is a principality – hence the heir to the throne, since 1301, is given the dynastic title 'the Prince of Wales'. This is a distinction which sounds unimportant but it may yet assume greater significance if the United Kingdom as currently constituted really does begin to fall apart. The events of 1603 were superficially a reverse takeover. The Scottish King James VI became James I of England. A Scot became top dog in the new relationship, and England was for more than two centuries ruled by 'foreign' monarchs – the Scottish Stuarts, then William of Orange and the German Hanoverians followed by the line of Victoria of Saxe-Coburg and Gotha, which changed its name to 'Windsor' during the First World War. Back in 1603 King James VI moved from Edinburgh to London because that's where the power and money were – and still are. He took with him some of the best-educated and most powerful people in Scotland. In that, too, not much has changed. As Samuel Johnson wryly observed, 'the noblest prospect which a Scotchman ever sees, is the high road that leads him to England'. Talented Scots emigrated to London for generations and to the outposts of the British (note: never

English) empire and served in the British (sometimes *English*) army and *Royal* Navy and the British Foreign and Commonwealth Office, formerly the Foreign, India, Home, and Colonial Offices.

Every century or so since that 1603 union of crowns, the United Kingdom has been reformed, rethought, renewed, reinvented and sometimes renamed, almost always after a crisis. In 1603 the crisis was an English one – how to find a suitable Protestant monarch to succeed the childless Elizabeth I. On matters of confusion about names, some Scots point out that our current monarch cannot reasonably be called Queen Elizabeth II of the United Kingdom, since the Virgin Queen, Elizabeth I, was Queen of England and Wales only. Beyond pedantry, the serious argument revolves around how far reforming the UK is once again necessary for the twenty-first century. It's been 100 years since the last big reformation, the Partition of Ireland and the creation of the Irish Free State, which became the Republic of Ireland in 1948. If a genuine reinvigoration is not now achieved, or if it is botched, then England's silent secession will lead to a noisier separation from Scotland and possibly Northern Ireland, and a full-blown political crisis. The end of Britain would then be much more complicated, messy, costly and bitter even than Brexit.

The UK leaving the European Union after forty-seven years remains contentious, difficult and at times bewildering. Imagine, therefore, deconstructing a union and intimate relationship stretching back more than 400 years, potentially creating an EU–England customs border somewhere between Carlisle and Dumfries and forcing Britain's Trident submarine fleet to seek a new home when it is finally ejected, as the SNP promise, from its base at Faslane on Gare Loch north of Glasgow. The nuclear deterrent may either have to be scrapped or be berthed on the English coast, if residents of Portsmouth or some similar naval base are prepared to tolerate the arrival of a throwback to the Cold War.

In the event of separation, Wales may tag along with England. Whether under those circumstances a continuing England-and-Wales union could legitimately be described as the 'Rest of the United Kingdom' or the 'Remainder of the United Kingdom' (rUK) is a matter of debate. Since Wales is not by itself a kingdom, whether rUK is a reasonable name – it is certainly not an elegant one – is a question we can leave to pedants and constitutional experts. More importantly, in the event of the UK as currently constituted ceasing to exist, there is no reason why England alone or England-and-Wales would automatically retain Permanent Five (P5) status on the United Nations Security Council with the same power of veto that it currently enjoys. That seat was granted to the United Kingdom in perpetuity since the state represents one of the victorious powers at the end of the Second World War. If the UK dissolves then presumably that P5 status will be reassessed. Brazil, India, Nigeria and perhaps even the European Union as a bloc might demand reform. France might consider relinquishing its P5 seat if an EU place on the Permanent Five were to be guaranteed. This is all speculative, but it has been discussed in diplomatic circles. I once put this scenario to a top British diplomat at the United Nations. After a moment's thought he replied: 'I can assure you that if we were threatened with losing our veto on the United Nations P5, well, we would… veto it.' He smiled. That response may work as an example of British mandarin humour at the Foreign Office, but in the realm of practical diplomacy the diplomat conceded there would be difficulties ahead with other nations coveting the permanent position on the Security Council held by the country formerly known as the United Kingdom. Nothing can be taken for granted.

An End of an Old Song

In 1707 the union of the United Kingdom was renewed again. Once again renewal came after a crisis, and more power shifted to London. Formally the Scottish and English parliaments decided to unite. Scots sometimes see this moment sentimentally in the words of the Earl of Seafield as he signed the Act of Union: 'Now there's ane end o' ane auld sang' (an end of an old song). More negatively this was (and by some still is) seen an act of national betrayal by the Scottish aristocracy, gentry and business leaders. Almost a century after the Union of Parliaments Robbie Burns reflected this bitterness in 'Such a Parcel of Rogues in the Nation' (1791):

Fareweel to a' our Scottish fame,
Fareweel our ancient glory;
Fareweel even to the Scottish name,
Sae famed in martial story...
We're bought and sold for English gold –
Such a parcel of rogues in the nation!

The English Treasury did pay a price to bail out Scottish debts. The Scottish aristocracy and merchant classes were desperate to be rescued from the self-inflicted economic and political disaster known as the Darien scheme. This was a badly thought-out attempt in the 1690s to create a Scottish 'empire' beginning with a colony in Panama. The Scots were seduced into thinking that a faraway tropical land was a rich and hospitable place just waiting to be colonized by Presbyterians with their Bibles and heavy tweeds. The Company of Scotland behind the scheme is estimated to have sucked up about 20 per cent of the money circulating in Scotland at the time. It was a reckless gamble. Some 2,500 bold pioneers set off and fell prey to heat, hunger, exotic diseases and the indifference of indigenous people who, they found to their surprise, were uninterested in bartering food for Scottish baubles, gewgaws and gimcracks. Only a few hundred survivors returned. This was a national humiliation. The failure of the Scottish harvest in 1698–9 compounded the misery. An estimated 5–7 per cent of the Scottish population died from starvation. The bodies of poor crofters were found with half-eaten grass in their mouths.

Beyond English money paying off Scottish debts incurred by the Darien scheme, north of the border merchants, traders and the political classes had other reasons to welcome the Union of Parliaments. Some Scottish Protestants – the majority of the population, especially in the more populated southern areas of Scotland – hoped that the closer parliamentary union with England would extend protection against

Catholic-inspired and French-supported insurrections. After all, 1707 was less than twenty years after the Battle of the Boyne (1690) and the Battle of Aughrim (1691) in which William of Orange's Protestant forces finally defeated the Catholic army in Ireland and guaranteed that future British monarchs would have to embrace Protestantism. Even after the Union of Parliaments, Scottish Protestants did not always feel secure. Catholic insurrections continued, although the 1707 parliamentary union helped ensure that the 1745 Jacobite rebellion was brutally and thoroughly defeated by British forces at Culloden. That battle lasted barely an hour. The Jacobites and Bonnie Prince Charlie are figures of a romantic past, and they continue even now to endure in song and sentimental folklore, but Culloden – despite the myth-making – was in military terms the Jacobite equivalent of the Charge of the Light Brigade: hopeless.

Daniel Defoe and the Unionist Sales Pitch

The Union of Parliaments was also sold to Scots as a way of strengthening Scotland's voice in London and ensuring Royal Navy protection for Scottish traders. It meant that Scots were involved in the three key areas which were central to the United Kingdom's historical success – ensuring that Protestantism had no serious rivals, expanding the business of empire in India and elsewhere, and prosecuting wars against foreign foes. The interests of England and Scotland in these three areas were broadly congruent – keeping the 'true' faith, making money, and keeping our islands secure from foreign invaders. But there was a catch. From the beginning there was a feeling that Scots were being outvoted by English interests in a geographically and culturally remote Westminster parliament.

Ambitious Scots would still continue to serve in London and grab opportunities presented by the ever-expanding and successful colonies. But despite the advantages on offer, despite increased security and opportunity, there was resentment among poorer and especially Catholic Scots long before Robbie Burns put those feelings into verse in 1791. Daniel Defoe, the author of the first English novel, *Robinson Crusoe*, was English born but a strong Presbyterian. He was also a brilliant journalist and polemicist. He wrote *A Tour Through the Whole Island of Great Britain* and spent time in Edinburgh in 1706, just as the ferocious debate about the Union of Parliaments was in full swing. Defoe – a prolific writer and a bit of a chancer – was at the time indebted to Robert Harley, the Earl of Oxford, who was one of the government ministers pressing strongly for the amalgamation of the two parliaments. Defoe became a propagandist and unionist cheerleader. His journal, *The Review*, tirelessly advocated the union, and Defoe is also credited with writing *The History of the Union of Great Britain*, published after the marriage had been consummated.

In his travels he reached the Highlands where he met such hostility to the English that 'we also found it much for our convenience to make the common people believe we were French'.[2] France, of course, was the perennial enemy and rival of England and therefore of the British state. Travellers pretending to be French in England would have been foolhardy, but by Defoe's account, pretending to be England's enemy in the north of Scotland was a wise precaution. Meanwhile in the Scottish capital, Edinburgh, riven with discontent over the union, Defoe 'found the city in a most dreadful uproar and the High Street full of the rabble… shouting and swearing and crying out all Scotland would stand together. No Union. No Union. English dogs and the like.'

The Scottish ruling classes who assented to the union were also abused. The Earl of Mar wrote: 'I am not very timorous and yet I tell you that every day here we are in hazard of our lives. We cannot go on the streets but we are insulted.'[3] Perhaps the Scottish national mood about the union could best be summed up by the response of the bell ringers of St Giles Cathedral, situated in the heart of the Old Town, on the Royal Mile between Edinburgh Castle and the Palace of Holyrood. When the Union of Parliaments act was signed the bells rang out a tune called 'Why should I be sad on my wedding day?'

*

The Irish Question

In 1801 Ireland joined the union. For England it was a shrewd move. Ireland was potentially the weakest flank in the military defence of the United Kingdom. In 1798 a rebellion initiated by the non-sectarian democrats of the United Irishmen had collapsed into chaotic violence, with Protestants massacred by Catholic rebels in the south of the country and savage repression carried out by British forces. England's great enemy, the French, landed a force of 2,000 men in support of the rebels in the west of Ireland, and, although it was too small to influence the rebellion, the implications were obvious in London. The British prime minister William Pitt was rightly concerned that Ireland posed a security risk as it had done for centuries, turning England's flank. The back door to Britain had to be closed.

The Irish poet James Clarence Mangan's inspired nineteenth-century reworking of the old Irish ballad 'Róisín Dubh' as 'My Dark Rosaleen' gives a flavour of British concerns seen from another angle. Mangan's Rosaleen is Ireland preparing to rebel and awaiting rescue from the British by an invasion from Catholic Europe:

> O the Erne shall run red
> With redundance of blood,
> The earth shall rock beneath our tread,
> And flames wrap hill and wood,
>
> And gun-peal and slogan-cry
> Wake many a glen serene,
> Ere you shall fade, ere you shall die,
> My Dark Rosaleen!
> My own Rosaleen!

The 1801 union was forced through, to England's advantage but with much less support among the Catholic Irish population than even the contentious union of the Scottish and English parliaments a century before. For the government in London the union meant that the western flank of the British Isles was more secure, although the issue would never completely disappear, right through to the Second World War. The Irish parliament was dissolved, and, with echoes of Scotland 100 years previously, there was rioting in Dublin. But again, like Scotland, Protestants rejoiced, and many merchants and wealthier Irish people hoped that the result of union would be full Catholic emancipation. Despite some optimism, assimilating an island in which the vast majority of people were Irish-speaking Catholics into an English-speaking, Protestant-dominated political culture at a time when Catholics in Britain were denied fundamental rights proved at first difficult and then impossible.

It took another twenty-eight years, under the leadership of the charismatic lawyer Daniel O'Connell, to achieve Catholic Emancipation. He then launched a movement for the repeal of the Act of Union, and the granting of Home Rule. His campaign mobilized vast numbers of supporters in mass meetings of a size that had no historical precedent – one was said to have attracted a million people. Westminster refused to consider any reform of the union, and O'Connell's movement collapsed during the Great Famine of the 1840s, when the British government failed to offer significant humanitarian relief. This was an outrage then and remained a raw wound which nearly 200 years later has yet to heal. The failure of O'Connell's resolutely peaceful campaign sparked a despairing belief that only armed action would force the British to make concessions, giving birth to a long tradition of militant Irish republicanism, especially with the rise of the conspiratorial Fenian movement in the 1860s.

In 2019 the British home secretary and Conservative politician Priti Patel suggested using food as a weapon against Ireland in future Brexit negotiations. The anger and astonishment in Ireland at her insensitivity and ignorance was profound. About a million Irish men and women died in the Great Famine. Another million or more emigrated. I blundered into this historical morass many years ago. Working as an inexperienced correspondent for the BBC in Northern Ireland, I found myself in Buswell's pub in Dublin, just across from Dáil Éireann, the

Irish parliament, spending a delightful evening drinking Guinness and whiskey with a group of Irish politicians. One of them was the then Irish foreign minister, the affable Brian Lenihan. We discussed how historical events could achieve mythical significance way beyond the facts – the 1745 Jacobite rebellion in Scotland, Crécy, Agincourt and Ireland's Great Famine. Very unwisely I tried to put the Famine 'into context' by pointing out that Ireland was not alone in suffering in the 1840s. Across Europe these years were known as the 'Hungry Forties'. France was hit by several famines. The 1840s of Dickens's London was a far from pleasant place. My drinking companions went silent. Brian Lenihan patiently and politely 'had a word with me'. I was in my early twenties and ignorant. He generously forgave my bad manners. I learned something and apologized. Ms Patel, a senior British government minister, hasn't and didn't.

The Irish Answer?

Unsurprisingly, the union constructed in 1801 rapidly became unworkable. After years of agitation for Home Rule, first under the leadership of O'Connell and later in the century the remarkable Protestant landlord Charles Stewart Parnell, Irish discontent turned bloody with the Easter Rising in 1916. Both men had led mass movements focused on parliamentary reform, but 1916 was the work of a minority who believed, with the Fenians, that only physical force could realize the will of the people. The armed rebellion was seen in the rest of the United Kingdom as an act of treason in wartime; its leaders were executed, turning their comprehensive defeat into a kind of moral victory. The unilateral declaration of a separate republic by a clandestine Dáil (parliament) elected, in the south, by an overwhelming majority, led to brutal repression in Ireland once Germany was defeated. The struggle was only concluded with the surrender by both sides to reality in the Anglo-Irish Treaty of late 1921. Ireland was partitioned. Most of the island, the twenty-six counties in which Roman Catholics were in the majority, became the Irish Free State, nowadays the Irish Republic. Six mostly Protestant counties, part of the historic province of Ulster, became what we now call Northern Ireland, resulting in the current designation on British passports, the United Kingdom of Great Britain and Northern Ireland.

Fast forward almost another hundred years. Renewed pressure for devolution in Scotland and Wales in the late 1990s and the Good Friday Agreement at last bringing peace (more or less) to Northern Ireland led to a new dispensation in the new century. Devolution meant that the Scottish parliament returned to Edinburgh in 1999 after a break of almost 300 years. The veteran Scottish National Party politician Winnie Ewing opened the parliament, which now sits at Holyrood, with a wry reference to the past: 'The Scottish Parliament, adjourned on the 25th day of March 1707, is hereby reconvened.' A new song replaced the deferred old song, and in Scottish nationalist sentiment it was as if 300 years of history were merely a break for refreshments. The National Assembly of Wales also began sitting in the 1990s. It had its powers enhanced in 2011. And the Northern Ireland Assembly began to meet – constructively, for the most part, at least at first – in the old Stormont parliament building on the outskirts of Belfast.

Stormont had a chequered existence. Its roots were in what was called in the 1920s by Northern Ireland's first prime minister Sir James Craig 'a Protestant Parliament for a Protestant state' (often misquoted as a 'Protestant Parliament for a Protestant People'). Nowadays, after a gap of three years, the parliament on the outskirts of Belfast is back working again. The hiatus followed rows about – among other things – the status of the Irish language. This is a signature cause of the nationalist and almost entirely Catholic party Sinn Féin, and official recognition of Irish has been strongly resisted by the unionist and almost entirely Protestant Democratic Unionist Party. But Stormont is by law a power-sharing institution. That means Catholics and Protestants, unionists and Irish nationalists try for the most part to cooperate despite their differences, or, if that is not possible, the parliament can be suspended and replaced by 'direct rule' from Westminster. The threat of 'direct rule' from London was supposed to be a wonderful unifier for Northern Ireland politicians, although it hasn't quite worked out like that. Instead it has empowered the most intransigent parties on both sides (Sinn Féin and the DUP) and squeezed the middle ground. Now that the local administration has been restored after a three-year gap, the hope is that the politicians in Stormont will in future prefer to argue among themselves than try to educate yet another generation of often ignorant English functionaries put in to settle their native quarrels.

The ignorance of English politicians in Ireland is legendary. Boris Johnson's comments on the border between the Irish Republic and Northern Ireland attracted particular derision. Johnson, foreign secretary at the time, pointed out that in London there was 'no border between Islington or Camden and Westminster' and yet traffic fees known as the congestion charge were easy to collect. He therefore concluded that customs and regulatory differences would not be a problem when the Irish border became the UK's land border with the EU. Irish stand-up comedians had plenty of material as a result. One meme popular on social media showed the iconic location in Northern Ireland's second largest city, Londonderry, marking Republican resistance to British troops from 1969 onwards known as 'Free Derry Corner'. It was photo-shopped with the words 'You are now entering Free Camden'.

Mr Johnson was not the only butt of Irish jokes. The Conservative MP Karen Bradley served as the British government's Northern Ireland secretary in 2018 and 2019. Despite thirty or more years of bitter disagreements, terrorist atrocities in both islands, and fighting between unionists and nationalists which resulted in more than 3,600 deaths, Ms Bradley admitted in an interview in 2018 'that when I started this job, I didn't understand some of the deep-seated and deep-rooted issues that there are in Northern Ireland. I didn't understand things like when elections are fought for example in Northern Ireland, people who are nationalists don't vote for unionist parties and vice-versa.'[4] The hashtag #ThingsKarenBradleyNeverKnew started trending on Twitter. When Ms Bradley finally left office, Deirdre Heenan, professor of social policy at Ulster University, commented: 'Attracting widespread and sustained criticism, Karen Bradley united the political classes in their belief that she was inept, ineffectual, gaffe-prone and completely out of her depth.'[5] Uniting unionists and nationalists in Northern Ireland was quite a feat.

The point here is not merely to reflect on the intellectual narrowness and incompetence of the British governing class, although that in itself complicates the strains and divisions within the current UK. The real point is that Northern Ireland's unionist and nationalist politicians together began to recognize that for all their differences they have more in common with each other than with English outsiders parachuted in at moments of political stalemate. The Stormont assembly has at times been successful. Its main achievement has been helping keep a kind of peace, largely taking the gun out of politics and marginalizing violent republican groups. Unfortunately, that has also entailed the normalization of criminal rackets, a ludicrous scandal over heating subsidies and the continuing row over the Irish language. Symbolically the language row assumes high importance despite the fact that (Irish language experts say) some of the politicians arguing most strongly for Irish are themselves unable to hold even a basic conversation in the language they advocate so passionately.

Nevertheless, the positive changes in Northern Ireland are important to recognize.

As a news journalist I visited Gerry Kelly and Brendan 'Bik' McFarlane, senior members of the Provisional IRA, in a Dutch jail after they had broken out of the Maze prison in Belfast and were later arrested in the Netherlands. Men like these, whom I came to know as senior members of a proscribed terrorist organization in the 1980s, and others who flirted with and stirred up paramilitary gangsters on the loyalist side, eventually chose a different path. They and their organizations began to campaign for votes. Gerry Kelly and others entered Stormont and have pursued their political ends constructively and by peaceful means, although former loyalist paramilitaries were less successful at the ballot box, and some resentment about this persists in working-class Protestant communities. Nevertheless, to turn Carl von Clausewitz's famous dictum on its head, war may be the continuation of politics by other means, but politics in Northern Ireland has proved to be a means of avoiding war. As we consider what the next century of change may hold for the United Kingdom, and whatever the deficiencies of the Northern Ireland Assembly, its politicians and its parties, removing the shadow of the gunman from one part of UK politics should be cherished.

London as the UK's 'Fifth Nation' and Its Resentments

While the component parts of our political union have been re-arranged several times, the people of the four nations of England, Scotland, Wales and Ireland/Northern Ireland have seized the advantages of freedom of movement within the union to rearrange themselves within the UK. Since 1801 there has been a massive shift in population, economic, cultural and political power, mostly to England. Within England the shift has decisively been to London at the expense of the other nations and English regions. The 1801 census showed some 54 per cent of the UK population living in England. (Ireland was excluded from that census.) By 1871 England made up 70 per cent of the population of the UK. In the latest census, 2011, the percentage of the population living in England had increased enormously to 84 per cent of the whole. Scotland's people made up just a tenth of that (8.4 per cent), Wales's a twentieth (4.2 per cent) and Northern Ireland's population accounted for 2.9 per cent.

By 2011 the 8.8 million people in Greater London made up 13 per cent of the total UK population – more than the population of Scotland and Wales put together. But even that is a significant under-estimate of London's power. In 2020 the World Urbanization Project estimated London's population at 9.3 million. It is the biggest city in the European Union, twice the size of its nearest rival, Berlin, and almost ten times as big as England's second city, Birmingham. Many more London commuters live in suburbs and satellite towns outside the city but travel into London for work – from towns such as Reading or Guildford, Brighton, Cambridge, Tonbridge or elsewhere.

The London 'metropolitan area' (variously defined, but taking into account commuters with work in London and their families) can stretch to include 18 million people. Beyond population, the full impact of London in economic terms makes it an astounding success story. The nominal GDP of Scotland in 2018 was $237 billion. The GDP of all of England and Wales was $2.8 trillion. But the nominal GDP of London alone that year was $1 trillion, a third of the GDP of the entire United Kingdom, and four times that of Scotland. London has become so powerful that by itself it could easily rank as our fifth nation within the UK alongside Scotland, Wales, Northern Ireland and the rest of England. In our lopsided union, this city-state within a state is in political and economic terms by far the dominant part. Yet London was not always so successful. The population declined from 1939 onwards. The city's economy was reinvigorated by Mrs Thatcher's reforms to the financial sector in the 1980s – the so-called 'Big Bang' (the sudden deregulation and modernization of financial services which almost overnight made London a trading rival to New York) – and by joining the Common Market in 1973.

As the European Union developed and the British economy integrated more efficiently with that of the major countries of the continent, London boosted itself as the English-speaking 'point of entry' to the EU for American and Japanese banks, and the European headquarters for other businesses from all over the world. By 2011 London's population had risen by 16 per cent since the previous census a decade before. Taken together these changes inevitably have had profound political implications and create their own tensions and irritations. Within London these include resentment about spiralling house prices, increased rents, crowded roads, overloaded public transport and other facilities. Outside London anger is directed towards the out-of-touch 'metropolitan elite'.

London is certainly different. It is much more racially diverse than other parts of the UK. The Greater London Authority reported in 2015 that almost half (44 per cent) of London's population were BAME – black and minority ethnic – compared to just 28.9 per cent in 2001. While a majority of people across England are likely to describe themselves primarily as 'English' rather than British, the opposite tends to be the case in BAME families, who see themselves as British, not English. London also represents power, money, politics, government, the media, banks, big businesses and the core of cultural life from music and theatre to the visual arts. This concentration of culture causes its own resentments. Friends of mine who are composers providing music for TV and film attended a conference in London where the most successful composers passed on advice to aspiring musicians. A Scottish musician asked if it was necessary to be in London to be really successful. The answer was yes. London is the place for British TV and film, otherwise the Scottish musician should consider LA or New York. There are related resentments within England about London's dominance leading to the marginalization of the north, the West Country and rural districts. This is most obvious in the constant (and justified) complaints about under-investment in infrastructure connecting great cities such as Liverpool, Newcastle, Manchester and Leeds. The former chancellor of the exchequer George Osborne talked endlessly about a 'Northern Powerhouse' in the north of England without directly helping to create one. This kind of talk has produced as much irritation in these northern cities as 'The Vow' did in Scotland, and it continues. In 2020 Boris Johnson promised to 'level up' Britain. It's a handy little phrase but without the burden of having any clear meaning. Part of that 'levelling up' included a one-day meeting in February 2020 of the UK cabinet in Sunderland. It was one of those photogenic stunts at which Mr Johnson excels, although the symbolism was marred by the reality. The then chancellor of the exchequer Sajid Javid Tweeted about his excitement at visiting 'north England', a phrase no one in the north of England would ever use about their geographical location.

Two surveys give a sense of why London's success can be an irritant elsewhere. One, by the Joseph Rowntree Foundation, examined the fortunes of seventy-four UK cities with populations of more than 100,000. They found that the 'most declining' UK cities were all in the north of England. Rochdale, Burnley and Bolton were the top three, followed by Blackburn, Hull and Grimsby. No city in the south of England featured in the top twenty-four of the 'most declining' index.[6] These cities have all lost population, especially young people, and seen declining economic activity, including boarded-up shops on their high streets and often poor health outcomes.

In a separate report published in 2019 the think tank Global Future found that, without the arrival of immigrants, nine local areas, including four areas in southern England – Southampton, Barking, Dagenham and Slough – would have suffered at least 5 per cent population decline, and as many as 130 local authorities would have suffered a working-age population decline. At a business event for the construction industry in one of London's iconic skyscrapers, the Shard, the CEO of a large UK property company made the same point in a more striking way. He took me over to one of the windows with a magnificent view of the London skyline and pointed to the glorious sunset reflecting upon gleaming new glass and steel buildings. 'If you want to know why London voted to remain in the EU,' he said, 'and millions of people in the north of England voted to leave, just count the number of cranes you can see at building sites around here. Then do the same in Liverpool or Leeds or Manchester. There are more cranes on more prestige projects in central London than you will see in two or three English cities combined.'

Take the train out from Waterloo and you can count these cranes for yourself. Or, if you want other hard facts about division of wealth, you can also look at the government figures which are a result of the Barnett Formula, the complex set of calculations through which British governments channel taxpayers' money to the nations and regions of the United Kingdom. Follow the money, and by any measure the areas which voted 'no' to Brexit and wanted to remain in the EU do much better than those which voted to leave. Perhaps not surprisingly, those who do better out of the status quo tend to vote for the status quo, including membership of the European Union. The British government website is clear who are the winners and losers in terms of public spending across the UK. Scotland, Wales, Northern Ireland and London all have higher than average levels. England-outside-London receives less than average: 'In 2018/19, public spending per person in the UK as a whole was £9,584. In England, it was £9,296 (3 per cent below the UK average). This compares with Scotland: £11,247 (17 per cent above the UK average); Wales: £10,656 (11 per cent above the UK average); Northern Ireland £11,590 (21 per cent above the UK average). Among the English regions, public spending per person was lowest in the south-east and East Midlands at £8,601 (10 per cent below the UK average) and highest in London at £10,425 (9 per cent higher than the UK average). The data shown are for public expenditure per person and are taken from HM Treasury's *Country and Regional Analysis: 2019*, which contains more detailed information including spending by function (health, education, etc.).

Taken together all these factors – differential benefits, new and historic resentments and competing nationalisms – mean that the next few years will demand a great deal of flexibility and cunning from Westminster governments if the United Kingdom is to remain united. Part of the task will be to manage the success of London and metropolitan England while somehow listening to the cries of help from failing smaller English cities and towns which have seen a decline in population, and to do so while attempting to revive an economy suffering the serious dislocation caused by the coronavirus pandemic. All this will require something much more substantial than vague slogans about 'levelling up' and gesture politics stunts such as the cabinet away-day to Sunderland.

We began this chapter by asking who 'we' mean by 'us'. The answer, as the Iranian revolutionaries attacking the British embassy and chanting 'death to England' demonstrate, can be quite complex. England is not Britain. Britain is not the United Kingdom. And – to the surprise of many, including some who live there – technically Northern Ireland is not Ulster. British passports tell Ulster folk that they are citizens of 'the United Kingdom of Great Britain *and* Northern Ireland', and that these are therefore two distinct entities. And that's only part of the story. While many Protestants in Northern Ireland claim to be 'Ulster Unionists' that's not quite right. Northern Ireland has six counties – Fermanagh, Armagh, Tyrone, Londonderry (or Derry), Antrim and Down. But Ulster is an ancient Irish province of nine counties. Three Ulster counties – Monaghan, Cavan and Donegal – are part of Ulster but not in Northern Ireland. They are in the Irish Republic. It's hardly surprising that we all get this wrong. While reporting from Washington, DC during the presidencies of Bill Clinton, George W. Bush and Barack Obama, countless well-informed US officials, congressmen and even Vice President Al Gore, were confused about Britishness. Vice President Gore on one occasion laughed at something I said and congratulated me on my 'English sense of humour'. I told him I was Scottish. He paused for a moment and said, thoughtfully, 'Braveheart, right?' In the former Yugoslavia I once spent twenty minutes explaining to a very cheerful train guard that being British was not the same as being English, while he explained to me that being a Yugoslav had been identical with being a Serb. He, of course, was indeed a Serb. Thinking back on that conversation, I find it instructive that the former Yugoslavia could survive Croat, Bosnian, Slovene or Kosovar nationalism, but it could not survive the nationalism of the biggest player, Slobodan Milošević's Serbia. Perhaps a lopsided union becomes especially vulnerable to collapse when nationalist passions grow strongly in the most powerful component. We are not, assuredly, heading down the Balkan route to, well, Balkanization. But our current crisis does demand that we take English nationalism and English identity more seriously. And yet when we speak of English identity, what and who exactly do we mean?

4

Another English Question: England, Which England?

'Having argued for long that states are artificial
constructions, intellectuals have failed to confront the
issue that England exists, and that its role and character
are being pushed to the fore as the stability of the United
Kingdom comes under increasing pressure, notably from
the ambitions of Scottish nationalism. English nationalism
is too important to be left to the extremists.'

Jeremy Black, English Nationalism

'A true-born Englishman's a contradiction,
In speech an irony. In fact, a fiction.'

Daniel Defoe, The True-Born Englishman

'History is a set of lies agreed upon.'

Napoleon Bonaparte

Tracking down that elusive beast, English identity, is like hunting for a unicorn. We know roughly what it should look like, but finding it is impossible. Daniel Defoe got part of it right when he joked that 'a true-born Englishman's a contradiction'. The English, even if some do not recognize it, are a mongrel lot, and nobody is 'true-born', whatever that means. In England, as in most developed countries, we have been enriched by foreign migration, intercultural marriages and interconnection with the rest of the world. The *Dad's Army* theme tune got another part of English identity right. The song was composed for the BBC in 1968, and yet Bud Flanagan's laconic singing makes it seem as if it genuinely sprang from the depths of the Second World War. Flanagan celebrates the resilience of 'old England' standing up to the greatest villain of the twentieth century. But the tone is pure English genius. The German chancellor is not the omnipotent Führer but just some delusional lunatic addressed with mock-politeness as 'Mister' Hitler:

Who do you think you are kidding, Mister Hitler,
If you think old England's done?

The English economist Sir Dennis Robertson hit on another note of Englishness, at least as many English people have come to regard it, when he told an American audience in 1953 that 'the Englishman has long been used to living in a certain haze as to what his country is'. These comments about Englishness by Englishmen strike me as, well, very *English* in their tone. They represent in various witty ways Englishmen laughing at their countrymen and at themselves, yet they also contain the serious suggestion that searching for something called an 'English identity' or 'British identity' (again the two are often elided) is a fool's errand. Many of the more serious politicians, thinkers and writers searching to define this identity often end up with a series of clichés. They reinforce backward-looking stereotypes by painting a tiny part of a much more complicated picture, leaving out much of the richness and diversity of what modern England really looks like to those of us who live here.

To take a famous example, the former Conservative prime minister John Major offered his thoughts on Englishness and English exceptionalism in 1993 when trying to see off the perpetual rebellions within his own party over Europe. From the moment he replaced Margaret Thatcher as prime minister he had to deal with right-wing elements within the Conservative Party, English MPs he came to call the 'bastards', who tried to undermine him. The 'bastards' argued in the 1990s and continued to argue during the 2016 Brexit debate that Britain would in some way no longer be Britain because it was being subsumed into a sinister 'European Project', an ever-closer union with other EU countries. The 'bastards' ostensibly were speaking of Britain, but they were always speaking to, and about, Middle England. Mr Major tried to point out – quite reasonably – that being part of the European Union did not make Germans less German, French people less French or – and this was the point of the speech – the British any less British. He claimed that fifty years into the future Britain would be 'unamendable' and 'will still be the country of long shadows on county grounds, warm beer, invincible green suburbs, dog lovers and pools fillers'.

Mr Major's charming nostalgia here was – again – ostensibly for Britain, but he meant England. There are no county (cricket) grounds in Scotland. Moreover, Scots after 400 years of union with England do not feel any less 'Scottish', quite the reverse. Worrying about some phantom dilution of a national identity within the EU is not a Scottish problem. But it is an English nationalist obsession. In the twenty-first century, Scottish identity is more confident than at any time in my life. When I was a child, the kilt was worn by some soldiers and what my father would have called 'professional Scotsmen', the entertainers of the White Heather Club, a few slightly eccentric lairds and Edinburgh lawyers and rarely by anyone else. Now Scots wear the kilt to sports events, family parties, formal dinners – whenever they feel like it. England does not have a national dress in that way. Nor does it seem to have such a self-confident national identity, at least for now. That's why one of John Major's other insights about Englishness invited much derision. It was of 'old maids bicycling to Holy Communion through the morning mist'. The old maids rolled into the prime minister's speech from George Orwell's essay 'The Lion and the Unicorn: Socialism and the English Genius', which was published at the bleakest time in the Second World War, February 1941. Orwell was thinking hard about 'English civilisation' and decided it was:

> somehow bound up with solid breakfasts and gloomy Sundays, smoky towns and winding roads, green fields and red pillarboxes. It has a flavour of its own. Moreover it is continuous, it stretches into the future and the past, there is something in it that persists, as in living creatures… the suet puddings and red pillar-boxes have entered into your soul.

By the twenty-first century, and even back in 1993, when John Major delivered his speech, the suet puddings were long gone, the red pillarboxes were being overtaken by faxes and eventually by email, and the smoky towns were a lot less smoky since they had banned toxic coal and the most highly polluting road vehicles. In 1941 such lyricism about the eternal core of England might have been appropriate but by 1993, as one newspaper leader column commented, John Major's recycling of all this was simply 'tosh… ah yes: that solid breakfast known as muesli, that winding road called the M25, that gloomy Sunday spent in Tesco, that bright-yellow field of rapeseed, that old mill town where the only smoke is on bonfire night, that pillar-box which may be privatised'.[1]

The sarcasm of the attacks on John Major were not surprising – English humour can be vicious – but Major was no fool. He personally was not swallowing all this sentimental tosh. He was using it to speak about and appease English nationalism in his own party, by reflecting back to the nationalists their own clichés, and insisting that they constituted an 'unamendable' self-image. It was a political message that 'English identity is safe with me'. But what is interesting even now is how John Major's speech hits on the constant notes of England's own song about itself, a series of themes which stretch back centuries – that England is not what it once was; that beloved England is disappearing, under foreign threats; and that the English in the past were better, stronger and more patriotic than they are now. The tune can be arranged differently, but the key notes are always the same: nostalgic pessimism.

Nostalgic Pessimism

Declinism and nostalgic pessimism are two of England's oldest traditions. The English writer Hugo Young in his book *This Blessed Plot*, published in 1998, dissected the United Kingdom's tortured relationship with Europe by concluding it was the story 'of fifty years in which Britain struggled to reconcile the past she could not forget with the future she could not avoid'. Brexit means that struggle for reconciliation has failed. The book's title comes from one of Shakespeare's most famous soliloquies, from one of his most famous Englishmen, John of Gaunt. The monologue from *Richard II*, Act 2 Scene 1 is also one of the most beautifully patriotic found anywhere in literature. It is a speech that every English schoolchild knows, often by heart, and it sets even my Scottish flesh tingling. But there is something quite strange about it which, as a student, I could not quite put my finger on. England, John of Gaunt tells us, was once great, but has made a mess of things in 'a shameful conquest of itself'. The sense is that the country had a great past 'she could not forget' but has now gone to the dogs. It's worth quoting in its entirety:

This royal throne of kings, this sceptred isle,
This earth of majesty, this seat of Mars,
This other Eden, demi-paradise,
This fortress built by Nature for herself
Against infection and the hand of war,
This happy breed of men, this little world,
This precious stone set in a silver sea
Which serves it in the office of a wall
Or as a moat defensive to a house,

Against the envy of less happier lands,
This blessed plot, this earth, this realm, this England,
This nurse, this teeming womb of royal kings,
Feared by their breed and famous for their birth,
Renownèd for their deeds as far from home
For Christian service and true chivalry
As is the sepulchre in stubborn Jewry
This land of such dear souls, this dear, dear land,
Dear for her reputation through the world,
Is now leased out – I die pronouncing it –
Like to a tenement or pelting farm.
England, bound in with the triumphant sea,
Whose rocky shore beats back the envious siege
Of watery Neptune, is now bound in with shame,
With inky blots and rotten parchment bonds.
That England that was wont to conquer others
Hath made a shameful conquest of itself.

This morose declaration of love of country must have seemed especially resonant in the year it was written, around 1585. It was a time of great uncertainty for England, just before the threatened invasion of the Spanish Armada, which was beaten back in 1588. It was also a time when the Protestant English Queen Elizabeth I stood alone against the vast Catholic powers of Spain and France as well as reckoning with the hostility of her rival to the north, the Catholic Mary Queen of Scots. There was uncertainty about the royal succession and even perhaps about whether 'this other Eden, demi-paradise' could survive as a beacon of the one true faith when surrounded by enemies in thrall to the pope. But forget if you can for a moment the poetry and dramatic genius of the speech. Instead look at the more banal question of geography and personal identity. Who was this John of Gaunt, this quintessential Englishman whose patriotic voice has resonated in England for centuries? He was Jean de Ghent – Belgian Johnny, a chap who had fetched up from the great medieval city in east Flanders. Jean de Ghent was no Englishman but a migrant who historically (if not dramatically) would have spoken in French, not the English of Shakespeare and the King James Bible. Among his achievements, Jean de Ghent introduced to the English a Poll Tax, a tax which every adult person over the age of fourteen was supposed to pay. Rather than a symbol of English glory, John of Gaunt and his Poll Tax were loathed by many ordinary Englishmen and women. Attempts to collect the hated tax became one of the contributory factors to the Peasants' Revolt of 1381.

None of this historical trivia would matter were it not for the way in which history has been misused and confused in our complicated twenty-first-century debates about our nations and British national identity in relation to Europe. History, as Napoleon Bonaparte once said, is a set of lies agreed upon. A conversation I had a decade or more ago with an English taxi driver, makes the point anecdotally in a different way. I had completed a BBC Radio 4 series on Britishness, in which I suggested in Benedict Anderson's phrase that nations are 'imagined communities'. We belong because we feel we belong, and we imagine what we mean by our national identity, especially in respect of being 'British', since the shape of Britain had changed so much over the years and would change again.[2]

The taxi driver, an avid radio listener, took exception to what he had heard in the broadcasts. In a tetchy conversation he told me that Britishness might be 'imagined' but Englishness was real. Britishness had no meaning for him because he was English 'through and through'. As a red-blooded Englishman he was 'fed up' with foreigners and immigrants 'taking over the country'. He went on to criticize the number of people of colour (although he did not use those words) on the BBC when he wanted to see 'English' faces. He meant white people. ('It's supposed to be the *British* Broadcasting Corporation for goodness sake.') The taxi driver also wanted what he called English jobs for English people, because migrants and foreigners were in some way 'taking over' the country. Pubs were closing because London was 'full of Muslims' who 'didn't drink' alcohol, which for him was a signifier of them not being English. In all this he said he wasn't being racist. I suppose in some ways that observation was correct. He was a xenophobe. He disliked equally all whom he considered foreigners, including some white people. Since I have lived more out of Scotland than in it, he probably did not clock that I was part of the Celtic hordes who had settled in England but who he wished had stayed at 'home'.

'We are all migrants,' I said. 'Everyone in Britain has roots somewhere else, including you.'

'Not me,' he protested. 'Pure English. Born in God's own country. English raised for generations. 100 per cent.'

I looked again at his taxi-driver ID card on display on the dashboard.

'But your last name is Fleming,' I said.

'So what?'

'That means your family at some point migrated to England from Flanders. They were called Fleming because they were Flemish. You are Belgian somewhere in your past.'

The driver did not have the fluency of Shakespeare's Jean de Ghent 400 years ago but he did have the same Belgian background and a similar attitude to England – a country he loved but which was now not as good as it should be. National identity as an act of imagination means that the nation we love is not always what we think it is. Daniel Defoe was correct when he wrote that 'A true-born Englishman's a contradiction / In speech an irony. In fact, a fiction.' But that's true of almost any country you can think of – especially since the phrase 'true-born' doesn't have any clear meaning. And yet the fiction persists.

The Tebbit Test

In April 1990 the former Conservative Party chairman Norman Tebbit approached the question of English identity from another angle, as a test. Tebbit wasn't worried about white people with Belgian names thinking they were true-born Englishmen. He was worried about people of colour from former British colonies who did not fit into his idea of British nationality. He decided that there was a simple way of finding them out. He came up with a question which became known as the Tebbit Test, and although he spoke of Britain he was (again) really thinking of England. He said that 'a large proportion of Britain's Asian population fail to pass the cricket test. Which side do they cheer for? It's an interesting test. Are you still harking back to where you came from or where you are?'

The obvious irony here is that it is Norman Tebbit doing the 'harking back' to an England in which he did not regularly come across people of a different skin colour to his own. Moreover, there is no British cricket team to cheer for, and so he was speaking only of England in remarks that constituted part of the 'othering' of sections of the British population in ways that have real consequences. When I have asked British friends of an Asian background whether they regard themselves as English, the reaction from many is a degree of incredulity. As one friend, whose family has been in London since they escaped the Partition of British India in 1947, put it to me, 'Would I see myself as English? Of course not! Don't be stupid! English people do not consider me English either.'

This friend has never expressed any interest in cricket, and if pushed to define her identity she would say she is a 'British Asian'. For her, 'British' is an inclusive identity in a way 'English' is not. Her parents and grandparents were citizens of the former British empire in British (not English) India. Moreover 'a large proportion' of Scots, Asian or otherwise, would also fail Tebbit's cricket test. Some Scots do play cricket, but it is not a national obsession as it is in parts of England, and when it comes to competitive sports most Scots would rather support small green monsters from the far side of the solar system than cheer on an English football team.

Another Conservative politician, the former party leader William Hague, offered in 1999 a personal, inclusive and more up-to-date list of things that he believed could reasonably be seen as part of a British identity. We were, he said,

the Britain of big industrial cities and housing estates, the Britain proud of its world-class designers and good restaurants, the Britain where hundreds of thousands go to the Notting Hill

Carnival and the Eisteddfod, the Britain which watches MTV and *Changing Rooms*, and which is fascinated by Ricky and Bianca's ups and downs, the Britain which turns to the sports pages before the political news, where more people go on holiday to Florida than Butlins, the Britain, in other words, that has always been Britain too: urban, ambitious, sporty, fashion-conscious, multi-ethnic, brassy, self-confident and international.

Mr Hague's list is certainly an attempt to capture some of our strengths and diversity. The former prime minister Gordon Brown did something similar with his own list:

In any survey our most popular institutions range from the monarchy to the army to the NHS... Perhaps Remembrance Day and Remembrance Sunday are the nearest we have come to a British day – unifying, commemorative, dignified and an expression of British ideas of standing firm for the world in the name of liberty... The union flag should be a British symbol of unity around our values... and we should assert that the union flag is for tolerance and inclusion.

William Hague, incidentally, is a Yorkshireman but his wife Ffion is Welsh, which may explain the appearance of the word 'Eisteddfod' in his list. Gordon Brown, as a Scot, was the least likely of these political leaders to confuse Britishness and Englishness, although his attempt to create a British National Day has disappeared without trace. Yet, as these examples show, defining national identity for any modern nation is fraught with difficulty, especially a diverse nation in which some feel tandoori chicken is a national dish as much as fish and chips and where 'warm beer' still exists but alongside Asahi, Peroni, prosecco, tequila shots and Aperol Spritz. Moreover Google, Facebook, Apple, Microsoft, Twitter, Netflix, Instagram, Uber, AirBnB – all American innovations – have internationalized modern culture along with Hollywood movies, pop music and access to holidays abroad for all but the least well-off Britons. Youth fashions are international to such an extent that a Korean boy band, England football supporters, grime stars, William Hague himself (at the Notting Hill Carnival) and even American presidents may all wear baseball caps without ever showing much interest in baseball. Casual sports fashion accessories worn while eating McDonalds washed down with the same brand of sweet fizzy drink are no bar to retaining a sense of national identity, but England has few overt signifiers of this. There is, for example, no obvious English national dress. Nevertheless, the search for an English identity repeatedly throws up two common themes that Shakespeare's Belgian John of Gaunt pitched so perfectly. The first is a sense of English exceptionalism, an island race blessed by God – 'this other Eden'. The second is a tone of loss and regret about the passing of England's greatness, the idea of the Fall from Grace. Taken together, these amount to the English talent for nostalgic pessimism which has become a debilitating affliction.

England's Ancestor Worship

From the very beginning of his *England: An Elegy* the conservative writer Roger Scruton is driven by nostalgic pessimism. 'What was England: a nation? A territory? A language? A culture? An Empire? An idea? All answers seem inadequate … the English enjoyed the strange privilege of knowing exactly who they were but not what they were.'[3] Scruton wryly notes that despite the English confusing their identity with Britishness 'only one group of Her Majesty's subjects saw itself as British: … immigrants'.[4] This is not quite right, as Scruton himself must have known. Even with the rise of English nationalism many English people, and plenty of Scots, Welsh and Northern Irish folk, still cling to a sense of British identity, from the marching bands and Orange Lodges of Ulster to those who remember the fallen on Remembrance Sunday. But part of Scruton's own under-scrutinized Englishness is that he is often willing to sacrifice factual accuracy and intellectual rigour for a quip or a neat turn of phrase. This is a vice shared with Prime Minister Boris Johnson. Here's another Scruton example: 'William the Conqueror was accepted as King because he promised to uphold the laws of England.'

The clue as to why William the Conqueror was 'accepted' as King of England is probably in the name by which he is remembered. He was called William the Conqueror by the English even though in Normandy he is better known as William the Bastard (Guillaume le Bâtard). William the Conqueror conquered. That ensured his 'acceptance'. The subject people of England did not have much choice. Scruton then goes on to say (for many, many pages) that the English 'instinctively knew who they were, without concepts like nationhood, Volk and culture'. This generalization about 'instinct' is another long-running delusion in English nationalism, as we will see. It is also demonstrably false, as my taxi driver Mr Fleming – 'instinctively' English since neolithic times despite his Flemish name – demonstrates. So does John Major's sentimental regurgitation of George Orwell and even Norman Tebbit's cricket test. And as for the English lacking concepts like 'Volk', Mr Scruton was simply wrong. Before his death in 2020 he lived through the Theresa May years, when the then prime minister constantly, insistently and eventually plaintively informed the world that Brexit was 'the will of the people', a phrase which translates nicely into German. For Mrs May, at least, a scant 52 per cent of the voting population constituted *Volksgemeinschaft* and *Triumph des Willens*. Perhaps Mr Scruton would have been closer to the mark had he written 'the English instinctively know who they are supposed to be, based on who they were told they were, but all that bears little or no resemblance to who they actually are'.

The most revealing part of Scruton's *England: An Elegy* is not the content. It's the fact that it is composed in the past tense. It is an obituary for a nation. His first sentence asks 'what *was* England?' He then goes on to say that the English 'knew' who they 'were', and that they 'bumbled on' and 'required so little explanation of their customs and institutions'. An elegy, as Scruton was well aware, is a tribute to the dead. Scruton's own Englishness is the self-pitying nostalgic pessimism of John of Gaunt, Norman Tebbit and the leading proponents of Brexit. It is sentimental tears shed for the loss of this other Eden. What Scruton and the others really demonstrate is the fear of change, the end of England as their own 'imagined community'. This fantasy England – white, upper-middle-class, rural, warm-beer-drinking, conservative, church-going – has for decades been replaced by the real England of kebab shops, Cool Britannia, *Kes*, *I, Daniel Blake*, Damien Hirst, grime, trans rights, Mo Farrah, the enlargement of university education beyond the narrow ground of Oxbridge, Tinder, Extinction Rebellion, Greggs vegan sausage rolls, Jürgen Klopp, and a list of thousands of cultural changes which make England what it is in reality – a complex, diverse, wonderful country where anything you can say about England is probably true.

The observations from Scruton and others who share his brand of complacent intellectual conservatism are the usual clichés which describe the narrow band of Englishness he sees when he looks in the mirror – white, male, public-school-educated and emotionally constipated. He and other English nationalist writers routinely observe that 'the English' are a 'reserved people'. Mr Scruton presumably never made it to Leeds, Manchester or Newcastle city centre on a Saturday night, or visited Glastonbury Festival or a Millwall or Liverpool home game. Then there is the idea that the English have hot-water bottles instead of a sex life. Not, presumably, the ones who end up shocking the locals in Ibiza and Ayia Napa by copulating on the beach or who end up on *Love Island*, or who become prime minister of the United Kingdom without being entirely clear about how many children they have fathered. England, in other words, is not exceptional in its belief in its own exceptionalism, but in reality it is quite like everywhere else in that it is a work in progress, a nation of constant reinvention and full of contradictions in which, unfortunately, the past is misremembered and regurgitated as myth. This can be harmless enough. But nostalgic pessimism, pining for the past, has the habit of blocking out rational consideration of the present and therefore the realities for the future. The *Dad's Army* theme song was right. Old England isn't done. It has been engaged upon a reinvention of Englishness, and that has created a new and at times problematic attachment to national – that is, English – symbols and emblems.

Which Flag?

Like all matters rooted in national identity, the English-British confusion is trivial until suddenly it is serious. A national flag can seem little more than a sheet of multicoloured cloth, until someone decides to desecrate it or wipe their feet on it or try to burn it. Then it becomes a symbol of something bigger, a lack of respect towards the 'imagined community' of a nation or national group. During the Vietnam War in 1968 Congress tried to outlaw flag burning in the United States. The US Supreme Court ruled that, however offensive it might be, flag burning was a protected form of free speech. In Northern Ireland flags are a constant source of friction with the red, white and blue of the Union Jack and the green, white and orange of the Irish tricolour constantly in contention. Fly the wrong flag in the wrong place and you may start a riot. Driving around West Belfast or Portadown in summer during what locals call 'the Marching Season', you can immediately spot which area you are in. The kerbstones in Protestant areas are often painted red, white and blue. Those in republican areas may bear the Irish national colours, green white and orange. Beyond Northern Ireland, an Ipsos Mori survey back in 1999 showed that national flags were of great importance in Wales and Scotland but *not* in England. For English people at the end of last century it was the British emblem, the Union Jack, which was much more significant. The survey concluded:

> In England, 88% identify with the Union Jack and only 38% with St George's Cross; but in Wales the dragon outscores the Union Jack by 85% to 55%, and while 75% of Scots identify with the Saltire only 49% do with the Union Jack. This 'Britishness', if not exactly an English invention, is now primarily an English survival.

If two decades ago England was the last bastion of the survival of Union Jack flag-waving Britishness, that bastion has now fallen. Until recently English people were often hesitant at the idea of identifying with England's St George's Flag, since it had become associated with the far right and racist groups. But that has changed. In *The Dog That Finally Barked: England as an Emerging Political Community*, the IPPR:

> presents evidence which suggests the emergence of a new kind of Anglo-British identity *in which the English component is increasingly the primary source of attachment for English people.* It also suggests that English identity is becoming more politicised: that is, the more English a person feels, *the more likely they are to believe that the current structure of the UK is unfair* and to support a particularly English dimension to the governance of England. It has long been predicted that devolution to Scotland, Wales and Northern Ireland would provoke an English 'backlash' against the anomalies and apparent territorial inequities of a devolved UK state. The evidence presented here suggests the emergence of what might be called an 'English political community', one marked by notable concerns within England about the seeming privileges of Scotland in particular and a growing questioning of the capacity of the current UK-level political institutions to pursue and defend English interests, and one underpinned by a deepening sense of English identity. (My italics.)

The evidence is here for all to see, literally. England's St George's flag is now much more widely in evidence than in the past, when it was often confined to England football matches and could be regarded with a degree of suspicion. Politicians who blunder into discussions about the English flag nowadays do so at their peril. Emily Thornberry is the Labour MP for the quintessentially metropolitan north London constituency of Islington South. In 2014 she was forced to resign as shadow attorney general after posting on Twitter a picture of a house in Rochester, Kent draped with three large England flags and with a white van parked outside. The Tweet was criticized as snobbish and out of touch, and seen as a symptom of why the Labour Party was losing English working-class votes. A Welsh Labour Party candidate for the Ceredigion constituency, Huw Thomas, was also forced to apologize in 2015 for suggesting (some years earlier) that Tippex be thrown on cars displaying English flags. He had claimed that the flags were displayed by people who were simpletons or casual racists. Mr Thomas was making an offensive generalization about a symbol whose popularity has grown even if – in the view of some English commentators – what they call the 'detoxification' process for St George's flag still has a long way to go.

'The English as the Unspoken People'

Labour's haemorrhage of support in English working-class communities proved decisive in the December 2019 General Election. The party lost a string of so-called 'Red Wall' seats in mainly working-class areas of northern England. Under Jeremy Corbyn the party appeared to former Labour voters as if it were incapable of understanding any kind of patriotic feeling for Britain, the British military and British foreign policy, or for the pride many people take in the nations of England and Scotland. Corbyn's 'solidarity' with the IRA and Middle East terrorist groups meant that he was attacked even within his own party for his sympathy for every kind of nationalism except that of ordinary people in his own country. Labour paid the price. As well as suffering disastrous losses in working-class English constituencies, Labour was once again almost wiped out in Scotland.

In an attempt to address part of the perceived problem with Englishness and identity, activists within the Labour Party in 2017 formed the English Labour Network. The ELN called for a specific manifesto for England aimed at understanding and addressing the growing sense of English identity. In February 2020, following the party's catastrophic defeat at the ballot box, the ELN produced a damning report, *General Election 2019: How Labour Lost England.* The report said the party had 'for many years… gone out of its way to alienate voters who emphasise their English identity' and had failed even to consider the existence of the English Question. The report highlighted the fact that:

> the Conservatives' election victory was almost entirely in England and amongst voters whose *primary national identity is English*... Labour has a long-standing and deepening crisis in its relationship with English voters that must be addressed if the party is ever to win again... in 2019 the party failed to make any attempt to address English voters or the governance of England.' (My italics.)

The report concluded that 'there is no path back to power that doesn't run through England and English voters'.[5]

Two of the ELN activists, John Denham and Gareth Young, went even further, writing that:

> where once politicians spoke of England when they meant Britain, motivating calls for devolution and separation in Scotland and Wales, they now speak of Britain when they mean England, leaving the English as the unspoken people. Four out of five residents identify strongly as English, but much of the liberal left insists that Englishness belongs to the far right. For both left and right, acknowledging that England is a nation and a democratic political community raises uncomfortable questions about why England is governed by the UK Parliament and not by its own elected MPs. The Conservative Government depends on the DUP. The last Labour government used Celtic MPs to pass English laws.[6]

England Speaks Up

England's 'unspoken people' have now spoken, at least about what they do not want, and that included the Corbynite Labour Party. Those on the Labour left and English Marxist intellectuals more generally have often proved incapable of understanding the genuine passion English, Scottish, Welsh and Northern Irish people feel for their own sense of national identity, while showing empathy for the nationalist feelings of states and armed groups that have been enemies of their own nation, including the IRA. Jeremy Corbyn's key adviser, Seamus Milne, was formerly a prominent journalist on *The Guardian* newspaper. As an opinion writer he even defended the legacy of Stalin, noting that 'the number of victims of Stalin's terror has been progressively inflated over recent years', and omitting to remind readers that Stalin and Hitler were acting together at the start of the Second World War, carving up another sovereign nation, Poland, between them.[7] When the Scottish political theorist Tom Nairn wrote of the break-up of Britain in 1977 and advocated Scotland's place in a more integrated Europe, his most strident critics were also on the Labour and communist left, those who find nationalist sentiment politically awkward. If the left consigns those increasing numbers of people who feel themselves strongly English to the political right, then it is hardly surprising that those same people will reject at the ballot box those in Labour who have rejected them and their values. They will turn, indeed they have turned, to UKIP, the Brexit Party and the Conservatives instead.

While English nationalist sentiment has grown, it lacks some of the coherence of the other nationalisms on these islands, perhaps through lack of practice. Most Scots can tell you when Burns night takes place, 25 January, or that St Andrew's Day is 30 November. Most Welsh people will know when to celebrate St David's Day, 1 March. Everyone Irish – and millions of us who are not – know St Patrick's Day falls on 17 March. In an interview with me a few years ago the former Essex Conservative MP Teresa Gorman once claimed that English people needed to be much more proud of their Englishness. When I agreed with her sentiments but asked how that could be achieved she suggested creating a new holiday on St George's Day. I then asked her when she would celebrate it.

'On St George's Day.'

'But when is St George's Day?'

'March sometime,' she replied with the vague confidence of a veteran politician.

St George's Day falls on 23 April.

I was struck at the time that an English nationalist Conservative MP didn't know when she should celebrate her own national day. How very English, you might say. Incidentally, England's St George was a dragon-slaying Greek. Ireland's St Patrick was a Roman Briton from what we now call Wales. Scotland's St Andrew was one of the (Jewish) Apostles and brother of St Peter. He'd have had a hard time reaching Scotland. England is not the only nation which has a lazy sense of national identity and a fairly random selection of supposed heroes who may have been 'true-born' somewhere, but nowhere near the countries they have come to symbolize.

The Race Question: Where Are You From?

The underlying question for the United Kingdom in the twenty-first century, then, is what Britain, British or Britishness mean. Do people in these islands consider themselves primarily English, Scottish, Welsh, Irish, Ulster or some other signifier of identity? And whatever your personal preference, is Britishness a significant part of the mix? If so, what does that mean in practical terms for how we can bring the United Kingdom together, given that nationalism is a feeling as much as a set of characteristics?

The changing figures on identity reveal a change in mindset. In the 2011 census, 80.5 per cent of people in England and Wales declared they were White or White British, and 19.5 per cent said they were from ethnic minorities. 'White' according to the UK government website means:

English / Welsh / Scottish / Northern Irish / British
Irish
Gypsy or Irish Traveller
Any other White background

(The censuses in Scotland and Northern Ireland had a different ordering and nomenclature for ethnic groups.) The most ethnically diverse region was London, where almost half, 40.2 per cent, of residents identified with either the Asian, Black, Mixed or Other ethnic group. London had the smallest percentage of White British people, at 44.9 per cent, while the north-east of England had the highest percentage, at 93.6 per cent.

The Office for National Statistics commented on the 2011 census results (England and Wales only):

English identity (either on its own or combined with other identities) was the most common identity respondents chose to associate with, at 37.6 million people (67.1 per cent). English as a sole identity (not combined with other identities), was chosen by 32.4 million people (57.7 per cent). British identity (either on its own or combined with other identities) was a common identity chosen by 16.3 million people (29.1 per cent). 10.7 million people (19.1 per cent) associated themselves with a British identity only. Welsh identity (either on its own or combined with other identities) was chosen by 2.4 million people (4.3 per cent). 2 million people (3.7 per cent) associated themselves with a Welsh only identity.[8]

A number of things are clear from these figures, even though the census is now out of date. First, there has been a significant growth in the numbers of people in England who consider that Englishness is their 'sole identity'. This group is three times greater than those who consider their sole identity as 'British'. But it is also clear that of the 19.1 per cent of people in England and Wales who consider themselves British, a very significant number are from ethnic minority or migrant communities. Surveys talk of Black British, Asian British and White British as identities, but do not speak of Black *English* or Asian *English* – perhaps because English officialdom considered at least until recently that to be 'English' meant to be white. The website openDemocracy noted among other things that 'the 2011 National

Census… is something of a misnomer, as the Census has in fact been devolved: there are separate Censuses for England and Wales, Scotland and Northern Ireland', and, as the writer David Rickard pointed out:

> In England and Wales, 'non-white' persons are not offered the option of including 'English' or 'Welsh' as part of their ethnic-group identity: they're classified only as 'Black British' or 'Asian British', and not 'Black English' or 'Asian Welsh', for instance. By contrast, black and Asian persons living in Scotland are permitted to identify as 'Black Scottish' and 'Asian Scottish'.[9]

Where Are You From?

In *BRIT(ish)*, her memoir of growing up in a mixed-race family in Wimbledon, a predominantly middle-class area of London, the writer Afua Hirsch speaks of her own confusion over Britishness and the challenges which come with it:

> everywhere I went I was other… as British people ours are identities that have played themselves out as a nation where these things are not talked about openly… It's the muting of the conversation – the fact that we cannot in Britain today cope with exploring and accommodating these identities in a healthy way – that is the issue… I do believe that, as an example of an intense, unrelenting search for a kind of Britishness I can belong to, my experience may offer an insight into where we are headed as a nation.[10]

She then points out what she calls a 'daily ritual of unsettling', in which people of colour are constantly asked 'the Question' – where are you from?:

> The Question is both a symptom and a cause. It's a symptom of the fact that we don't really know what it is to be British.

Is someone like me included? Don't know, people think, better ask. And there goes The Question. It's also the cause. The more you get asked The Question the more confused you feel about the answer. I can't be British, can I, if British people keep asking me where I'm from? I must be something else.[11]

However confused the answer then becomes, neither Afua Hirsch nor any people of colour I know personally describe themselves as 'Black English' or 'Asian English', preferring Black British and Asian British. Hirsch's search is 'for a kind of Britishness', not Englishness. And people from ethnic minorities may of course be 'othered' or made to feel not English or un-British in even more unpleasant ways, being yelled at in the street and told to 'go home', when 'home' is Peckham or Birmingham or Glasgow or Cardiff. And there is a different type of 'othering' when people of colour – and only people of colour – are accused of 'playing the race card'. To take one example, in May 2018, after the royal wedding of Prince Harry to Meghan Markle, the journalist Yasmin Alibhai-Brown Tweeted: 'Is it safe to be back on Twitter? Have people – including royal wedding journalist junkies – run out of breath yet? Proof again that GB is an infantilised, escapist nation.'

Yasmin Alibhai-Brown's family are British Asians. They escaped from Idi Amin's Uganda and settled in the UK. The Conservative MP and later government health minister Nadine Dorries responded: 'Yasmin, why don't you just try to be nice? Maybe appreciate just a little the country and the people you have chosen to live, work and benefit from all of your life.' This quickly degenerated: 'Seriously, Yasmin, the last time you and I were together you apologised to me for being so "hateful". Below you to play the race card, you're better than that. Have a nice day.' The Conservative writer Tim Montgomerie joined the row by again repeating the phrase 'playing the race card'.

As someone who knows all three of these interlocutors, I asked Nadine Dorries and Tim Montgomerie why it was only people of colour who were accused of 'playing the race card'. Didn't the Conservative government of Theresa May 'play the race card' over the

Windrush scandal, or when they sent 'Go Home' vans round some areas of Britain's inner cities telling supposedly illegal migrants that they could be thrown out? Nadine Dorries replied to me with a polite private message. Tim Montgomerie did not respond. Yasmin's comments about the royal wedding were perhaps ungracious, but she is entitled to her opinion and anyone – including Nadine Dorries and Tim Montgomerie – are entitled to challenge her on that opinion. But suggesting 'the race card' is being played has an unspoken yet clear message. In the world of increasingly febrile English identity politics, Yasmin Alibhai-Brown (M.Phil. from Oxford, one-time Columnist of the Year, author, self-described 'leftie liberal anti-racist, feminist, Muslim') has a British passport but she is apparently not British enough to criticize a British institution and will never be English enough for some people, or perhaps never considered English at all. You could conclude that some white people play the 'race card' all the time in defining who they regard as 'one of us' and who they think is therefore qualified to criticize 'our' institutions.

Afua Hirsch writes of race in terms of an integration which depends upon the erasure of 'otherness':

Britishness, as an identity, is in crisis. It is still linked in the imaginations of people of all races to the concept of whiteness. A 2017 poll found that more than half of the British population felt the presence of people from ethnic minorities threatened their culture. Not surprisingly, there is widespread distrust in the language of integration. It's the only answer political leaders currently have to offer and represents the unspoken hope that eventually these visible 'others' will have their otherness neutralised by British culture. They will eventually disappear, leaving nothing more than a trace of curly hair, a splash of extra freckles, a liberal, harmless version of a foreign faith, or the memory of a funny-sounding name, their culture blending seamlessly into the mainstream British experience.[12]

The former Conservative government minister Baroness Sayeeda

Warsi suggested that Scots may have been more successful than the English at integrating black and Asian groups within an inclusive national-ethnic identity. There are certainly racists in Scotland, as well as religious and sectarian bigots, but Scotland has tried to act positively to encourage integration. To take one example: since the year 2000, Sikh tartans have been registered in Scotland. The comedian and broadcaster Hardeep Singh Kohli is one of a number of tartan- and kilt-wearing Scottish Sikhs, with his tartan matching his turban. Chinese, Polish, Jewish and other groups have explored the idea of registering their own tartans. But in England, devoid as we noted, of a distinctive national dress, such a symbol of the inclusivity of 'Englishness' is lacking. What would we choose? Bowler hats? The uniforms of Morris dancers? And there is also the surprising lack of availability of more inclusive categories of identity in the English 2011 census. But there is something worse. On the fringes of English nationalism there exists a growing sense of grievance that has raised the profile of a racist and sometimes violent minority. These nationalist extremists blame immigrants for what they see as the decline of their traditional communities. Nostalgic pessimism has slipped into tribalism and racism.

Extremism and Intellectual Failure

Jeremy Black, professor of history at Exeter University, argues that the phenomenon of English nationalism has become so significant that it deserves much more thoughtful study, but this is often lacking:

Having argued for long that states are artificial constructions, intellectuals have failed to confront the issue that England exists, and that its role and character are being pushed to the fore as the stability of the United Kingdom comes under increasing pressure, notably from the ambitions of Scottish nationalism. English nationalism is too important to be left to the extremists.[13]

The importance of English nationalism, the rise of extremism and the sense of Britain in decline has echoes elsewhere. A similar process is clearly visible in the rise of populist and far-right parties in Eastern Europe, Germany, France, Italy and also the United States. Donald Trump built his political career on tapping into America's nostalgic pessimism in four words – 'Make America Great Again'. This begs the obvious and unanswered question, when did America cease being great? The USA remains the world's largest economy, by far the world's biggest military power and has the world's most sought-after consumer products and technical innovations.

In the late 1990s I travelled around forty-eight of the fifty US states and wrote a book called *The United States of Anger*. It was an exploration of a very obvious paradox of the years of the Clinton presidency. As the United States became even more dominant as the last remaining superpower, with the collapse of the Soviet Union in 1989, very many middle-income and working-class Americans that I met were angry or unhappy with their personal lives and disappointed with the way things were turning out for their children and families. This feeling seemed at first very odd. America in the 1990s was the core not just of the global economy but also of the world's cultural life, with its Hollywood movies, rock and hip-hop music, its vastly popular TV programmes, and American products from Boeing aircraft to Apple computers and Microsoft operating systems. American innovations such as Google and Facebook were taking over the world. Yet the mainly middle-income Americans I talked with felt that the system was in some way rigged against them and that their lives were not as good as the lives of their parents in the 1950s and 60s. The fact that on the evening news they heard that the stock market was booming, home ownership was up and unemployment was low in those late Clinton years didn't make them feel better about their own lives; quite the reverse. There was a conflict between the wonderful statistics they heard about their nation and the lives they actually were living. America in the aggregate didn't chime with the anecdotal America of their real experience.

A police officer in Annapolis, Maryland – a man with a US flag proudly displayed over his house – summed up the difference for me: 'Bill Clinton says he has created 11 million new jobs since he became president,' the police officer told me. 'Sure he has. And I have four of them.' He worked six days in a row in uniform then in his three days off he worked as a security guard at a bingo parlour, a marina and a business complex, then went back to work for the police department. Work never stopped. His wife also worked. This patriotic American had a profound sense that life for him was not as good as it had been for his parents, and the statistics of the stock market and low unemployment did not cheer him up. In fact, they made him even more angry about what he thought was his loss of a share of the American Dream.

In Britain in the twenty-first century something similar has been occurring. There is a disjunction, especially noticeable in working-class areas of England-outside-London, between the lives people lead, their memories of how things were for their parents in their towns and communities and what they are being told by experts. The better the statistics – low unemployment, booming house prices – in some cases the greater is the anger in communities where the sense of decline and loss of status is real. The left-wing writer Owen Jones recounts stories that bear out this phenomenon. In his 2011 book on the demonization of the English working class, *Chavs*, Jones offers an insight into a very different England from the clichéd stiff upper lips and gentlemanly reserve of Roger Scruton's elegiac portrait of country house England or John Major's long shadows on the county cricket grounds. Jones's focus is relentlessly on working-class English people who have reasons to be angry not just about the struggles of their daily lives but at the way they are laughed at and portrayed as feckless, lazy and hopeless by those in power and in vast swathes of popular culture. Jones points out that John Lennon's 'working-class heroes' are no longer 'something to be'. Often working-class English men and women are not even given the opportunity to find meaningful work. Jones points to the profound consequences of deindustrialization and the marginalization of groups of people who in the past had played such a central role in the British economy. The steel workers, miners and shipbuilders who literally built Britain have seen their industries eclipsed by foreign competitors, their communities impoverished by the lack of skilled work, and they themselves have been demonized as unthinking uncultured ruffians – chavs. The jobs which are available – in fast-food shops, as delivery drivers, Uber drivers or in Amazon warehouses – are precarious, often unskilled and less prestigious. The statistics of life in the UK tell them unemployment is low, but so is the pay. These jobs are unrewarding in every sense.

Worse, in Jones's analysis, is a lack of self-worth. Key figures in the political classes have a habit of blaming the victims for their multiple problems. Here's former prime minister David Cameron:

> We talk about people being at risk of poverty or social exclusion: it's as if these things – obesity, alcohol abuse, drug addiction – are purely external events like a plague or bad weather. Of course circumstances – where you are born, your neighbourhood, your school and the choices your parents make – have a huge impact. But social problems are often the consequence of the choices people make.[14]

People do make bad choices. But this empathy-free lecture on self-reliance and personal responsibility was delivered by a politician who described his own background in these terms: 'I have the most corny CV possible. It goes: Eton, Oxford, Conservative Research Department, Treasury, Home Office, Carlton TV and then Conservative MP.' As Jones wryly points out, Cameron describes his wife's upbringing as 'highly unconventional' because 'she went to a day school'. David Cameron's father was a stockbroker and controlled investments worth millions of pounds in a number of offshore tax havens. Cameron inherited a great deal of money. His wife, the daughter of a hereditary baronet, is also extremely wealthy. Cameron's CV is not 'corny', but it is disconnected from the England in which most people live.

And yet David Cameron was quite sympathetic to the woes of the English working class in comparison with his more right-wing colleagues. A year after Jones's book was published, in 2012 a group of English Conservative MPs including future high-flyers Dominic Raab, Elizabeth Truss, Priti Patel and Kwasi Kwarteng, published a book claiming that British workers are 'among the worst idlers in the world'. Britain, they claimed, 'rewards laziness', and 'too many people in Britain prefer a lie-in to hard work'. Taken together – cultural ridicule, nasty tropes about English working-class culture, shocking contempt from right-wing Westminster MPs, failed traditional industries and poor educational opportunities to prepare for a high-skilled information economy, the rise of English nationalism is not just understandable. It is inevitable. What is also understandable is why on the fringes it tips into political extremism.

Defending England

In *The Rise of the Right*, a book published in 2017, the sociologists Simon Winlow, Steve Hall and James Treadwell examined how English nationalism, in their words, is responsible for 'the transformation of working-class politics'. Their central thesis echoes that of Owen Jones in *Chavs*, stating that English working-class communities have lost economic power and a degree of self-respect over the past thirty or so years, hollowed out when neo-liberal economic orthodoxy was embraced by the British Labour Party. A reader doesn't have to buy into either the authors' political message or their at times clumsy jargon to find value in the interviews they conducted with far-right working-class activists from the English Defence League (EDL).

In the interviews two trends are apparent. The first is that age-old idea that in some past Golden Age everything in England was better. In the EDL's case the other Eden was a time before people of colour and especially Muslims arrived in England. England's nostalgic pessimism and sense of decline therefore runs in an unbroken line from John of Gaunt to Roger Scruton and on to EDL Islamophobes grumbling in the pub and fighting on the streets. They are negative towards all traditional democratic political activity. They deride political leaders, in particular in the Labour Party, the party almost certainly supported by their fathers and grandfathers. These EDL supporters appear however to contradict the basic thesis of the book – that it is Labour's adoption under Tony Blair of neo-liberal policies that has led to the rise of right-wing extremism. In fact, the EDL supporters were most appalled by Jeremy Corbyn's Labour Party, which appears irrelevant to their concerns. Corbyn's focus on cultural issues rather than traditional left-wing core values centring on economic injustice were of no interest to them. Mr Corbyn did, of course, make speeches on economic injustice, but his views on cultural and international injustices – trans-rights, the plight of the Chagos islanders, solidarity with the Venezuela of Chávez and Maduro, with Sinn Féin in Ireland, his reluctance to criticize Vladimir Putin and other matters – are not simply the creation of a hostile media. He cared deeply about such subjects but in ways these working-class EDL activists clearly do not. Despite the idea that Tony Blair's economic policies in government were to blame, as the authors write, 'The truth is that they saw Jeremy Corbyn as a do-gooding, weak-as-piss hippy pacifist.'[15]

It's worth quoting some of the interviews at length. Among the most obvious themes are loathing of people who go to universities – the 'elite'; hatred of politicians, the kind of hatred that led to the 2016 murder of the Labour MP Jo Cox; fury at the mainstream media and the educated middle class. The EDL has, in Michael Gove's phrase, 'had enough of experts'. Above all, there is a sense of loss and decline permeating all the interviews. Here's a selection:

> Steppy: 'We're the poor man of Europe now. We used to have an Empire, for fuck's sake… You've got people in Labour and the Conservatives that used to go to school together. They went to university together, lots of them. Then you find out that the news reporters and all the people on TV actually know each other, know the politicians, their kids go to the same schools, stuff like that. It's a stitch-up, mate… they're all pals.'[16]

Jake: 'The people in power and the middle class are ashamed to call themselves English. If you listen to them, they expect you to identify as British, liberal and tolerant. If you call yourself an English nationalist some people see that as a provocation and a badge you're racist and intolerant... I'm English. I see England as my country, not Scotland... or Wales... I'm not British. I'm English. I don't follow the British football team. I believe in keeping English jobs for English people first.'[17]

Damien: 'English nationalism is opposed by middle-class pricks that don't know what life is really like when you live on a shitty fucking estate where everything is disappearing except the fucking foreign faces.'[18]

The authors concluded that their many interviewees 'were concerned mostly with values and traction and they could see no evidence that Muslims were willing to commit to the basic principles of the English way of life. The "English way of life" was also poorly sketched out. Our contacts certainly could not agree on what it was, beyond the idea that Muslims refused to adopt its principles.'[19] This is an important point. These EDL supporters have a world view divided between 'us' and 'them'. They have absolutely clear views about 'them' – Muslim men who don't go to the pub; Muslim women who wear hijabs; people of colour. But they cannot define 'us' or the supposedly 'English way of life'. They are filled with prejudice about others, and yet their lives are a vacuum of understanding about the Englishness their 'league' is trying to defend. It is as if they have organized to protect unicorns. The anger and bigotry is nasty, but it is also rather sad, even if – as we will explore in more detail later – their sense of grievance is real, and there is some truth in their assumption that many politicians and journalists are part of the same elite, with similarly privileged backgrounds, including private education and study at elite universities.

The anger and bigotry of those of a similar mindset to the EDL supporters burst into view after the Black Lives Matter demonstrations following the killing of an African American man, George Floyd, by white police officers in Minneapolis in May 2020. The demonstrations which took place across the United States were echoed from Belgium to Australia. In England in June 2020 activists in Bristol removed the statue of the entrepreneur and slave trader Edward Colston and dramatically threw it into Bristol Harbour. There were some further acts of vandalism on statues, including spray paint on that of Winston Churchill in London's Parliament Square. A mob of angry white men, no doubt some of them connected with the English Defence League, descended on London claiming to 'defend' the Churchill statue. One of their number was arrested and sentenced to fourteen days in prison for urinating beside a memorial to a police officer who had died protecting parliament from a terrorist attack. Others faced off with the police and offered Nazi salutes, without apparently recognizing the incongruity of doing so near Churchill's statue, the Englishman who did more than any other to defeat Hitler.

The *Rise of the Right* authors suggest that English nationalism is a reflection of Sigmund Freud's theory of the difference between mourning and melancholia. Mourning is an acceptance that a loved one has gone. We are sad but we move on. Melancholy is very different. Freud defined melancholia as a *refusal* to accept that something or someone has gone. It therefore becomes a pathological attachment to something which is dead, and, unlike mourning, no amount of time will heal melancholia. Freud asserts that the melancholic projects a kind of destructive death wish into him- or herself, resulting in 'an impoverishment of the ego on a grand scale'. This is a profound feeling of worthlessness, partly because the melancholic doesn't know precisely what he has lost but is sure that he has lost his self-respect and value, and more or less explicitly blames someone or something else for this loss. The authors believe that:

> supporters of the EDL display a fetishistic attachment to the lost historical object of traditional English proletarian culture. They refuse to accept the loss of their traditional way of life. Their decaying communities and dilapidated neighbourhoods

are enshrouded in melancholy. They know that this lost world cannot be brought back into existence. However for the moment this knowledge is too disturbing to be accepted consciously... The anger these men carry with them springs from sadness and fear.[20]

Who Are You?

EDL supporters have no membership lists, no political programme and a ramshackle organization. But they do have one big interest – football. They are men who have joined a 'league' to 'defend' England. The EDL was founded in 2009 and remained quite prominent until 2013, when it began to decline. This decline came as Nigel Farage, UKIP and subsequently the Brexit Party gave voice to the previously unvoiced fears of English nationalism before losing that role to the Conservative Party in 2019. The EDL began around groups of football hooligans, essentially as a far-right Islamophobic hate group. Its political activism involved mainly street demonstrations and the threat of violence, although they were also energetic keyboard warriors, nasty anonymous trolls on YouTube, Twitter and Facebook. On Twitter they can be easy to spot – an obviously phoney name, football references in their biography and quite often a Twitter picture of flags and a hallowed football ground. In their street demonstrations, supporters at times conform to precisely the 'chav' stereotype Owen Jones tried to overturn – violent, drunken and tribal. Their public demonstrations peaked at around 2,000 people, but many EDL events were simply a few hundred strong, the equivalent of attendance at an English non-league football club game on a wet Saturday in February.

Turned off from traditional politics, alienated by Jeremy Corbyn's Labour Party, ridiculed, despised and feared in the media and popular culture, the EDL and similar groups epitomized the wilder reaches of English nationalism. Nevertheless, in working-class communities the flags and symbols of their kind of English nationalism became increasingly prominent, lending visual coherence to their views as well as their fanatical loyalty to the English national football team.

They were driven, as Jeremy Black puts it, by a nationalism which was 'a feeling as much as a principle'.[21]

Sam Tarry, an east London anti-racism campaigner, spoke of the phenomenon as he'd watched it develop in Barking and Dagenham:

> We've seen a switch to a sort of English nationalism and you'll see a lot of white families deliberately hanging out the English flag from their windows almost as though they are staking out the territory in a slightly aggressive, non-inclusive way. For me there is an element which I can't quite put my finger on about this sense of what it means to be from a working-class background: what it means to be English and where your sense of identity and purpose and direction actually now come from.[22]

The (Bad) Health of the Nation

It's worth noting that this division within England between rich and poor, privileged and under-privileged, educated and less-well-educated was exacerbated by a political decision – the austerity enforced on Britain after the financial crash of 2008. These divisions had consequences beyond the increase in English nationalist sentiment and the growth of the far right. A health-care study published in 2020 suggested that for many English people life expectancy in the twenty-first century was going into reverse. The report, by Professor Sir Michael Marmot, one of Britain's leading experts on health inequalities, said life expectancy in England had stalled over the previous decade, for the first time in a century. Among women living in the poorest communities in England life expectancy had declined since 2011, and health outcome inequalities were growing.

'England has lost a decade,' Professor Marmot concluded. The damage to the nation's health was 'shocking'.[23]

While the largest decreases were in the most deprived areas of north-east England, some areas saw increases. The biggest increases in positive health outcomes were in the richest parts of London, a place where you rarely see the flag of St George hanging from windows. The rich–poor life-expectancy gap in England has become a difference of 9.5 years for men and 7.7 years for women. The rich–poor divide was equally true of the coronavirus pandemic. A pandemic – a global epidemic – affects everyone, but it is not an equal opportunity killer. In preliminary figures published in May 2020 the Office for National Statistics, Britain's most trusted source of facts and figures, reported 55.1 deaths per 100,000 citizens in the 10 per cent most deprived areas of England. The figures in the 10 per cent least deprived areas were 25 deaths in 100,000.

There is nothing new in the idea that rich people will live longer than the poor, but the map of declining health outcomes again more or less coincided with areas where the majority of people expressed their discontent with their lives by voting to leave the EU, for Nigel Farage's UKIP and for its successor, the Brexit Party. Poverty, one might conclude, results in a poverty of opportunity and also a poverty of expectations.

The key question underlying all of this – flags, census categories, the rise of far-right English nationalism – is whether the idea of an inclusive Britishness persists. The evidence for such a sentiment is thin. If EDL activists appear somewhat confused about the English-ness they were defending, Britishness in the twenty-first century is even more difficult to define. Perhaps the rhetoric of Boris Johnson demanding that we all pull together against coronavirus as if in a war will ultimately reinforce some sense of Britishness as a struggle against a common enemy, but if it takes a pandemic to rebuild a sense of a national identity, you may conclude that Britain really is in trouble.

Why This Matters

The backward-looking pessimism of commentaries about England, from Roger Scruton's elegy to the whingeing in the pub, are full of something much worse than fear-of-change sentiments and nostalgia.

They are also profoundly complacent. This complacency stretches to the top of the Westminster government and consequently blights the possibility of creatively setting a course for a better future for the United Kingdom. One striking example is provided by the man chosen by Prime Minister Boris Johnson to lead British negotiations with the European Union, David (now Lord) Frost (St Johns, Oxford, MA in French and History). David Frost's career was as a civil servant, Foreign Office official and former UK ambassador to Denmark, chief negotiator with the EU and then promoted by Mr Johnson to become his national security adviser.

In February 2020 David Frost – the key player in the biggest and boldest political decision taken in Britain since 1945 – delivered what he clearly thought was a speech of considerable intellectual heft at ULB Brussels university. It was a model of a certain kind of Englishness at work in public life. Mr Frost outlined the principles guiding his and the British government's thinking in the negotiations over a deal with the EU. Frost began by quoting Edmund Burke (born, incidentally, in Dublin) and a passage from Burke's *Reflections on the French Revolution*:

> The state ought not to be considered as nothing better than a partnership agreement in a trade of pepper and coffee, calico or tobacco, or some other such low concern... It is to be looked on with reverence... It is a partnership in all science; a partnership in all art; a partnership in every virtue, and in all perfection.

Frost goes on to set out what he sees – and supports – as the impetus behind the 2016 Brexit vote, the rise of nationalism, or, as he puts it:

> the reappearance on the political scene not just of national feeling but also of the wish for national decision-making and the revival of the nation state. Brexit is the most obvious example for that, but who can deny that we see something a bit like it in different forms across the whole continent of Europe? I don't think it is right to dismiss this just as a reaction to austerity

or economic problems or a passing phase, or something to be 'seen off' over time. I believe it is something deeper. Actually, I don't find it surprising – *if you can't change policies by voting, as you increasingly can't in this situation – then opposition becomes expressed as opposition to the system itself.* (My italics.)

It is true that nationalism and the revival of ideas about the nation-state have indeed been in the ascendant across Europe. So has anti-EU sentiment, and 'opposition to the system itself' in populist revolts from Italy to Hungary and in the Tea Party movement and Trumpism in the United States. But the 'national feeling' behind Brexit is *English* national feeling, not British. The 'revival of the nation state' is not the same as the revival of a United Kingdom of several nations. Frost does not reflect on the fact that 'opposition to the system itself' has also become a key factor in Scottish, Welsh and Irish nationalist opposition to the Westminster system. Nor does he mention that the 4 million English nationalist voters who supported Nigel Farage and UKIP in 2015 could not 'change policies by voting' because the outdated British electoral system would not let them do so and unfairly left them with just one seat in parliament. This systemic unfairness had nothing whatsoever to do with being in the European Union. It had everything to do with being part of Britain. But then Frost goes completely off-piste.

He speaks of the EU's development as a series of deliberate and agreed designs to create new mechanisms to bring its members together. That's true. But then in a blast of English exceptionalism he claims that somehow the United Kingdom doesn't really work that way, and that the UK 'evolves' rather than designs its political systems. The tone is one of arrogant complacency, as if the English are gifted amateurs who have stumbled across the secret of a much better way of governance than Johnny Foreigner with all his clever schemes:

So in a country like Britain where institutions *just evolved* and where governance is pretty deep-rooted in historical precedent, it was always going to feel *a bit unnatural* to a lot of people to be governed by an organisation whose institutions seemed *created by design* more than by evolution, and which vested authority outside the country elsewhere. (My italics.)

Frost speaks as if designing the institutions of government is some kind of unnatural vice to which foreigners are prone and the English are immune. Then towards the end of his speech he returns to the principles upon which he will base his negotiating strategy with the EU:

One of those fundamentals is that we are *negotiating as one country*. To return again to Burke, his conception of the state was and is one that allows for differences, for different habits, and for different customs. It is one which means that our own multi-state union in the UK has grown in different ways across the EU – each playing unique roles in its historical development. It is actually rather fashionable at the moment amongst some to run down that state which has been very successful historically. We cannot be complacent about the Union in the UK, but I nevertheless believe that all parts of the UK are going to survive and thrive together as one country. In particular, I am clear that I am negotiating on behalf of Northern Ireland as for every other part of the UK. (My italics.)

Mr Frost cannot be 'negotiating on behalf of Northern Ireland' to leave the EU, since Northern Ireland voted to remain. He may declare that he is not 'complacent about the Union' but he appears to be complacent about almost everything else. The speech was roundly welcomed in sections of the London-based press as if it were a heavyweight intervention in the continuing British debate about Europe. When an Englishman quotes Burke, many English commentators seem to lose their wits. Thankfully, not all of them. The former Conservative MP Matthew Parris, writing in *The Times*, challenged Frost's description of Burke as a 'philosopher' and called him instead an 'agitator and a crusader' and, one might say, rather like a heavyweight newspaper columnist. More significantly Parris excoriated the English exceptionalism of the argument. While Burke (and Frost) praised the concept of the state as 'a partnership in every virtue and in all perfection' the assumption has to be that both were talking of British national identity. Parris asked: 'Does he [Frost] think the French, Germans or Swedes have a stunted sense of national identity?' The answer to the rhetorical question is that it would seem unlikely, even if Frost falls into the supreme complacency of assuming that the British have a finer sense of this 'partnership in every virtue and all perfection' that others lack.[24]

This is where the English–British elision is particularly dangerous. The phrase 'in a country like Britain where institutions just evolved' is simply nonsense. The Union of Crowns, the Union of Parliaments, the Revolution Settlement, the Protestant ascendancy, the Union with Ireland, the 1832 Reform Act, the Partition of Ireland, the agreement over power-sharing in Northern Ireland, the creation of devolved parliaments and assemblies and other institutions including the NHS did not 'just evolve'. They were the product of crises, in some cases of riots and bloodshed, or an attempt to forestall crises, riots and bloodshed. Every one of these massive changes (and many others) within the United Kingdom was 'created by design' by humans working together to build or maintain some kind of union based on shared values. The creation of NATO did not 'just evolve', nor did Britain's role in the European Space Agency and Galileo programme, the European Medicines Agency (formerly based in London), the Erasmus programme, the United Nations (of which the UK is a Security Council Permanent Five Member) the WTO and numerous other international bodies.

Parris concludes that 'having added cod history to cod philosophy, Frost moves on to cod economics' and scathingly dismisses much of the rest of the speech. But in terms of the search for British identity, Frost's complacency – reflecting the prevailing complacency within the British government – is even more extraordinary. Remember: this is the key player in negotiating Brexit. He has swallowed the nostalgic Kool-Aid of English history, English exceptionalism and nostalgic pessimism, despite – or perhaps as a result of – studying history at Oxford University. On that delusionary basis, whatever the source, claiming to be 'negotiating as one country' is something that is prima facie impossible given the different interests and different politics of different parts of the United Kingdom and the rise of the competing nationalisms which Frost, in one moment of clarity, does appear to notice, even if he disregards its potency. This too is complacent. In Scotland, to take an obvious example, the Holyrood government wants Scotland-specific work visas to ease labour shortages in the Scottish economy. Westminster says no. How can Frost then negotiate for the whole of the UK? Then he claims to be 'negotiating on behalf of Northern Ireland as for every other part of the UK' when Northern Ireland – according to Boris Johnson's agreement with the Irish prime minister Leo Varadkar in October 2019 at the Wirral – was not to be treated like 'every other part of the UK'. Johnson – astonishingly – conceded that the UK customs border with the EU does not include Northern Ireland. Indeed, plans were put in place to create customs facilities for goods entering Northern Ireland from Britain, including extra facilities at the County Antrim port of Larne and in Belfast.

Mr Frost's thesis is not merely nonsensical, it is dangerous and torpedoed by his own words. He does correctly argue that 'if you can't change policies by voting, as you increasingly can't in this situation – then opposition becomes expressed as opposition to the system itself'. But that is the position not just of those formerly rejected UKIP voters in England but also of most Scots and potentially both unionists and nationalists (for different reasons) in Northern Ireland along with at least some of the citizens of Wales, and most certainly considerable numbers of Remain voters in England, especially in London. The partnership of the UK does not exist 'in all perfection' or anywhere near it. It may not in future exist at all. Mr Frost is at the sharp end of a government composed of English men and women who in the words of the economist Sir Dennis Robertson have 'long been used to living in a certain haze' as to what their country is. Mr Frost may soon find out what the country is not. We are not in reality an 'island race', even though this part of the English nationalist haze is a persistent idea. John of Gaunt said that England was a 'precious stone set in a silver sea', which in many ways is true. But he then claims that the sea 'serves it in the office of a wall'. As we will see next, far from being the barrier beloved of English nationalists, a rampart defending the island race from the tribulations of an increasingly interconnected world, the sea is more like a highway, a transport route, a connection, while the familiar yet erroneous myth about the English as an 'island race' befuddles any kind of clear thinking about the future.

5

God's Chosen People

'An Englishman thinks he is moral
when he is only uncomfortable.'

The Devil, speaking in George Bernard Shaw,
Man and Superman

W. E. Henley's poetic declaration of love for his nation, 'England, My England', was written during the heyday of the British empire. It is a statement full of the peak imperial confidence of the late Victorian era, which means the hubristic tone can sound comic today. Henley, to modern ears, is channelling 'Ozymandias', with the British empire that once saw itself as king of kings no longer triumphant and more like the 'colossal wreck' of Shelley's verse:

What have I done for you,
England, my England?
What is there I would not do,
England, my own?
With your glorious eyes austere,
As the Lord were walking near,
Whispering terrible things and dear
As the Song on your bugles blown,
England—
Round the world on your bugles blown!

Mother of Ships whose might,
England, my England,
Is the fierce old Sea's delight,
England, my own,
Chosen daughter of the Lord,
Spouse-in-Chief of the ancient Sword,
There's the menace of the Word
In the Song on your bugles blown,
England—
Out of heaven on your bugles blown!

England, Henley tells us, is blessed by God, and blessed by the strength and patriotism of its people while the bugles of the empire are heard round the world. A contemporary of Henley's, the great imperialist Cecil Rhodes, was even more assertive: 'Ask any man what nationality he would prefer to be, and ninety-nine out of a hundred will tell you that they would prefer to be Englishmen.' Rhodes also advised, 'remember that you are an Englishman, and have consequently won first prize in the lottery of life'. Other English poets, dramatists, writers and politicians have joined Henley and Rhodes in implying that God himself, if not demonstrably an Englishman, has singled out England for special favours.

They have a point. England is an extraordinarily inventive country in which one Cambridge college is said to be associated with more Nobel prizewinners than China and Japan put together. Even after the collapse of the British empire, the English language continues its colonization of the world. If the dollar is the world's reserve currency, English is the world's reserve language. English creativity in the arts and culture, from Shakespeare to the world wide web, Dickens to the Beatles, Kate Bush and Adele, along with a delight in eccentricity and individuality, are some of the country's great assets. Despite occasional rioting and domestic unrest, compared to our closest European friends, Spain, France, Germany and Italy, English history suggests that change often comes after argument and reason rather than violent conflict, at least since the religious wars of the seventeenth century. Walk into Canterbury Cathedral or through the Yorkshire Dales, to Buttermere in the Lake District or on the cliffs near Port Isaac on the coast of Cornwall and it does not take much imagination to understand that those of us lucky enough to live in England are entitled to brag about a land and a people, exceptional and blessed. Even as a boy at school in Edinburgh I sang lustily along with William Blake's famous affirmation of English exceptionalism, in which England is the New Jerusalem:

> And did those feet in ancient time
> Walk upon England's mountains green:
> And was the holy Lamb of God,
> On England's pleasant pastures seen.

Generations of British schoolboys understood that the common-sense and literal answer to Blake's questions was 'no', Jesus did not walk here. Indeed, Blake himself had a touch of the English disease, nostalgic pessimism. In the same poem he saw the land blighted by one of England's great economic achievements, the Industrial Revolution and its 'dark, satanic mills'. But that was not the point. England, for Blake and W. E. Henley, Jez Butterworth in his play *Jerusalem*, Cecil Rhodes and others, is so blessed one could presume that Our Saviour did indeed walk upon the land, even if Blake's rousing words are clearly a critique of the materialistic, industrial and imperial obsessions of his age.

One of the most poignant expressions of English exceptionalism thanks to the grace of God, is that of the clergyman and historian Laurence Echard. Writing during the reign of George I, Echard noted the 'wonderful and providential' history of his country: 'England in an especial manner has been such a mighty and distinct scene of action (that) there seems to have been more visible and signal instances of judgements and punishments, mercies and deliverances from above than perhaps can be paralleled in any other part of the Western world.'[1] This is a proud clergyman's take on Edmund Burke's 'partnership in every virtue and all perfection' and David Frost's miraculous 'Britain where institutions just evolved'. Truly, throughout the centuries the English are – or were – God's chosen people. But the English are far from exceptional in their exceptionalism. Nor are they unusual in the multiple contradictions and hubris inherent in the variants of their nationalism. The former Conservative cabinet minister and one-time candidate for the leadership of her party Andrea Leadsom put it this way: 'You see, I am an optimist. I truly believe we can be the greatest nation on earth… I believe we have a great future ahead of us… we are a remarkable people and we have so much more to give.'[2] It's classic nationalist boilerplate, and she could have lifted the words more or less verbatim from the speeches of Donald Trump, Russia's Vladimir Putin, Hungary's Viktor Orbán, Brazil's Jair Bolsonaro or indeed from the man who did become prime minister of the United Kingdom, Boris Johnson. His take on it all was that 'by 2050, it is more than possible that the UK will be the greatest and most prosperous economy in Europe'.[3] By 2050 it is more than possible that the United

Kingdom will have ceased to exist in anything like its present form, and that Boris Johnson and Andrea Leadsom will be among those whose actions have encouraged it to change, although perhaps not in the way they have planned.

England's Unexceptional Exceptionalism

There are many examples of nationalistic pride in Scottish, Irish and Welsh literature, and that of the French, Germans, Russians and every other nation you can think of. In 2019 Abdolali Ali-Asgari, the head of Iran's broadcasting authority, noted that Persians had replaced Jews as God's Chosen People, because they were the countrymen of the Prophet Muhammad's companion Salman the Persian. Iranians were chosen to 'shoulder the heavy burden of truth and progress in the world' after the Jews 'pursued worldly ornaments and behaved unjustly'.[4] In the United States Walt Whitman's lengthy love poem to his vast country 'Leaves of Grass' is in a line of American love-of-country writing. It leads to sentimental country music ballads along the lines of 'I'm Proud to Be an American' and the beautifully written oratory provided for President Ronald Reagan by the speech-writer Peggy Noonan and others.

Reagan's speech-writers used stirring biblical imagery to describe the United States as a 'shining city on a hill'. Even one of the greatest anti-war songs of the past thirty years, Bruce Springsteen's 'Born in the USA', has – despite the lyrics – at times been co-opted by patriotic Americans to justify or celebrate military action. In a bar in Washington DC during the Gulf War, I heard a group of US Marines (out of uniform) lustily singing Springsteen's chorus with no apparent recognition that the song is about a foreign conflict in which working-class Americans were sent out to die in a country about which they understood very little. Nationalism, in other words, is a filter. We sing the words of anthems that make us proud, and hear the poetry of what we want to hear. Those US Marines must have missed the Springsteen lyrics:

Got in a little hometown jam
So they put a rifle in my hand
Sent me off to a foreign land
To go and kill the yellow man

I had a brother at Khe Sahn
Fighting off the Viet Cong
They're still there
He's all gone

Or perhaps Walt Whitman had an insight about all nationalisms when he wrote in 'Song of Myself': 'Do I contradict myself? / Very well then I contradict myself, / (I am large, I contain multitudes.)'

In all our competing nationalisms there is a further contradiction requiring us to sublimate the idea of 'our' nation with that of the multinational British state. Henley performs the same sleight of hand. He writes of the military bugles, the might of the navy and the power of the British empire. As we have noted, no one speaks of an 'English' empire, nor in Henley's time were there bugles of the 'English' army, and Britannia ruled the waves thanks to the Royal Navy not the English navy. Yet even in the time of Henley and Cecil Rhodes it is difficult to believe that millions of people round the world would have preferred 'to be Englishmen'. Ask that question in a Glasgow, Cardiff, Belfast or Dublin pub a hundred years ago or on any Saturday night in the twenty-first century and – this is a guess – you would receive a broadly negative response. Besides, 'to be Englishmen' would appear to be impossible unless you are already English. The Hungarian humourist and émigré George Mikes observed: 'A criminal may improve and become a decent member of society. A foreigner cannot improve... There is no way out for him. He may become British, he can never become English.'[5] Mikes settled in England and felt welcome. He relished what he saw as the peculiarities of the English, including their sense of humour, which he understood with perfect pitch. Yet even Mikes sometimes confuses the English with the British, and – adopting the habits of his new home country – he too never lets the facts get in the way of a witty comment. It was Mikes who claimed that continental people have a sex life, while the English have hot-water bottles. Perhaps at the time he began writing, just after the war, he had a point – although for some reason the generation conceived during that period are known as the Baby Boomers.

The English attitude to sex, we are led to believe, is typified by David Lean's 1945 film *Brief Encounter*, which sizzles with repressed passion. Trevor Howard's 'good chap' doctor helps Celia Johnson remove a speck of dirt from her eye as they wait for a train. Both are in what we would now call joyless marriages and yet they exercise self-control because 'we are not put on earth to enjoy ourselves'. Even though the film is a moving demonstration of Lean's creative genius, the claustrophobia of the setting, the painfully stiff dialogue and the passion which is kept on a tight leash make it an uncomfortable period piece from a postwar England used to sacrifice. As Philip Larkin famously put it in *Annus Mirabilis*:

Sexual intercourse began
In nineteen sixty-three
(which was rather late for me) –
Between the end of the 'Chatterley' ban
And the Beatles' first LP

Larkin's own personal life suggests that sexual intercourse may have reached England a little earlier than the Beatles. So does the estimate that in Victorian times as many as 80,000 women worked as prostitutes in London alone. In 1869 the social campaigner Francis Newman, brother of Cardinal Newman, wrote of prostitution: 'Under the name of the Great Social Evil our newspapers for years have alluded to an awful vice, too evidently of wide prevalence.' George Bernard Shaw wrote of it with considerable understanding in *Mrs Warren's Profession*. From Chaucer's *Wife of Bath* to the Porter at Hellgate scene in *Macbeth*, reflecting on how alcohol increases sexual desire but reduces performance, to Charles II and Nell Gwynn, to

Daniel Defoe's *Moll Flanders* and onward to *Love Island* and the expanding family of children without number attributed to Prime Minister Boris Johnson, *Brief Encounter* is not a reliable signifier of sexuality in England of all classes for all time. Its emotional repression tells us nothing about 'the English'. It tells us a great deal about middle-class angst and the uncertainties and duties of war, in which a dull but settled life is preferable to adventure.

The cliché of the English refusal to recognize the amount of sexual activity in their own country despite the evidence all around, may be summed up by the old English name for syphilis, 'the French disease', which could perhaps be avoided by the use of other foreign importations, French letters, or Dutch caps. The British diplomat and Brexit negotiator David Frost may have been unconsciously channelling the idea that foreigners are the source of maladies and perversions when he suggested that the European way of designing a political system was 'a bit unnatural'. However, reflecting on Cecil Rhodes's strain of ultra-Englishness, George Mikes went on to say:

> It has still never occurred to one single Englishman that not everybody would regard it as a step up, as a promotion, to become English... And if Britannia does not rule the waves, very well, that is only and exclusively because the waves of the world do not deserve it any more.

Russians sometimes speak of their country not as Jerusalem or that other Eden but as 'Holy Russia' and the 'Third Rome' after the original Christian Rome and then Byzantium. Chinese exceptionalism includes the idea of China as a shining civilization in the centre of All-under-Heaven, endowed with a peace-loving culture. Australians sometimes see themselves as 'the Lucky Country', although the full original quote of this phrase from the historian Douglas Horne is not so flattering: 'Australia is a lucky country run mainly by second rate people who share its luck.' And the phrase 'God's Own Country' – with a touch of wry humour – has been used to described everywhere from Wicklow in Ireland to Yorkshire and the Indian state of Kerala.

God's chosen people, it seems, includes more or less everyone who loves their country, which is most of us. The problem for the British is that English exceptionalism complicates the meaning of 'our country', and the obsession with the idea of the English as an 'island race' who 'stood alone' simply does not stand up to scrutiny.

This Sceptr'd Isle

As a Scot who came to England to study English and then Irish litera-ture at two English universities, I always found Shakespeare a delight, a challenge and at times a puzzle. The puzzle was the history plays. I found them perplexing. You might blame the British education system, except that there is no such thing. The Scottish education sys-tem (as we will explore in more detail later in Chapter 8, focusing on supposedly 'British' institutions) is distinct. How and what we are taught inevitably affects how Scots view 'our' country and England too. History teaching is a good example. At my Scottish school we learned about the unification of Scotland, various wars with England and alliances with France. We turned to British history after 1603, to the Stuarts, Cromwell, then European history, the Reformation, the French Revolution and the American War of Independence. We paid scant attention – in my case almost none – to the English Wars of the Roses and various English monarchs who mostly seem to have been called Henry, although there was an Edward or two and a Richard who was good while another Richard and a John were probably bad. All these English-only matters were treated as ancient wars between foreigners. They were given less emphasis in my schooldays in Edinburgh than the struggle between Rome and Carthage – *Carthago delenda est!* – or the conflicts of the Greeks and Persians, the origins of the phrase 'Pyrrhic victory', and the rise of Napoleon, Hitler and Stalin.

In Edinburgh we were also surrounded by history, 'our' history. My school was built in the 1620s underneath Edinburgh Castle with money from a Scottish moneylender called George Heriot. He took the Scottish route to salvation and made his fortune by following King

James VI to London where the king became James I. Heriot loaned King James money at such a profit that he returned to Edinburgh laden with gold, presumably supplied by English taxpayers. He went on to buy a great deal of land in the centre of the city and to do charitable work, especially in education. George Heriot was called 'Jinglin' Geordie' by the burghers of Edinburgh because his pockets were supposedly so full of English money that they chinked when he walked around town. There is a pub in central Edinburgh hidden down Fleshmarket Close which bears the Jinglin' Geordie name. For the school he chose a site just inside the Flodden Wall. The wall was erected to keep the English out, after the battle of Flodden, another Scottish catastrophe, this time in 1513. King James IV along with the 'flower' of the Scottish nobility invaded England – the 'Auld Enemy' – to ease the military pressure on 'our' allies in the 'Auld Alliance', the French. It didn't work out very well. James IV led the 'Flowers of the Forest', as the Scottish song has it, to their slaughter, and the king himself was killed by the villainous English.

The reason this series of historical anecdotes retains significance even now is that when any Scottish or Irish person reads or sees one of Shakespeare's history plays or hears about the glories at Crécy or Agincourt from Jacob Rees-Mogg, a small voice at the back of the Scottish or Irish brain whispers that 'we' were not 'them', not the heroes of the story. In fact 'we' were the enemy. If the British art historian and former museum director Neil McGregor is correct in expressing German disappointment that the English have yet to move on from the Second World War, he might also care to reflect how the various nations of Britain have not yet entirely moved on from Flodden, Agincourt, the Battle of the Boyne, the siege of Limerick, the vanished Welsh hero Owen Glendower and the Great Famine – as well as Dunkirk and other battles or disasters of the past. Indeed, the Scottish anthem 'Flower of Scotland' is a 1960s creation that celebrates the defeat of 'proud Edward's army' sent home 'to think again'. It celebrates a rare Scottish win, the Battle of Bannockburn, fought against England's King Edward II in 1314. The song is full of the same nostalgic pessimism that characterizes English nationalism:

Oh Flower of Scotland
When will we see your like again?

The song does not reference the slaughter of that other 'flower' of Scotland – the king and the nobles who died at Flodden or in other military catastrophes. Instead, the final verse suggests that recalling the heroism of the past victory at Bannockburn may yet secure independence in the future:

Those days are past now,
And in the past
They must remain,
But we can still rise now,
And be the nation again,
That stood against him,
Proud Edward's Army,
And sent him homeward,
To think again.

As with John of Gaunt's supposed Golden Age of English nationalist dreaming, Scotland's greatest period is never here and now – it is always somewhere far in the past, when people were braver, and their stirring example may determine a better future if we can only live up to the heroism of those long dead. All nations have their own sentimental tunes and romantic ideas about their history. But there is one key and distinctive theme in English nationalism throughout the centuries. It occurs many times in Shakespeare, in John of Gaunt's speech and elsewhere, and it has echoes in the present. It is the idea that England is an island and the English are an 'island race' who 'stood alone'. England is not merely exceptional but also in some way cut off from others, especially foreigners.

Winston Churchill frequently spoke of defending 'our island' and wrote *This Island Race*, a book title that would not make much sense now in multi-ethnic Britain and probably did not accurately describe the Britain of Churchill's day either. John of Gaunt claimed that England itself was a 'sceptr'd isle'. Elsewhere in Shakespeare the Duke of Austria speaks of 'that England, hedged in with the Main / That water-filled bulwark, still secure / And confident from foreign purposes'.[6] And even if the rhetoric is not Churchillian and the poetry is not Shakespearean, here is Jean Rook, the *Daily Express* columnist at the time of entry into the Common Market in 1973: 'Since Boadicea we British have slammed our seas in the faces of invading frogs and wops who start at Calais... to know the British... will be Europe's privilege.'[7] Rook's xenophobic epithets are not merely offensive, they are wrong in suggesting that the sea is a 'slammed' door – and not just because the metaphor is ugly. The 'frogs' provided Britain with talented Huguenots fleeing from France. The wops, slang for Italians or southern Europeans, presumably include the Romans, and the families of Benjamin Disraeli, John Profumo, Barry Fantoni, John Galliano, Jim Capaldi, Anna Calvi, Sir John Barbirolli, Semprini, Jack Vettriano, Emilio Coia, Sir Eduardo Paolozzi, Dominic Minghella, the Rossettis, Francis Rossi of Status Quo plus a kitchen full of chefs, scientists, doctors, business people, footballers ice-cream makers and other adornments of British culture. But beyond the tabloid mixed metaphors, the glorification of Boadicea or Boudicca is the celebration of another disaster. The Boudicca-led rebellion of a pre-English tribe of Trinovantes or Iceni was a catastrophic defeat. It led to the destruction of towns on the sites of what are now London and Colchester, the consolidation of Roman power in what is now England and what may have been the suicide of Boudicca herself. Like the Charge of the Light Brigade or the Dunkirk Spirit, Boudicca is the English glorification of failure.

In terms of the 'island race' the key point is that despite the nationalistic myth-making the seas around our coastline historically were not just – and often not even – a defensive 'bulwark'. The seas were most often the opposite, a form of connection and travel route. The seas were (and still are) an open door, the main means of communication, and therefore the invasion route taken by outsiders. I am writing this near the beach in Kent where the Roman invaders commanded by Julius Caesar first landed. A few miles down the road on the outskirts of Sandwich the Romans created Richborough fort, the Dover transport hub of its day, to bring in their legions and supplies. The reason Canterbury Cathedral's Twitter handle is @No1Cathedral is that St Augustine brought Christianity to Kent by arriving across the sea and becoming Archbishop of Canterbury in 597. The sea allowed the invasions of Germanic tribes, of the Norman William the Conqueror, the Dutch William of Orange, and the arrival of generations of migrants including Jews, Huguenots, and the Windrush generation from the Caribbean, and in recent years refugees and asylum seekers who stow away on the backs of lorries or risk their lives in small boats to make the crossing from France illegally. A water-filled bulwark? Sometimes, but not often.

A Shared Island – Or 6,000 Islands

To state the geographically obvious, England is not an island. It is part of an island. England shares that island with Scotland and Wales. Yet the myth of the island race plays neatly into our contemporary politics and reinvigorated English nationalism, especially after Brexit. The facts are – as always – a bit more complicated than the feelings. The United Kingdom is made up of some 6,000 islands. These islands – Orkney, Shetland, the Isle of Wight, Scilly, the Inner and Outer Hebrides – include large and scattered parts of archipelagos. Others are tiny and uninhabitable. The key attraction of the modern use of the island myth is that reflected in Jean Rook's newspaper. It is the idea of the sea ensuring that England has been immune from foreign invasion since the Normans in 1066. But that depends what you mean by 'invasion'. And it also depends what you mean by 'foreign'. The Scots certainly invaded England numerous times after 1066 by heading south on foot or horseback. Armies raised in Ireland joined the Scots by sea and landed right up until the eighteenth century, with designs on marching south to London. It worked both ways. The Plantation of Ulster began under James I in the early 1600s. It was an invasion launched by sea, endorsed by London merchants (hence the city of London-Derry, originally the Irish *Doire*) though it was carried out mostly by Lowland Scots.

In the seventeenth century England and Ireland were *both* invaded by the Protestant forces of William of Orange. This fact is sometimes overlooked in popular histories of the 'Glorious Revolution' of 1688 and the Battles of the Boyne and Aughrim, which ensured the Protestant succession. The historian Linda Colley writes of the patriotic history books she read as a child in which King William 'featured unequivocally as a liberator who landed at Torbay on 5 November 1688 strictly by invitation. In cold reality William arrived after much planning and expensive preparation equipped with some 500 ships and over 21,000 Dutch, German and Scandinavian troops. So the English had limited choice in the matter.'[8]

History does belong to the victors. They shape the past for their convenience in the present. But Good King Billy landing 21,000 foreign troops, including mercenaries, on English soil even with the pre-arranged consent of some of the local nobility is, in common parlance, a foreign seaborne invasion. The 'Glorious Revolution' is a clever title which could more accurately be termed the 'Glorious Invasion' – except that invasion has unwelcome connotations of defeat. The 'island race' does not like to think in the language of defeat. The sea as a 'bulwark' or John of Gaunt's 'sceptr'd isle' is glorious poetry but it is far from perfect history and seriously flawed geography. And yet the poetry's grip on popular culture suggests that the 'island race' story remains the finest expression of an English sense of 'otherness', isolation and exceptionalism. Irish people, it's true, sometimes call their island the Emerald Isle, but neither they nor the Scots and Welsh fetishize the 'island race' the way that English popular culture so easily and frequently does. And when people in England say 'we stood alone', the evidence for that is also much more complicated.

*

With a Little Help from Our Friends

The combination of the island race myth, the idea that the sea is primarily a defensive wall, English exceptionalism plus nostalgic pessimism and the increasing disconnection of Englishness from Britishness all combine into a potent but very confused nationalist cocktail, especially when mixed with a streak of self-pity. This was most obvious during the first few years of the Brexit debacle. After the referendum in 2016, when negotiations soon ran into various practical difficulties, Brexit-supporting London tabloids used that most English of expressions to claim that Britain was constantly being 'snubbed' by Brussels. Reading sections of the British media on Brexit over the past few years has been like listening to an entire orchestra playing two discordant notes simultaneously. Britain was, at the same time, the victim of bullies and yet all powerful; we were being 'snubbed' by the EU and yet 'we hold all the cards'; we could 'have our cake and eat it', and yet the European Union gave us nothing but crumbs; Brexit was 'the will of the people', but perplexingly the United Kingdom remained thoroughly divided; Britain was a great world power, yet somehow supposedly lesser countries – especially Ireland – refused to do what they were told. For the English nationalist writers in the press it was all a bit confusing.

In October 2018, to take one example from many, the then foreign secretary Boris Johnson and part-time *Daily Telegraph* columnist told readers of that newspaper: 'There comes a point when you have to stand up to bullies. After more than two years of being ruthlessly pushed around by the EU, it is time for the UK to resist.'[9] The 'ruthless' bullying amounted to the European Union insisting from 2016 onwards that if Britain was not an EU member then Britain could not have the benefits of EU membership. In Mr Johnson's case 'standing up to bullies' meant that by October 2019 as prime minister of the country that held all the cards, he folded his hand after a few hours in conversation with the Irish prime minister Leo Varadkar, by agreeing that the customs border with Northern Ireland would be in the Irish Sea. In customs terms at least, Boris Johnson ended the partition of

Ireland and offered encouragement to Sinn Féin to wonder whether the full reunification of Ireland was fast approaching.

This odd cocktail of English exceptionalism and rhetorical arrogance combined with weakness and self-pity encompasses everything from the old Etonian silkiness of Jacob Rees-Mogg's oratory to the chants on the football terraces by England supporters of 'Two World Wars and One World Cup'. To those of us who cheered on England in the 2018 World Cup (in my case for lack of any Scottish team to support) this English football chant has always seemed especially sad. Are England supporters in the twenty-first century really celebrating a football match fifty years ago? (Yes.) Are they also celebrating victories in terrible wars stretching back 100 years? (Yes.) But in what sense did 'England' win a world war or, as the mythology goes, 'stand alone'? Not in the First World War, to begin with. In 1914 Britain – not England – and the British army (including many Irishmen) plus the forces of the entire British empire fought alongside the French and other allies against the Kaiser. Russia attacked Germany on the Eastern Front, and United States involvement from 1917 proved decisive.

In the mythology, the notion that England 'stood alone' tends to be connected to the Second World War after the fall of France. Even then it was not quite so simple. My father was a Dunkirk veteran, one of just sixty British soldiers to escape the siege of Calais in May–June 1940. While William John Esler survived to fight another day, 300 of his comrades were killed, 200 wounded and around 3,500 were captured. This sacrifice of several thousand British soldiers is commemorated in the film *Finest Hour*. I am therefore not minimizing either the dangers of the period nor the heroism of those who did the right thing and stood up to Hitler. But, as my father repeatedly pointed out to me, Britain – or England – never 'stood alone' in the Second World War, not even in 1940–1, nor did leaders at the time speak as if England was fighting alone. When Churchill used the phrase he was speaking of *the entire British empire* standing against occupied Europe without another European state as an ally. This in itself was a truly heroic achievement but it was not

England or Britain 'standing alone'. In those very bleak days during the Battle of Britain almost a quarter of the RAF pilots were from other countries, including Poland, New Zealand, Australia, Canada, Czechoslovakia, Belgium, France, the United States and South Africa. Beyond support from the Free French, Polish aircrews and others, as Linda Colley notes:

> the UK never fought alone... Right up to the summer of 1944 there were more Commonwealth troops in the fighting line than Americans... Some 2.5 million troops from the Dominions fought with the UK in the Second World War. So, too, did two million Indians, some 700,000 men from African colonies other than South Africa and 16,000 men and women from the Caribbean.[10]

As my father often pointed out to me, in the subsequent North Africa campaign against Rommel he personally fought as a British artilleryman alongside men from Bhopal in India and from what was then called the Bechuanaland Protectorate in Southern Africa, and eventually alongside Americans. As a member of the Dunkirk Veterans' Association, he despised – that is not too strong a word – those politicians who did not fight in the war and yet used terms like 'stand alone' and 'Dunkirk spirit' as if they were part of a great victory. Despite the heroism of so many involved, as my father had cause to remark, Dunkirk was a catastrophic defeat which should be remembered and reflected upon, not used to rouse a mindless patriotic cheer.

The historian David Edgerton also emphasizes the misleading nature of claims of standing alone:

> The Second World War was at its beginning also a war presented as one in which the empire fought as a whole. After the fall of France in June 1940 if anything was alone it was the entire empire, not the 'island nation'. No one in authority could or would have said 'Britain stood alone' – that was a phrase from

post-war nationalist history books… The empire had allies even in 1940–41… When Princess Elizabeth addressed the nations of the Empire from South Africa on her twenty-first birthday in 1947 she spoke in terms of empire not nation. It was the 'British family of nations' she said which had the 'high honour of standing alone seven years ago in defence of the liberty of the world'.[11]

It is worth remembering the historical accuracy of Princess Elizabeth's speech. By the time she was crowned Queen in June 1953 the empire of nations of which she and Winston Churchill had spoken was in the process of dismantling itself. And yet the 'stand alone' myth persists even if in reality we stood with millions of non-British allied troops in uniform fighting on our side. It has become one of the seriously myopic delusions of those who several generations after the war have no direct ancestral memory of what it was like in reality, and no curiosity about the real history as opposed to that of the befuddled imagination.

A Sense of Humour

One gloriously English characteristic acts as a corrective to all this: the ability to laugh at the distortions of fact-free nationalism. From *Monty Python* to *Blackadder*, comic TV versions of posh army officers have instructed the lower ranks that the time has come for an utterly pointless sacrifice. Henley's 'England, My England' inspired a number of other versions with similar titles but reflecting very differently what the reality of England meant to English men and women. D. H. Lawrence's collection of short stories also called *England, My England* (written 1913–21) turns a withering gaze on the country. In Orwell's 'England Your England', beyond his own version of what Englishness meant, Orwell wrote acutely of how differences between the nations of the United Kingdom can rapidly melt away faced with even a non-threatening outsider:

It is quite true that the so-called races of Britain feel themselves to be very different from one another. A Scotsman, for instance, does not thank you if you call him an Englishman. You can see the hesitation we feel on this point by the fact that we call our islands by no less than six different names, England, Britain, Great Britain, the British Isles, the United Kingdom and, in very exalted moments, Albion. Even the differences between north and south England loom large in our own eyes. But somehow these differences fade away the moment that any two Britons are confronted by a European.

Orwell then continues:

Economically, England is certainly two nations, if not three or four. But at the same time the vast majority of the people feel themselves to be a single nation and are conscious of resembling one another more than they resemble foreigners. Patriotism is usually stronger than class-hatred, and always stronger than any kind of internationalism.

Orwell is undoubtedly correct in much of this, at least for the time at which he wrote, but it is debatable how much these observations still hold true now. Post-Brexit Britain is not a country at peace with itself. We are not an 'island race', we are numerous islands of many races. The question of which nation we feel 'patriotism' towards in the United Kingdom of the twenty-first century is for many of our citizens very different from twenty years ago, and therefore undeniably different from the united front of a United Kingdom leading an empire and facing the Nazis in 1941. War or threats of conflict really have been the glue by which Britain was created, which kept us together, and which acted as the catalyst for renewal. In 1603, the crisis of succession brought two previously warring nations in Scotland and England together in the face of foreign enemies, the Catholic armies of France and Spain. In 1707 fear of the French again helped solidify the union. In 1801 fear of the French once more was the decisive factor in forcing the Act of Union on the Irish. In the twentieth century it was fear of Germany and two European wars which helped keep most of the United Kingdom together, despite the secession of Ireland. That sense of a foreign threat continued after the war through the Cold War until the collapse of the Soviet Union. But now? The post-Brexit crisis with our European neighbours, including Ireland, appears to have had precisely the opposite effect on our own union. Despite the rhetoric of bullying and snubs, Brexit is not a foreign threat. It is a self-inflicted wound, self-harm upon the unity of the United Kingdom by the most powerful part of it. If a nation is an 'imagined community', then since the Brexit vote the British nation is suffering a profound failure of imagination. England in particular, when it imagines itself, appears obsessed with a series of flashbacks. Here's an example.

Back to the Future

The magazine *This England* was founded in 1968. It claimed it was 'as refreshing as a cup of tea'. For years it produced the kind of material the editor said appealed to:

> not just dukes but wonderful dustmen as well, and pensioners from the East End and judges and ferry boatmen and vicars' wives in remote missionary stations and royalty and showgirls and lads and lassies from all over the globe... decent, God-fearing plain-speaking crusaders whether they wear mitres or mini-skirts.

It wasn't revealed what the magazine's readers were crusading for, but it was abundantly clear from an editorial in 1997 what they were crusading against:

> We are in the middle of a carefully crafted plot going back many years which is designed to create an easily manageable, European super-state to be run like a socialist republic. That means one

overall (but unelected) government, one puppet parliament, one federal army, navy and air force, one central bank, a single currency and one supreme court of law. Our precious monarchy will be replaced by a President on the Continent, the Union Jack will be banned in favour of that horrid blue rag with those 12 nasty yellow stars and we shall have to sing the new Euro anthem to the tune of Beethoven's *Ode to Joy*... except that its title will really mean 'Goodbye Britain'.[12]

This sense of victimhood and of being bullied infuses popular culture in England well beyond the dukes and wonderful dustmen who supposedly read the magazine. (Its circulation is put at around 40,000 and it is claimed to be a favourite with English expatriates.) In speaking at public meetings across England in the aftermath of the Brexit vote I have heard the rhetoric of victimhood recycled in various ways. At a literary festival event in Rye in Sussex in 2019 a man complained to me that the European Union was an undemocratic bully which had 'imposed its laws' on Britain without our consent. When I asked him which laws he had in mind, he could not name any. In Chester a woman told me that the European Union had 'taken away our sovereignty'. When I asked her which parts of 'our sovereignty' she most missed, nothing came to mind except – and I am not making this up – 'the Queen'. The audience laughed. While I was canvassing in central London during the European elections of May 2019 a voter told me she was voting for Nigel Farage because the European Union was 'pushing us around' and was 'completely undemocratic'. I asked her how, if she was *voting* in an *election* for a *parliament* and for someone who had been a *member of that parliament for twenty years*, she could think it completely undemocratic. She seemed stumped. In terms of the lack of democracy, nothing, again, came to mind.

'Oh, I hadn't thought of it that way,' she said as she turned away.

In 1997 the journalist Jeremy Paxman went to meet the editor of *This England*, Roy Faiers, and noted that 'the enemy of course is really the march of time – not a single article looks forward to the future'.

Paxman asked Faiers for his own definition of what it meant to be English. The answer was utterly bizarre:

> The actor James Stewart, for example, he was American but he had Englishness. He didn't brag about himself. He wasn't pushy. He had one wife all his life. You could trust him with your wallet. That's English... Englishness is very deep. It's a spirit. The spirit of St George, the idea of St George is a fight against evil.[13]

Defining Englishness as a spirit exemplified through the lifestyle of a deceased American Hollywood actor is a considerable leap even for the editorial imagination of *This England*. By Mr Faiers's definition it is difficult to see Boris Johnson or Nigel Farage or much of the cast of *EastEnders* or *Coronation Street* as being 'English', having one wife all their lives and being able to trust them with your wallet. The roughly 90,000 couples every year in England who obtain a divorce, including the heir to the throne and many other members of the extended British royal family, would presumably be barred from 'being English' too. And yet it is clearly a self-image of Englishness that readers of *This England* found appealing, and no doubt others do too. Even more striking is the sense throughout the magazine that England is inevitably doomed in an even more apocalyptic fashion than that feared by John of Gaunt. Perhaps the final irony is that, while John of Gaunt turned out to be Belgian, in 2009 *This England* was bought up by the Dundee-based publisher D. C. Thomson; another treasured English jewel undermined by foreigners, in this case the Scottish publishers of the *Beano*.

What is striking is how so much of the Brexit debate and English political discourse is still conducted in the terms of *This England* – the foreign threat, the European superstate waiting to pounce, the replacement of the monarchy, the unelected oppressors and the sense of a defiant country standing 'alone' as an island of democracy against the undemocratic bullies over the Channel. In terms of our self-image as a beacon of democracy, the United Kingdom is one of the few nations in Europe, indeed in the world, to have as head of state an unelected monarch and an unelected upper chamber of parliament in the House of Lords. We also do not have a written constitution, and yet these arguments about other nations acting undemocratically still have traction.

Nigel Farage's Brexit Party MEPs – elected as part of the apparently undemocratic European superstate – reacted to the playing of Beethoven's *Ode to Joy* in the European parliament exactly as the editor of *This England* might have liked. They turned their backs in protest. Beethoven's great work was not retitled 'Goodbye Britain' for the occasion, although for the Brexit MEPs it might as well have been. It is also difficult to see that particular anthem as a symbol of foreign oppression once you discover that the *Ode to Joy* was commissioned by Englishmen of the Philharmonic Society of London in 1817.

Blitz Spirit and Coronavirus

Scots, Welsh, Irish and other nationalities all have their own beloved nationalist myths and the cock-eyed view of history these myths entail. Americans 'Remember the Alamo', or at least the Hollywood version of it, and recall Paul Revere's ride in the historically inaccurate poetry of Longfellow, verses which bear only a passing resemblance to the real events. The faux-historic fantasies which have been most potent in British public life since the Brexit referendum in 2016 are English at their core rather than British. These English nationalist tropes undermine Britishness. They have eaten away at the coherence of the United Kingdom by reminding Scots, Welsh and people in Northern Ireland that in these discussions 'we' are actually 'them', still on the side of the French (or EU) rather than this sceptr'd isle and the New Jerusalem. The rhetoric from the magazine *This England*, the resonance of John of Gaunt's speech as opposed to the reality of who he was, the underlying themes of W. E. Henley's poetry and Cecil Rhodes's brand of severe Anglophilia resonate powerfully in our public life, in political speeches and in the imaginations of many in the imagined community we call our nation. Those English nationalistic tropes from the past – the Blitz spirit, the Dunkirk spirit, even the Charge of the Light Brigade – have been invoked repeatedly since 2016 as part of the debate about the future of the United Kingdom, despite attempts by serious historians to prick the mythical bubble.

It happened with coronavirus too. Writing in the *Financial Times* in the early stages of the outbreak, amid further calls for the 'Blitz spirit' to combat the pandemic, Steven Fielding, professor of political history at the University of Nottingham and co-author of *The Churchill Myths*, quoted the British national treasure Dame Vera Lynn. In March 2020, as Boris Johnson's government ordered social distancing and shut down pubs, clubs, restaurants and gyms – measures even tougher than those seen in wartime – the 103-year-old Dame Vera invoked the spirit of the Blitz as a time 'when we all pulled together and looked after each other'. From Dame Vera this was a welcome corrective to the coronavirus panic and the selfishness of some British citizens determined to stockpile more toilet rolls than any human could expect to use. But Fielding asked the obvious question. How much was the famed Blitz spirit truly evident in pulling us all together and looking after each other during the Second World War itself? Up to a point, but perhaps not quite as much as we might imagine. Professor Fielding noted that in September 1939 the evacuation of 1.5 million British working-class children to the countryside provoked, to take one striking example, a Berkshire Congregational journal to question the 'necessity for the spoliation of decent homes and furniture (or) the corruption of speech or moral standards of our own children'. In the face of 'such Christian fellowship', Fielding says as many as 90 per cent of mothers and children decided they would rather risk the bombs in London and other cities than submit to the snobbery and grudging hospitality of fellow Britons supposedly 'pulling together'. All but 10 per cent returned home by Christmas 1939 to endure the Blitz instead. Fielding concluded: 'Like today's coronavirus crisis, the Blitz was largely experienced privately or within families: collective sacrifice and altruism was of the enforced sort through rationing of food and clothes.'[14]

The idea of the Blitz spirit lives on as a useful piece of mythology, even if it was less in evidence in reality than is convenient for modern politicians and their speech-writers. Much of the human capacity for myth-making is harmless. Napoleon's observation that history is merely a set of lies agreed upon is unfair to professional historians, who often confront us with inconvenient truths. England and most other nations all have their own stories of self-sacrifice. But in the twenty-first century the constant English rhetoric of grievance and the exceptionalist myth of 'stand alone' isolation coupled with the idea that a declining nation is not living up to the greater standards of the past, has a dangerous destabilizing influence in our politics. The internal danger is that some English politicians actually believe the myths and act accordingly, in a political culture which manages to be both arrogant and condescending while – as Boris Johnson proved at the Wirral – fundamentally weak. The external danger is that those outside England regard these actions as symptomatic of an England that is stuck in a delusionary past and has therefore lost its way. If England really believes it 'stood alone' in the past, some true believers think that maybe it could easily 'stand alone' in future. One of them is the English writer famous for *Captain Corelli's Mandolin*, Louis de Bernières.

Captain Corelli's Maudlin Whinge

As these threads of English nationalism come together, the English elephant is becoming more assertive and more consumed with a sense of having a unique identity. Its Scottish, Northern Ireland and to some extent its Welsh partners feel increasingly beleaguered and crushed. The question is whether to get out or to try somehow to remake the communal bed by reviving and reconfiguring a renewed United Kingdom. It won't be easy. And it may be too late. This sense of separation, the silent secessions, from Britishness, have already had profound political consequences for the United Kingdom. Scotland's government is demanding another chance to get out of the union in a second referendum. This call has not yet been answered, but neither will it go away. Irish nationalism may yet find a peaceful democratic route to closer relationships on the island of Ireland. These demands have not gone away either. Louis de Bernières is relaxed about all this and even enthusiastic about the idea of England truly standing alone.

Writing in the *Financial Times*, de Bernières argued:

The logic of Brexit should take us further. It has been increasingly obvious to me and fellow Leavers for years that the English would be better off on their own. It seems ever more obvious that Ireland can be reunified because all the very good reasons for the North resisting this have gone; the Republic is no longer a corrupt, backward country, it is an energetic vibrant place where anyone would love to live, including me. We are an important trading partner; if Ireland were being *strictly rational it would also leave the EU and opt for an Anglo-Irish economic zone*. England has no good reason to want to cling on to Northern Ireland or to Scotland either. The English attachment to Scotland is a sentimental one, but the Scots have fallen out of love with us, and inevitably the English will sooner or later have had enough of the grandstanding of the nationalists. The English have noticed that their own nationalism is the only one that is routinely denigrated and despised, and that also grates. The English have developed their own 'cultural cringe'.[15] (My italics.)

Note the idea – resonant throughout English literature and culture – that in some way the Irish are not being 'strictly rational' in failing to follow England's lead. In this case the presumptuous Irish have refused to leave the European Union just because England has done so. Numerous right-wing Conservative MPs of the so-called European Research Group have expressed similar sentiments, as has Nigel Farage. They even coined a word for it – 'Irexit', Ireland's putative exit from the European Union. The problem with this argument goes beyond de Bernières' condescension, given that he does accept that modern Ireland is a successful small country which (as we will examine later in more depth) has thrived within the EU, and in which writers such as he himself could easily feel at home.

Even before the relative prosperity Ireland has enjoyed since joining the Common Market in 1973, in the twentieth century it managed to produce James Joyce, Samuel Beckett, W. B. Yeats, Sean O'Casey, George Bernard Shaw, Paul Muldoon, J. M. Synge, Seamus Heaney, Flann O'Brien and many other writers, although admittedly some of these writers, including Joyce and Beckett, could not bear to live in Ireland, which they saw as an introverted theocracy and cultural backwater. But de Bernières thinks the Irish have problems being 'strictly rational'. This appears to be what psychologists call 'projection'. De Bernières is projecting his own inability at being 'strictly rational' as he joins those English men and women who unaccountably think Ireland is about to cut itself off from one of the sources of its recent success and prosperity, the European Union itself.

On the contrary, membership of the EU, according to opinion polls, has never been more popular in Ireland than since Britain's Brexit debacle. Most Irish people recognize that the economic and cultural transformation in their country is in great part due to Ireland's self-confidence as a result of being a member of the world's most successful trading bloc. This self-confidence was boosted immeasurably when Ireland was wholeheartedly supported by the rest of the EU throughout all the negotiations with the United Kingdom over Brexit. The great imperial power was bested by its former colony – even if that is not how it is seen in England.

The idea that Ireland would 'also leave the EU and opt for an Anglo-Irish economic zone' is a modern version of George Bernard Shaw's goodhearted yet ridiculous Englishman Tom Broadbent in his 1904 play *John Bull's Other Island*. Broadbent chastises his Irish colleague with the words: 'Never despair Larry. There are great possibilities for Ireland. Home Rule will work wonders under English guidance.'[16] Shaw recognized, as de Bernières doesn't, that the English capacity for making themselves comic figures in Ireland – 'under English guidance!' – has a long tradition. It is alive and well in some parts of the English nationalist imagination. Seamus Heaney also captures this sentiment. In the brutal imagery of his 'Act of Union' from the 1975 collection *North*, Ireland is the victim of an act of union which is the rape of a small nation by a larger aggressor:

> A gash breaking open the ferny bed.
> Your back is a firm line of eastern coast
> And arms and legs are thrown
> Beyond your gradual hills. I caress
> The heaving province where our past has grown.
> I am the tall kingdom over your shoulder
> That you would neither cajole nor ignore.

If de Bernières is in cloud cuckoo land about sentiment in Ireland, his is however an eloquent statement of self-pitying English nationalism. He notes that in Scotland the Saltire flies everywhere, whereas the English intellectual class to which he belongs remain embarrassed by 'chanting, rioting, racist rightwing oafs' who wave the flag of St George. He observes that 'the English don't even know their country geographically. Most southerners have little interest in what goes on Up North, and most northerners wouldn't be able to find Guildford on a map.' For the other nations of the United Kingdom – Scotland, Wales and Northern Ireland – he then concludes that 'England's attitude should be like that of any sensible lover: if you love me, stay; if not, I am better off without you.' Perhaps this tone works in some romantic relationships (though I doubt it) but it is definitely not going to work in the complex politics of the United Kingdom. England seen as a spurned lover is a revealing simile in its contradictions, especially as a counterpoint to Heaney's sexually charged sense of England as an abuser. De Bernières accepts, rightly, that many English people have no knowledge of or interest in other regions of their own country. Presumably he also then accepts they have the same or even greater indifference towards Scotland, Wales and Northern Ireland. And yet the Scots and the others are supposed to 'love' the English and 'stay' or else be booted out of the bed of the United Kingdom. In the de Bernières account we are dealing with a one-sided relationship. One of the partners is narcissistic and believes that those in whom he has no interest are nevertheless supposed to love him. This is the rhetoric of the old Bette Midler gag in the movie *Beaches*: 'Anyway, that's enough about me. Let's talk about you... what do YOU think of ME?'

Reading de Bernières – whom I respect and with whom I have discussed in admiration his novel *Birds Without Wings* for its humane treatment of Greeks and Turks and their competing nationalisms as the Ottoman empire breaks up – inspired me to write this book. Until I read his *Financial Times* article I had not realized just how emotional, irrational and confused nationalism in England had become. But as the historian Jeremy Black puts it: 'Britishness is a time limited, essentially political concept and of value within a state shaped by very different historical legacies and with individuals and communities holding multiple identities.'[17]

Louis de Bernières may be articulating the inchoate sentiments of a large section of Middle England, in which case Middle England is a rather sad place. Like the Greeks and Turks in the 1920s the peoples of the United Kingdom may be witnessing the final disintegration of a once-great empire. Individuals and communities which once happily and unthinkingly held multiple identities are now choosing to focus on one separate identity – English, Scottish, Welsh, Ulster or Irish – rather than that inclusive identity we call being British. The end of Britain, under such circumstances, is only a matter of time.

In Ernest Hemingway's *The Sun Also Rises* one character asks another: 'How did you go bankrupt?' His friend answers: 'Two ways. Gradually, then suddenly.' The United Kingdom is already well into the gradual phase, a slow unwinding not merely of devolved institutions but of the way in which we imagine our nation and how it will be in the future. One day we may wake up and find this unwinding has suddenly accelerated. It seems clear that Scotland has already departed the union culturally, in its mind and in its heart if not yet in its political system. Scotland has already been comprehensively 'othered', as we will explore next. England may yet achieve its own independence and be happy and liberated as de Bernières believes, although this is unlikely to happen because it 'just evolves'. The worst part of reading de Bernières' essay is that its tone is that of resentful victimhood, like that of someone within a marriage who cannot believe it is their own neglect and boorishness which has caused a once-valued partnership to collapse.

England Stands Alone – For Real, at Last

Whether and when Scotland takes the final step – 'suddenly', in an independence referendum – cannot be predicted, but it seems now inevitable that such a vote will take place. The date of exit depends upon – ironically and inevitably – the parliament and government that most represents England, Westminster. That fact in itself sums up another aspect of Scotland's perception of its own 'democratic deficit'. The more a predominantly English government resists an independence vote, the more a vote for Scottish independence seems in the end inevitable. Rather than Ireland emulating the 'common sense' of England, the real story is that Scotland's nationalists see hope in emulating Ireland. But first it's worth considering a more coherent view of the future of Englishness from David Edgerton, professor of history at King's College London. He is one of the few English academics who have taken the prospect of the break-up of Britain seriously. Writing in the *New York Times*[18], Professor Edgerton suggested – in tune with de Bernières – that the break-up of the UK could be good for the most dominant nation, England itself. Such a break-up isn't an outrageous idea because the United Kingdom as currently constructed is 'neither ancient nor stable'. Before 1945, Irish, Welsh, Scottish and English identities 'were for many not local varieties of national Britishness but part of something much bigger', namely an imperial identity: 'British World War II propaganda explained that the United Kingdom was just one equal element of a British Commonwealth of Nations that, along with India and the colonies, made up "the British Empire". It was the empire that fought the war, not the United Kingdom.'

After 1945, the United Kingdom reinvented itself and:

from then into the 1970s, the United Kingdom existed as a coherent economic, political and ideological unit, distinct from the rest of the world. There was a national British economy, a national British Army and a national British politics dominated by two national, unionist parties. It was a brief period of British nationhood. In fact, it was the only one. This national United Kingdom was broken up economically starting in the 1970s by the closely related processes of globalisation and deepening economic integration with Europe. It is this decaying British nationalism, a leftover from the 1970s, that is now disrupting the union, not the self-conscious Scottish, Irish and Welsh versions... The Brexiteers wrongly believe that independence from the European Union will make the United Kingdom great again. But Brexit and the delusions of the United Kingdom's grandeur that go with it are the politics of the aged, of those who remember that brief experience of a united, national United Kingdom. The young people of England, like those in the rest of Britain, overwhelmingly supported remaining in the European Union. They also understand we need liberation from the practices of Westminster and Whitehall, not Brussels, and from the self-defeating rage of the old.

England may indeed seek a new future, liberating itself from the practices of Westminster and Whitehall. Scotland has already done so, at least in the way that many Scottish people now think of themselves. It's the endgame for Britishness.

6

Othered and Scunnered

'The news where you are comes after the news where we are.
The news where we are is the news. It comes first.'

From 'The News Where You Are' James Robertson

'There are no two nations under the firmament that are more
contrary and different as Englishmen and Scotsmen, although
they be neighbours living in the same island and speaking the
same language. For Englishmen are subtle and Scotsmen are
facile. Englishmen are ambitious in prosperity and Scotsmen
are humane in prosperity... To conclude, it is impossible that
Scotsmen and Englishmen can remain in concord under one
monarch or prince because their natures and conditioning
are as different as the natures of sheep and wolves.'

The Complaynt of Scotland

Two old Scots words are useful when trying to understand not just the Scottish Question but also a much wider dissatisfaction with the United Kingdom's institutions in the twenty-first century. One of the words is 'scunnered'. The other is 'thrawn'. Scunnered is always negative. It means being sickened or utterly turned off by something. Thrawn means stubborn, with the sense of being stubborn perhaps beyond your own best interests, although the word can sometimes be used almost as a compliment. Some of my fellow countrymen are at times proud to be described as thrawn. (Me included.) If a nation of 5 million people can be summed up in two words right now it is these two. Most Scots are scunnered by events at Westminster since 2016, notably by Brexit, and by what they see as the incompetence of Boris Johnson and his government. As with every Westminster election since 2005, in December 2019 Scotland overwhelmingly did not vote for the party that formed the British government. Mr Johnson is often regarded (and not just in Scotland) as Donald Trump's Mini-Me. With his usual verbal inventiveness President Trump himself saw the similarity, and liked it. In July 2019 he said: 'We have a really good man who's going to be the prime minister of the UK now. He's tough and he's smart. They're saying, "Britain Trump". They call him "Britain Trump" and people are saying that's a good thing.'

Not in Scotland. An opinion poll survey in June 2019 found that only 13 per cent of Scots thought 'Britain Trump' would make a good prime minister, whereas twice that number of English voters expressed some confidence in Mr Johnson.[1] The coronavirus pandemic was a common struggle against a common enemy, but from the beginning Scots expressed more confidence in the first minister, Nicola Sturgeon, and her team than in the Westminster government. There was considerable Scottish press criticism of what was perceived to be at first a lackadaisical attitude and then dithering from Johnson, particularly his early mis-steps, when he seemed to accept the notion of 'herd immunity' without the availability of a coronavirus vaccine. The Scottish government website in April 2020 presented Ipsos Mori polling which showed that when it came to trust in information about coronavirus roughly 70 per cent of Scots trusted the World Health Organization, just short of 70 per cent trusted the Scottish government, whereas a little over half trusted information from Boris Johnson and the UK government. Even more striking, a Survation poll that month found that the same number, about 70 per cent, of people across the entire UK gave the highest trust score to the Scottish government, whereas only 54 per cent of the UK population said they were likely completely to trust the UK government. People were more likely to trust their local council, *Channel 4 News* and friends and family than the messaging from Number 10.

There were good reasons for this loss of trust. When Boris Johnson took sick with the virus, after boasting that he had continued to shake people's hands despite clear recommendations from scientists not to do so, to many Scots (and others) it appeared evidence of his unbearable lightness of blathering. His chief adviser, Dominic Cummings, while sick with the virus, drove from London to Durham with his family during the lockdown and thereby drove a hole in government lockdown rules. Mr Cummings did not resign. Mr Johnson did not fire him, although he did castigate those English people who went to the beach and in doing so were apparently 'taking too many liberties with the guidance'. For many people all across the United Kingdom this suggested that those in charge of the coronavirus response were showing elitist contempt for rules that they devised but did not feel any obligation to obey.

One other revealing and trust-busting incident occurred when the top civil servant at the Foreign Office, Sir Simon McDonald, told a committee of MPs that government ministers had been briefed on 'what was on offer' in terms of cooperation with the European Union to obtain ventilators for the sickest coronavirus patients. Sir Simon revealed that Johnson government ministers, who as a group had been chosen for high office by the prime minister because they accepted the principle that Britain should, if necessary, crash out of the European Union without a trade deal, had refused the offer of cooperation with the EU 'for political reasons'. In the row which ensued, Sir Simon immediately retracted his statement. Telling the truth in British politics had become dangerous for senior civil servants. In 2019 the UK ambassador to Washington, Sir Kim Darroch, had been forced to resign for daring to suggest in private emails that the Trump White House was dysfunctional (a revelation that had been obvious since Mr Trump's inauguration in January 2017). By April 2020 the row over failure to join the EU in a bulk purchase of ventilators meant that the Johnson government appeared to be putting Brexit ideology ahead of people's lives. By June 2020 Sir Simon McDonald announced he would be leaving his post. The UK's top civil servant, Sir Mark Sedwill, and the former chief civil servant at the Home Office, Sir Philip Rutnam, joined the roll call of those unable to continue working with the Johnson government.

For many people in Scotland, the very existence of the Johnson government and the Brexit vote were practical examples of their democratic deficit, major decisions imposed upon them that they did not choose, demonstrably do not like and which they continue to resist. Scots are consequently thrawn – stubborn – about wanting to retain links with the European Union, refusing to accept being hauled out of the EU just because England has been having a 'nervous breakdown'. That phrase comes from a newspaper article by the English writer Tim Lott.[2] What Lott actually wrote was that Brexit had occurred because 'Britain embarked on its journey towards a full-blown nervous breakdown'. Tim Lott and *The Guardian* occupy a very different political space from Jacob Rees-Mogg, Boris Johnson, W. E. Henley or Shakespeare's John of Gaunt. Even so, this is another example of a London-centred Englishman confusing England with Britain. Scots, Londoners and people in Northern Ireland are not on a journey towards a 'nervous breakdown' over Brexit. Parts of England-outside-London, are on this perilous journey, dragging others along as unwilling passengers.

Another version of this same confusion was expressed by a different and equally highly regarded writer, Ben Macintyre of *The Times*. As one of our many supposed 'Brexit Days' arrived – this one was 31 January 2020 – Macintyre looked for historical comparisons and settled on Henry VIII's break with Rome. Henry VIII's marriage difficulties and his desire to ensure English money did not leave his kingdom through the Roman Catholic Church and end up in the hands of the pope were, yet again, an English-only affair. There is no comparison between the United Kingdom leaving the European Union and Henry VIII breaking with Rome, except to note that Scotland (and Ireland) had nothing to do with either event, although in different ways both nations suffered collateral damage from English decisions.

I admire Lott and Macintyre's writing, just as I also admire the novels of Louis de Bernières, but whatever their politics may be, they are among those for whom we need to repeat in our political vocabulary the term coined by the Palestinian-American writer Edward Said, 'othering'. Scotland increasingly feels 'othered' by the British establishment just as Ireland has often been 'othered' by England, or more precisely, by the London-based political and media establishment. Because the BBC is so important in our lives, as a cherished British institution, paid for by everyone through the BBC licence fee, it is very often in the firing line for exhibiting precisely this kind of unthinking metropolitan bias. Sometimes as a British national symbol the BBC is attacked as a surrogate for the British national government and the amorphous 'establishment' of which both are a part.

The BBC and 'Othering'

If everyone pays for something, everyone has the right to expect something in return. Everyone – more or less – pays for the BBC. People complain if they feel they are not receiving their money's worth. The BBC is, even now, both a national (that is, British) institution and the most influential news source in the UK, the place where we hear and see politics in action. That means that shouting at the TV can be a national safety valve for those who are critical of our failed political institutions and structures.

The BBC replicates some of the problems, flaws and cultural biases of the UK government itself. Nevertheless, the BBC, where I worked for many years, is a good thing. Warts and all, it remains one of the emblems of Britain, internationally renowned and therefore part of our soft power. The BBC's structure and ideology – to inform, educate and entertain the widest possible number of people – reflects its desire to reinforce a sense of British national cohesion in our peculiar union. Twenty-seven million of us watched Prime Minister Boris Johnson speak about the coronavirus lockdown in March 2020, mostly on BBC TV. Nevertheless, the BBC's role as the 'national' – that is British – broadcaster has been eroded by political, cultural and technological change and the explosion of new media competition. For some of my talented former colleagues, working-class England is much less familiar than the power centres of the United States or the trouble-spots of the Middle East. London-centric reporters in the broadcast media and newspapers – including me – paid more attention to events in Tehran and Tennessee than Tranmere, and Moscow rather than Mansfield. I have visited Brussels (dozens of times) much more often than Blackpool (about five times). Washington always makes more news than Workington. When the people of England who had not spoken started to speak many of us at first failed to listen, or chose to pay more attention to the noisy and sometimes violent English nationalist fringe.

I was once involved in a heated debate with an ambitious TV executive about putting a violent right-wing English nationalist on television in a panel discussion. The TV executive saw this person as a spokesman for English working-class angst. I saw him as a football thug with a crafty PR skill.

'Why him?' I asked. 'On a good day he attracts fewer supporters than a bad non-league football club. He makes a lot of noise but he is not important.'

'Fireworks,' was the immediate response.

Another BBC executive agreed with me. This second executive argued that showing a racist, a man with criminal convictions, on TV might be appropriate in a one-to-one interview in which I could directly put serious allegations against him, but giving him equal time with a distinguished panel of experts was inappropriate. The racist, this executive said, was not just like any other guest. Putting him on with two others gave him legitimacy – as if his views were just as acceptable as those of anyone else. This was a reasonable editorial to-and-fro between colleagues, not a matter of deciding policy for all time. In the end I would have reluctantly accepted the racist getting some airtime, even though the format of a panel discussion was a poor idea. Yet it wasn't the debate so much as the tone and language that was revelatory. The TV executive who wanted the violent activist on the panel discussion kept insisting that the man was 'an interesting phenomenon' and that 'it will be a great watch'. It was as if the working-class Englishman with racist ideas was part of some recently discovered exotic tribe from the Amazon rainforest. Maybe because in my childhood I had lived on two council estates, one in Clydebank, the other on the outskirts of Edinburgh, I felt I understood the difference between a genuine working-class voice and a big-mouthed mountebank yob.

This issue – how a national institution should reflect the nation, including its share of racists, anti-Semites and Islamophobes, as well as genuine nationalist sentiments – is always going to be tricky. The somewhat confected debate about singing 'Rule, Britannia' at the Proms is a recent potent example. But part of that debate also involves considering how the most important fault line in British society, class, touches on the cultural narrowness at the top of some British institutions, notably in the media. Only 7 per cent of British children attend fee-paying private schools, but research by the Sutton Trust in 2019 revealed that 'the media continues to be one of the UK's most elite professions… 43 per cent of the UK's 100 most influential editors and broadcasters, as per its News Media 100 list, went to private school'. That at least was progress – an 11 per cent drop since the previous study was carried out in 2014. But 'the proportion of newspaper columnists who studied at independent schools rose by one percentage point to 44 per cent'. Fewer than 1 per cent of the UK population have studied at Oxford or Cambridge, but among top journalists almost half (44 per cent) of newspaper columnists went to Oxbridge, down 3 per cent over the past five years, and more than a third (36 per cent) of the News Media 100 list of editors and broadcasters. That is down 9 per cent. The Sutton Trust found that both newspaper columnists and those on the News Media 100 list were 'among the ten professions with the most Oxbridge and private school graduates'. While the top BBC executives do show a strong bias towards private schools (29 per cent) and Oxbridge (31 per cent), the BBC is more diverse than the average for the industry and working hard to promote diversity.[3]

The reason the Sutton Trust figures are significant is that in the media, politics, business and other professions, diversity is not a gimmick. It's an asset. Lack of diversity means a lack of perspective and experience. The danger is that national newspapers, and opinion-influencing magazines like *The Spectator*, are indeed led by those of whom Louis de Bernières wrote that they 'don't even know their country geographically' and are often 'southerners (who) have little interest in what goes on Up North'.

How you see the world depends upon where you look, and many of us in important media jobs were not looking closely enough at the ways in which our country was moving apart. The BBC, to its credit, has tried to remedy this narrowness by widening its recruitment and appointing news correspondents to focus reports on what BBC jargon calls 'under-served' areas of the country. It meant that in the 2019 General Election there was considerable coverage of a phenomenon known as 'Workington Man' and also attempts to hear the views from strongly pro-Brexit areas such as Stoke-on-Trent. Yet even the phrase 'Workington Man' suggested that the metropolitan media had discovered the corpse of some long-extinct Neanderthal in the trackless wastes beyond the M25, the 'other' Britain where strange things were happening. In Scotland, this 'othering' has provoked a long-running series of rows.

Our *BBC*, Your *Country*

The BBC was founded in 1922 by a Scottish Presbyterian, John Reith. Nowadays the BBC in Scotland has its headquarters in Glasgow's Pacific Quay, one of the most beautiful sites on the River Clyde, a string of new developments where once there were thriving ship-yards and docks. Clydeside as a shipbuilding hub remains strong in the folk memory of Glaswegians, especially those from Govan and Clydebank. Before the First World War there were nineteen ship-yards on the Clyde, employing 70,000 people, including members of my family. Most of the shipbuilding has now gone, although a few of the huge cranes have been left to remind visitors of the past glories of 'Red Clydeside'. Clydebank was a Labour Party stronghold. During the 2014 Scottish independence referendum and 2015 General Election I knocked on doors and talked to people on the Clydebank council estate where I was born.

The one obvious fact from this limited personal survey was that the Labour Party had died in what had once been its Scottish heartland. Almost everyone I talked with supported independence. Most also said they would vote for the SNP, and many were critical of the BBC (although I was generally forgiven, a lost sheep welcomed back to the fold). I was, however, repeatedly informed that the London-centred British national broadcaster was disconnected from their lives and was at times merely a mouthpiece or a surrogate for the British govern-ment and the London-based unionist parties, the Conservatives, Labour and Liberal Democrats.

There were occasional anti-BBC protests. Demonstrators accused the corporation of unionist or government bias and took particular exception to some colleagues from the London newsroom, including Nick Robinson. Behind these disagreements there was one common complaint, a sense of 'othering' in the British national media which had eroded the idea of a common British identity. Some of these complaints might seem trivial, but taken together there was a constant sense in Scotland that the British media were increasingly disconnected from the important things in the lives of most Scots. To begin with an apparently minor example, some Scots, and not just SNP members and activists, told me they were scunnered that the London-based media too often called the SNP the 'Scottish *Nationalist* Party'. Its name is the Scottish *National* Party. The difference in those three letters is significant. Does anyone call the NHS the *Nationalist* Health Service?

I started to listen out for the misnaming of the SNP and began to hear it surprisingly often on various news networks (not just the BBC) in the 2014 independence campaign as well as in the 2015, 2017 and 2019 General Elections. It was mostly just a slip of the tongue or it stemmed from ignorance rather than bias. But to call the SNP 'Nationalist' suggests that they are exclusionary and even that they hate England and the English. This is a sore point with SNP activists because historically there was a strand of Anglophobia within the SNP. It hasn't entirely gone away, but the biggest change in Scotland's politics in the past twenty-five years has been the attempt by SNP leaders to stamp on xenophobic sentiment within the party and within Scottish culture. The aim has been to present Scotland's future much more positively than simply 'not liking the English'. Indeed, the SNP would be mad to do otherwise. England is and always will be Scotland's biggest trading partner and biggest source of tourism and investment.

In August 2017 at the Edinburgh Book Festival the first minister, Nicola Sturgeon, admitted that even the correct name, the Scottish National Party, is 'hugely, hugely problematic' because of the connotations of the word 'nationalism'. As she put it: 'The word is difficult. If I could turn the clock back… ninety years, to the establishment of my party, and chose its name all over again, I wouldn't choose the name it has got just now. I would call it something other than the Scottish National Party.' Ms Sturgeon's openness in these matters is refreshing. Super-sensitivities can become an obsession. But as we noted with English nationalism, such things remain trivial until they are not. Little slips or differences in language can come to reflect entirely different visions of what the 'nation' might mean because nationalism takes many guises, and some of them are extremely negative.

Why Scottish Nationalism is Civic, not Ethnic, Nationalism

George Orwell's essay 'Notes on Nationalism', written during the 1941 Blitz, was, as one might expect for the time, suitably scathing about the racist nationalism driving the Nazi Party. German bombs were falling on London as he wrote. He asserted that there were 'certain rules that hold good in all cases' of nationalism and govern what he called 'nationalist thought'. He included in this definition Scottish Nationalism and Zionism, anti-Semitism, Trotskyism and Nazism. (It's an odd list – Trotskyites are theoretically and resolutely internationalist, but such peculiarities are not our concern here.) Orwell's 'certain rules' of nationalism included obsession, instability, indifference to reality or truth. He might have added also the tendency to require enemies to define and measure 'the other' against 'the nation'. Orwell argued that preserving the independence of what was then called Eire, Scotland or 'even Wales' was a 'delusion' if it was 'unaided' by 'British protection'. In 1941, he had a point. Europe was occupied by German forces from Jersey to Poland. Ireland, Scotland and Wales could hardly stand alone against the most powerful army Europe had ever seen without the full might of the British empire. What Orwell called 'Celtic nationalism' in Scotland, Wales and Ireland was driven, he wrote, by a perceived enemy. That enemy required of the Scots, Welsh and Irish an 'anti-English orientation'. This, again, was undeniably true at the time, especially in Ireland. There was considerable hostility towards Britain in Ireland during the war. The IRA tried to collaborate with Nazi intelligence to invade Northern Ireland. On the basis that my enemy's enemy is my friend, the IRA leadership cosied up to the Nazis, and the IRA's chief of staff at the time died aboard a German submarine returning him to Ireland in 1940.

Even today 'anti-English orientation' can still be found on the edges of Celtic 'nationalist thought', if the chanting at football matches and casual bigotry on Twitter can be dignified by being described as 'thought'. At the Scotland–England match in 1970 in Glasgow some Scottish fans chanted 'Kill the fucking English bastards.' In 1999, again in Glasgow, Scotland and England fans started to fight. These games were seen by some cliché-prone Scottish journalists as encounters with what they called the 'Auld Enemy'. Fans on both sides have been deliberately offensive in this way. In Scotland's case there have been chants of 'If you hate the fucking English, clap your hands.' England fans have demonstrated a talent at conflating their racisms, chanting 'I'd rather be a Paki than a Jock.' The regular England–Scotland games stopped in the 1980s, not because of the occasional violence, but because there were greater opportunities for international competition.

Away from the darker side of football, Orwell's description of nationalism in 1941 does not work as a twenty-first-century evaluation of the competing nationalisms of the United Kingdom. Neither does the idea that independence from Britain is only possible if it is 'aided' by 'British protection'. That idea will bring wry smiles to the faces of Irish readers who see in Orwell a great English author falling into the de Bernières trap – the casual assumption that Ireland can look after itself only under English guidance. Shaw defined the joke with his stage Englishman Tom Broadbent in *John Bull's Other Island*. Irish readers get the joke listening to what they perceive as the astonishing arrogance of some English politicians (as we will see in later chapters). But Orwell and de Bernières in this instance are part of a joke, one that long ago ceased to be amusing.

The SNP did not win fifty-six out of fifty-nine Westminster seats in 2015 and lead successive Scottish devolved administrations at Holyrood merely on a protest vote based on ancient anti-English grievances and being resolutely negative about the United Kingdom. Scottish nationalism in the twenty-first century is *civic* nationalism, a definition used repeatedly by Nicola Sturgeon to contrast her party's ethos with the ethnic, cultural or racial nationalism of the far right in the United States, the English Defence League and some nationalist movements elsewhere. In his 1983 work *Nations and Nationalism*, the political theorist Ernest Gellner defines civic nationalism as a movement that arises in specific circumstances to address a perceived democratic deficit. He argues 'nationalism is primarily a political principle that holds that the political and the national unit should be congruent'. By this definition, British nationalism, in which four separate nations feel themselves in some way to be strongly British, would be extremely unusual. The main 'political unit' in our lopsided union is Westminster, with much of the government bureaucracy and other powerful institutions of our democracy, including the most influential media, the financial sector, prominent NGOs and professional organizations such as the Bank of England, all based in London. This London-centric political unit therefore is 'congruent' in Gellner's terms only with *British* nationalism. But, as we have seen, in England, Scotland and Wales, national identification with Britain is in decline, and in Northern Ireland it can be problematic. The British polity in which power resides with the Westminster parliament is not therefore 'congruent' with the developing nationalisms of the four nations which make up the UK, and that includes those parts of England in which there are growing numbers of people who feel wholly or primarily English rather than British.

In her remarks on nationalism at the Edinburgh Book Festival the first minister explained her own sense of what 'civic nationalism' means in Scotland in terms of Gellner's definition: 'If Scotland is your home, and you live here and you feel you have a stake in the country, you are Scottish and you have as much say over the future of the country as I do,' Nicola Sturgeon said.

And that is a civic, open, inclusive view of the world that is so far removed from what you would rightly fear. Secondly one of the great motivators for those of us who support Scottish independence is wanting to have a bigger voice in the world, it's about being outward-looking and internationalist, not inward-looking and insular.

Scottish nationalism, she insists, is different from the new English nationalism in its coherence, outlook and ambition.

Nationalism and the Irrational

We can all think of examples of Orwell's belief that nationalists are driven by obsession, instability and indifference to reality or truth. There are extremists, xenophobes and nationalistic bigots in every country. Within Scottish nationalism, on the fringes, there are also some brick walls against reason. Prominent members of the SNP despair over the conduct of some so-called 'cyber-nats', the rude boys of the internet who troll on behalf of their narrow view of Scotland. Insulting people does not make for converts. And in Scotland, as elsewhere, there are also examples of an almost comical acceptance of national mythologies and resistance to historical facts.

In Edinburgh a few years ago I was unwise enough to offend the owner of a kilt shop by suggesting that the codification of clan tartans is an invented tradition. Today's kilt was probably designed by an Englishman to encourage the agility of workers in his Highland lumber business. As Hugh Trevor-Roper writes in his essay 'The Highland Tradition of Scotland', the modern kilt was 'unknown in Scotland in 1726' but appeared shortly afterwards and was well established by 1746: 'Its inventor was an English Quaker from Lancashire, Thomas Rawlinson', who had leased a wood at Invergarry near Inverness. The traditional highland costume of belted plaid was inconvenient for the work he demanded, and a shorter kilt was created. The tartan codification which followed, the elaborate development of tartans for different clans, was greatly helped by British army regiments, and the 'free circulation of air' which 'so fitted the Highlander for activity'.[4]

I read the essay while I was a columnist for *The Scotsman* newspaper and excitedly told the kilt-shop owner about the contents, since it seemed a story which – to me at least – made wearing the kilt even more interesting. Sadly, the response was a short intake of breath and a gasp that such heresy could not possibly be true. Worse, in another *Scotsman* newspaper column I suggested that since Scotland had yet again failed to qualify for the football World Cup I would support the England team. Genuine outrage ensued. My favourite version was the gentleman who wrote to me, very politely, as follows: 'I would rather support Satan and all his minions gloriously arrayed than any England football team. I am not particularly proud of this. It is just the way I am.'

Within Irish nationalism, James Joyce satirized the 'one-eyed' nature of all extreme nationalist feelings in the 'Cyclops' chapter of

Ulysses. An Irish nationalist – a 'one-eyed' anti-Semitic pub drinker – rants about the superiority of Ireland, in which every great human being you can think of is Irish, including the following: 'Benjamin Franklin, Napoleon Bonaparte, John L. Sullivan, Cleopatra, Savourneen Deelish, Julius Caesar, Paracelsus, Sir Thomas Lipton, William Tell, Michelangelo, Hayes, Muhammad, the Bride of Lammermoor, Peter the Hermit, Peter the Packer, Dark Rosaleen, Patrick W. Shakespeare, Brian Confucius, Murtagh Gutenberg, Patricio Velásquez, Captain Nemo, Tristan and Isolde, the first Prince of Wales, Thomas Cook and Son, the Bold Soldier Boy, Arrah na Pogue, Dick Turpin, Ludwig Beethoven, the Colleen Bawn, Waddler Healy, Angus the Culdee, Dolly Mount, Sidney Parade, Ben Howth, Valentine Greatrakes, Adam and Eve, Arthur Wellesley, Boss Croker, Herodotus, Jack the Giantkiller, Gautama Buddha, Lady Godiva, The Lily of Killarney, Balor of the Evil Eye, the Queen of Sheba...' And so on.

Meanwhile in England during the months of Brexit debate I took part in many public meetings and repeatedly came across that obsessive strain of English nationalism indifferent to truth which resulted in ordinary, decent English voters believing things that a few seconds of reflection might demonstrate could not be true. At one event I was criticized by an irate Brexit enthusiast for 'going on about your bloody facts'. Fair enough, I admitted. I did go on about facts quite a lot. At another public event, in London's Conway Hall in the summer of 2019, a woman told me that when she voted for Brexit in June 2016 she was 'voting for a clean Brexit, leaving the EU without a deal on October 31st, 2019'. Neither the date, nor the phrase 'clean Brexit', nor the idea we would leave the EU without a deal were part of the discussions when this woman voted in 2016. No pro-Brexit politician was at that time suggesting or offering such an outcome. Theresa May did not push the Brexit button until 2017, and even then her two-year Article 50 timetable had to be extended. To say the woman was outraged when I pointed out that she could not have voted for what she said she had voted for would be a significant underestimation of her reaction. And to complete the picture with a piece of bizarre Ulster Protestant indifference to facts, a few years ago in Northern Ireland I asked a prominent member of the (Protestant) Orange Order in Portadown why marching in Orange regalia was so important to him. He replied that it was to commemorate the 'massacres' of Protestants by Catholics in the seventeenth century. There was indeed a massacre of Ulster Protestants during the 1641 rebellion. But when I responded that there were terrible killings on both sides, he exclaimed that the Protestants were most often the victims, and that he knew this for certain because 'I have seen the photographs.'

Today's competing nationalisms in Britain – as with any other kind of nationalist spirit – have on the fringes a minority of Cyclops-like oddballs and eccentrics, but mostly we are all normal folk who have swallowed some version or other of our national myths. These stories are important to us, and we are irritated – as the kilt-shop owner was – when our mythic views are challenged. Orwell's 'indifference to reality or truth' remains part of our post-Brexit nationalist discourse. Politicians selling Brexit argued for several years after the vote that the United Kingdom had to 'honour' and 'respect' the result of the advisory referendum of 2016, and that we would secure the 'easiest trade deal in history', find 'sunlit uplands' and the re-creation of a free-trading British Empire 2.0 which would become 'Singapore on Thames'. For advocates of these visions, the potential break-up of the United Kingdom, Britain becoming poorer than otherwise it would have been and the possibility of a return of violence over the Irish border were simply non-issues. Outside observers compared this strand of English nationalism to Alfred, Lord Tennyson's poem 'The Charge of the Light Brigade', a heroic determination obsessively to continue to do something which others see as objectively doomed and daft:

'Forward, the Light Brigade!'
Was there a man dismayed?
Not though the soldier knew
Someone had blundered.
Theirs not to make reply,
Theirs not to reason why,
Theirs but to do and die.

Into the valley of Death
Rode the six hundred.

Yet beyond the 'theirs not to reason why' fact-averse Brexit ultras and the far fringes of Scottish or Irish nationalism, or those Welsh activists who burned the holiday homes of English people in Wales, most Scottish, English, Welsh and Irish nationalisms do not fit into Orwell's scathing definition of obsessional nationalist sentiment. Instead, they fit into Gellner's more positive definition. English, Scottish, Welsh and Irish nationalists express various types of civic nationalism rooted in the sense that each part of the United Kingdom in the twenty-first century is driven by a 'perceived democratic deficit'. The most significant change, as we have noted, is that this is now true of England itself, and particularly obvious in great swathes of northern England, where Westminster government talk of 'levelling up' and creating a 'Northern Powerhouse' remains just that – talk. At the same public meetings I attended where people expressed English nationalist sentiments, there was also often an envious recognition that the Scottish and Welsh parliaments and Northern Ireland Assembly were indeed devolved 'political units' that are undoubtedly 'congruent' with 'national units' and that each of them attempts to address the 'perceived democratic deficit' of their nations. In the regions of England the only meaningful 'political unit' is Westminster, a Westminster seen to be out of touch, self-serving and at times corrupt. With no English assembly or strong local government structures, many English voters feel alienated by the political system. They channelled their energies into blaming Westminster or Brussels and the European Union, or both. They were angry, but not alone.

The 'Global Democratic Recession'

Two days before Britain finally left the European Union, at the end of January 2020, Cambridge University launched a new venture, the Centre for the Future of Democracy. Dr Roberto Foa, from

Cambridge's Department of Politics and International Studies (POLIS), summarized its first report by noting: 'Across the globe, democracy is in a state of malaise. We find that dissatisfaction with democracy has risen over time, and is reaching an all-time global high, in particular in developed countries.'[5] The report suggested that since 2005 there had been a 'global democratic recession' and that in the UK this was a reversal of a trend for some thirty years from the 1970s. During the Thatcher, Major and Blair years, satisfaction with British democracy rose markedly. This satisfaction peaked while Tony Blair was prime minister. By the time Blair left office in 2007 there was significant disillusionment over the Iraq War, when democratic protests against the war were ignored. It became apparent that the public had been lied to about intelligence claims offered as justification for the war. This was compounded by the massive economic shocks of 2008, the MPs' expenses scandal of 2009, government-imposed 'austerity' from 2010, the Scottish independence struggle, global warming, the supposedly 'advisory' referendum on Brexit and the incompetent ways in which leaving the EU was handled.

For the first time since the 1970s, that is, before membership of the Common Market and a time when the United Kingdom was seen as 'the sick man of Europe', by 2019 a clear majority of UK citizens were dissatisfied with British democracy. Dr Foa said the rise of populism may be 'less a cause and more a symptom of democratic malaise' and that Britain was not alone in having to face up to its implications:

> Without this weakening legitimacy, it would be unthinkable for a US presidential candidate [Donald Trump] to denounce American democracy as rigged, or for the winning presidential candidate in Latin America's largest democracy [Jair Bolsonaro of Brazil] to openly entertain nostalgia for military rule. If confidence in democracy has been slipping, it is because democratic institutions have been seen failing to address some of the major crises of our era, from economic crashes to the threat of global warming. To restore democratic legitimacy, that must change. (op. cit.)

One consequence of the 'weakening legitimacy' of British democracy is that voters began to look even more critically at the institutions which governed or appeared to govern their lives, casting a baleful eye over the workings of the Westminster parliament and the institutions of the European Union. Even though most voters across the UK would not speak in terms of Gellner's 'civic nationalism', they did appear to understand the concept, in particular the idea that 'the political and the national unit should be congruent'. And that in England they were not. In Scotland and Wales citizens could deride Westminster and yet see in their local assemblies institutions which, for all their shortcomings, were at least congruent with their sense of identity. (Northern Ireland was, as always, a special case here. A significant minority had never accepted, or accepted only grudgingly, the idea that the Stormont Assembly was congruent with their Irish identity.) Voters in England who felt increasingly out of touch with Westminster, had no England-only institution congruent with their increasing sense of English identity. Instead many of them turned their wrath on the European institutions in Brussels.

While these different parts of the UK pursued different paths, much of the invective used by English nationalists towards Brussels was similar to that used in Scotland against Westminster – out of touch, undemocratic, an unrepresentative elite, plus demands that 'we' assert our 'independence' from the distant bureaucrats, and so on. But the political solutions to these complaints in different areas of the UK were completely at odds. Brexit cheerleaders spoke of the great opportunities for Britain as a trading nation to reach out to the world beyond Europe, but in Scotland, Wales, Northern Ireland, London and much metropolitan England the Brexit impulse was regarded as the complaint of Little Englanders, turning inwards and the clock backwards.

Iain Macwhirter, a perceptive and well-connected Scottish political writer, had observed back in 2014 that in Scotland the independence debate 'has not really been between nationalism and internationalism as is often suggested by many unionists, but between two competing nationalisms, British and Scottish'.[6] In that debate,

British nationalism in Scotland with its 'weakened legitimacy' became the clear loser and victim of the 'democratic recession'. The same is now true in England, where the debate is between two further competing nationalisms, British and English, with British nationalism again losing out, but no positive outlet available for English nationalism, only the negative one of leaving the EU.

As Gellner's definition would have it, English nationalism could be seen as a civic nationalism which has grown to address a perceived democratic deficit caused by three upheavals – devolution to Scotland and Wales, the indifference of Westminster to the concerns of many areas of England and the apparent loss of sovereignty from being in the EU. But there is a major caveat here. Civic nationalism is generally contrasted with ethnic nationalism, the type of narrow nationalistic feeling characterized by xenophobia and the rhetoric of superiority. In this sense Scottish nationalism and that of the Irish Republic are demonstrably accepting of differences with minorities and other cultures and generally welcoming of migrants. English nationalism, as currently expressed by its loudest proponents – Nigel Farage for example – is a long way from this kind of civility. It is hostile to other cultures, dogmatic about its own superiority and inimical to newcomers. In June 2016, to take one well-known example, Nigel Farage posed in front of a poster which showed what appeared to be a long line of migrants destined for the UK with the words 'BREAKING POINT' garishly written across the front, a visual echo of a notorious Nazi Party poster from the 1930s. The migrants in the Farage poster were on the Croatia–Slovenia border, and the photograph was presented to show people of colour. Mr Farage was reported to the police for allegedly stirring up racial hatred.

The differences between Farage's English nationalist views and those of most people in Scotland were made plain after a police officer and a number of others were stabbed in a Glasgow city-centre hotel. Farage Tweeted[7]: 'Horrible tragedy in a Glasgow hotel housing illegal immigrants.' (This was factually wrong. The hotel housed asylum seekers and refugees.) Farage continued: 'All over the UK hotels are filling with young men coming across the Channel everyday. It's a massive risk to our well-being – yet the government does nothing.' There were very hostile responses from Glaswegians and across Scotland to what was regarded as a particularly nasty attempt to stoke up fear and racial hatred. Perhaps the best response was a sign and a meme which became popular in Glasgow, playing on the nickname for Glaswegians as 'Weegees'. The sign created a new word – 'REFUWEEGEE' – and defined such a person as follows: 'Refuweegee: A person who upon arrival in Glasgow is embraced by the people of the city, a person considered to be local.' Underneath was the tag-line 'We're all fae somewhere.' (We're all from somewhere.)

As a generalization, the further away from Westminster British citizens are geographically, the further away they feel emotionally and politically. The central positive argument which we will return to later is that if the nations of the United Kingdom can address *effectively* these various 'perceived democratic deficits' by changing the United Kingdom from within, then the UK may even now find a way to stay together and avoid the upheavals of dis-union. The common struggle against the coronavirus outbreak and pride in institutions such as the NHS may help. But there is a catch. Brexit remains a divisive force. It does not and cannot answer the English Question. That's because the Question is at its root about how to end the sense of detachment from Westminster, not about Brussels at all. Worse, while failing to ease feelings of *England*'s democratic deficit, Brexit has instead *increased* the sense of democratic deficit in Scotland and Northern Ireland by dragging them out of the EU when they voted to stay. Brexit has worked the double-magic of alienating voters who wish to remain, while appearing to be unlikely to offer real satisfaction to those who think leaving the EU will make their lives better.

Brexit, in other words, is the wrong answer to the right questions. In Scotland, in particular, Brexit is the wrong answer because Scottish nationalism is indeed international in outlook. That's why being taken out of the EU has made so many Scots both scunnered and thrawn in their determination to resist and eventually to rejoin the EU when Scotland becomes an independent nation. 'When' increasingly is the word Scots use, not 'if'. In Northern Ireland, Brexit is also the wrong answer. Northern Ireland has its land border with the Irish Republic. Now, thanks to Boris Johnson's capitulation in his October 2019 meeting with Leo Varadkar, Northern Ireland also has a notional customs border somewhere in the Irish Sea between Ulster and Scotland. One consequence of this disillusionment with British democracy is that some Scottish political leaders have suggested something which would have seemed far-fetched twenty or thirty years ago. Rather than Louis de Bernières' eccentric and patronizing idea that Ireland needs to see reason, leave the EU and join an Anglo-Irish union, politically engaged Scots talk enthusiastically about the Irish Republic as a progressive model of how an independent Scotland could develop. There are good reasons to consider this.

Ireland and the Inspiration for Scottish Independence

I was asleep in Edinburgh at 5 a.m. when the Brexit referendum result was announced. The telephone rang, and it was my wife telling me the result and wondering if our children should get Irish or German passports (my father-in-law is Irish; my mother-in-law German). I was staying near the Holyrood parliament, and after some eye-opening coffee I wandered down the Royal Mile in the blazing morning sunshine. The parliament sits at the other end of the Royal Mile from Edinburgh Castle, across the street from the ancient Royal Palace of Holyrood. The palace is the site of many Scottish and English dramas. It was attacked by Henry VIII's troops to try to force a marriage between his son Edward and the infant Mary Queen of Scots, a period Scots know as the 'Rough Wooing'. In May 1544 much of Edinburgh, except the castle, was occupied and destroyed. The Scots, however, living up to their self-image of being thrawn, did not give in to English violence. Mary fled to England's enemy, France, and married the Dauphin. The poor lad died at the age of sixteen. Mary returned to Scotland, where in the rebuilt Holyrood Palace she got married again, this time to Lord Darnley. In the palace, Darnley's accomplices murdered Mary's Italian secretary David Rizzio amid speculation that perhaps Queen Mary really was a lover of all things European and that she had been impregnated by the Italian.

In less tumultuous times in 2016, as I walked towards the Scottish parliament, a different kind of history was being made. Small knots of journalists and politicians were stunned at the Brexit vote. Edinburgh was, after all, Remain Central. The city had also been strongly against independence, but in June 2016 Scottish journalists and politicians immediately recognized that situation could change. 'The Vow', the promise that Scotland would have more powers if it stayed in the UK and that only by voting against independence could the country also remain in the EU, was immediately destroyed by Brexit. England was jumping off a cliff by choosing to break away from two unions – the European Union and the UK itself. Five hundred years after the Rough Wooing we were potentially about to enter into a Rough Divorce.

A leading member of the SNP with whom I was on friendly terms turned the corner towards me that morning. As we talked in the sunshine outside the parliament, he appeared almost in tears. This politician is a very thoughtful and passionate European; the embodiment of a Scottish nationalism which is internationalist in outlook. He had been appearing on various breakfast news broadcasts expressing his disbelief at the Brexit referendum result. His first words astonished me.

'We are going to have to sort out something with Ireland,' he said.

Ireland? I had no idea what he meant. I was thinking of the likelihood of another independence vote and he was talking about Ireland? He responded that there were already close links between the Scottish parliament and Dáil Éireann, the parliament in Dublin, and these – even before Scotland pushed again for independence – would have to be improved. He was very emotional, and the conversation was mostly one-sided as I listened to a torrent of words. As if thinking aloud, he said Northern Ireland had to be 'drawn into the mix' because there was an identity of interest with Scotland. He feared that the destabilization caused by Brexit might provoke a return to arguments about the border and a rise of violent sectarian tension again in Northern Ireland. The border would become an issue once more if there were discussions about installing a hard a border on the island of Ireland between the UK and the whole of the European Union. The closer Scotland drew to the Republic of Ireland the better, he said, because then Ulster Protestants would not feel so threatened.

There are strong cultural and historical bonds between Scottish and Ulster Protestants and between Scotland and Ireland. In eastern areas of Ulster, including County Antrim, where my parents lived for many years, they understand the words scunnered and thrawn and speak a dialect of Ulster Scots. Scotland has its own Catholic–Protestant sectarian divisions even now. Glasgow, Edinburgh and Dundee each have two major football teams, one traditionally Protestant, the other traditionally Catholic. If the governments in Dublin and Edinburgh drew closer together, the SNP politician said, this would help maintain peace in Ireland and encourage Scots to see that there was a future for a small country outside the UK. Scotland would become independent and rejoin the EU. Ireland might be a model.

'Is this a material change?' I asked my politician friend, nodding towards First Minister Nicola Sturgeon's assertion the previous year that 'something material would have to change' before another Scottish independence referendum could be contemplated. He nodded.

'But it's only an advisory referendum,' I said.

'We'll see.'

At the time, I confess I didn't pay much attention to his stream-of-consciousness about Ireland, because I had my story for that day, and it was more than enough. England voting to leave the EU meant Scotland would want to vote again on leaving the UK. Two unions were now in jeopardy. But the Irish connection was also worth pursuing. Scotland and Ireland have a lot more in common than great golf courses.

*

Erin Go Bragh and England's Hostile Environment

For centuries both Scotland and Ireland have waved goodbye to their most valuable export on quaysides, at train stations and airports. Talented young people have gone to England, the United States, to the outposts of the British empire and more recently to the European Union and all around the world. But in the twenty-first century Ireland's population has shown a significant increase. Mass emigration from Ireland has become net immigration to Ireland. In the early 1960s the population of the Irish Republic was just under 3 million. Nowadays it is almost 5 million, about the same population as Scotland. Some 90,000 people migrated to Ireland in the year up to April 2018 according to Irish government figures. Almost a third of these were returning Irish citizens, but many are EU migrants and talented people from outside Europe. That's because Ireland has prospered within the EU. The British prejudice about Irish immigrants has traditionally been the image of poor bedraggled labourers coming to Liverpool, London or Glasgow in search of work on building sites or as the old Irish song 'Muirsheen Durkin' goes, 'picking praties' (potatoes) while dreaming of 'digging lumps of gold' in California. The story was that they left to escape the grinding poverty of the priest-dominated and benighted Emerald Isle and were successful in every country except their own. That story has changed.

Ireland and the UK joined the European Common Market at the same time in 1973. That year Ireland's GDP per capita was $2,408, while UK GDP per capita was almost 50 per cent greater at $3,426. By 2018 that had reversed. UK GDP per capita in 2018 had risen to around $40,000 but Ireland's GDP per capita was almost double that of the United Kingdom at $78,750. Ireland's economy has developed out of all recognition in the last few decades. The guarantor of Ireland's independence turns out not to be the UK and the British army, as George Orwell suggested in his essay of 1941. The guarantor of Ireland's independence and prosperity turns out to be the fact that it is a small democratic independent state punching above its weight among the twenty-six other nations of the European Union. One caveat is worth mentioning. Ireland for a time thought of itself as a 'Celtic Tiger' economy. Reality set in with the 2008 banking crisis. But after years of austerity, and in agreement with the EU, the Irish economy turned around, although there remains a considerable gulf between the new rich and the poor. Such inequalities are reflected in anger about housing costs, inadequate health-care provision and other social ills. That anger helped boost the vote for Sinn Féin in the 2020 Irish General Election. But the overall point still stands. In economic terms measured by per capita GDP, the people of Ireland are now much richer than those of the United Kingdom, although you would not know this from the condescending attitudes towards Ireland from some English nationalist politicians. Ireland has a lot of friends around the world and few enemies. Scottish politicians have repeatedly told me that they were hugely impressed at the whole-hearted EU support for Ireland during the Brexit talks. Dublin was subjected to British rhetorical bullying over the Irish border, but it was Boris Johnson who was forced into his customs-border-in-the-sea flip-flop while Ireland and the EU held firm.

For Britain this was a remarkable moment. During the 2016 Brexit campaign the Irish border was never an issue for English nationalist politicians. It's simply not on their radar. But after the vote it became the key issue, the most important sticking point. The core of the Good Friday Agreement, which in 1998 largely brought an end to the sectarian conflict of some thirty years in Northern Ireland, was for unionists the recognition that a border did exist on the island of Ireland while for Irish nationalists it was the sense that the border might exist in theory but in practice it could be ignored. It was Schrödinger's border – existing and not really existing at the same time. Brexit risked destroying that idea, and peace itself, if the Irish border became a hard border between the EU and United Kingdom. The Irish government rightly feared customs posts would return, and that the IRA campaign – during which customs posts were bombed and shot at – might also reignite. At every stage of the Brexit withdrawal negotiations therefore the twenty-six other members of the European Union supported Dublin's stance against the UK on this issue, and, as we noted, after much complaining about Irish intransigence, the British side capitulated.

Since Scotland has also suffered from years of emigration, and has also been relatively poorer per capita than England or the British average, the Scottish government has paid close attention to developments on the other side of the Irish Sea. In rhetorical and presentational terms, the Holyrood administration has, like Ireland, publicly been very welcoming to returning Scots, even those of us on a short working visit. At Glasgow Airport I recall receiving a welcome when I exited the plane in the terminal building. ReturnedScot.com is a website highlighting information about and for the Scottish diaspora. New immigrants to Scotland have also been gratefully received, and the tone from Edinburgh has been very different from the mean-spirited rhetoric in Westminster on immigration.

England Awakes

When considering those seeking asylum, the former UK home secretary Theresa May promised to 'deport first, appeal later'. It's worth pausing a moment to reflect on that phrase, with echoes of 'shoot first, ask questions later'. The woman who was in one of the top jobs in British democracy and who would later become UK prime minister was threatening to deport without a legal appeal asylum seekers who should be considered, in Franz Fanon's phrase, as the 'wretched of the earth', unfortunate human beings who need help. The UK Home Office, under Mrs May's instruction, also engaged in a bizarre publicity stunt, sending 'Go Home' vans around some urban areas, urging illegal immigrants to deport themselves. Journalists were told that the 'pilot scheme' was supposed to encourage those living illegally in the UK to leave voluntarily. It was called Operation Vaken. Vaken is the Swedish word for 'Awake', a choice of code name that (like the Farage anti-migrant poster of 2016) was reminiscent of 1930s Germany. *Germany Awakes* – Deutschland Erwacht – was a

1933 Nazi propaganda film. Perhaps there is some other explanation for the peculiar title of the publicity stunt, although none springs to mind. At any rate the Go Home pilot scheme lasted for just one month, between 22 July and 22 August 2013, in six London boroughs. There is no reason why any illegal migrant hearing a loudspeaker yelling a recorded message from a van on a London street would pack his or her bags and immediately head for Calais. But of course the target audience wasn't migrants overstaying their visas. It was UKIP-leaning English nationalist voters. Mrs May and the government were in the time-honoured political tradition of those pretending to be 'doing something' to cut immigration without achieving anything except ensuring that her rhetoric was suitably xenophobic and tabloid-friendly. 'We are trying to create a much more hostile environment in this country if you are here illegally,' Mrs May boasted.

This 'hostile environment' proclamation came a year after the failed 2012 promise from Prime Minister David Cameron that net migration – the difference between those coming to the UK permanently and those leaving – would be limited to 100,000 a year or fewer. This neat round number, plucked from the skies, inevitably proved impossible for Mrs May to achieve. The best she could do was the publicity stunt of the Vaken campaign, although her 'deport first, appeal later' policy was eventually ruled illegal by the UK Supreme Court in 2019. When a policy is not working, politicians make a lot of noise and toughen their rhetoric to disguise the failure of their actual achievements. Mrs May followed that rule. When she became prime minister, in preparation for Brexit, the hostile environment towards migrants spread even further – to those from the European Union who had settled legally in the UK. Mrs May changed the rules, demanding a £65 fee for each person to register for the right to remain. The announcement was brusque: 'If you're an EU citizen, you and your family will be able to apply to the EU Settlement Scheme to continue living in the UK after 30 June 2021. If your application is successful, you'll get either settled or pre-settled status.'

This renewed hostile environment was much more divisive than the 'Go Home' vans, since it involved several million people who had come to the UK legally and who enriched the country by their hard work and expertise. It caused – and still causes – great irritation and disappointment for those EU citizens who had contributed to Britain for years as doctors, teachers, academics, vets, and other workers all over the country, and in the process often becoming husbands, wives, mothers, fathers, and friends of British people.

In 2017, to take one example, the House of Lords EU Environment Committee warned that the UK was 'overwhelmingly reliant' on EU workers to enforce animal welfare and food hygiene standards in abattoirs. The Lords committee asked that these workers on whom we are reliant stay after Brexit, despite Theresa May's efforts to make EU resident citizens feel unwelcome. The UK government's Food Standards Agency report was even more stark about the numbers of 'OVs', that is, official vets, working in the food industry: 'Latest FSA data shows that approximately 280 OVs are currently contracted by the FSA of which 97% are non-UK EU staff. The total number of OVs is approximately 330 of which 95% are EU nationals from out-side the UK.'[8] Stripped of jargon, this meant that all but 5 per cent of British vets certifying beef, lamb, pork and chicken fit to eat for British households are not British citizens. Nevertheless, the English nationalist impulse driving the Conservative government meant that even those qualified to declare our food safe to eat had to register and apply to stay.

A British Member of the House of Lords, Lord Wood of Anfield, who grew up in Kent, Tweeted that the new regulations meant he was expected to explain to his German-born mother, now in her eighties, a woman who had lived happily in England almost all her life after marrying an Englishman, that she was now an immigrant who would have to pay £65 to continue to live in the place she had called home for decades. It may seem odd that the octogenarian mother of a member of the upper house of the British parliament needed to find out if her application had been successful. Perhaps Orwell's 1941 characterization of obsessive nationalism requiring a perceived enemy – in this case, English nationalism seeing European Union citizens as potentially the enemy within – may still exist within the

Westminster government. If so, there are rather a lot of presumed undesirables.

At the latest estimate there were 3.8 million EU citizens living in the UK. Of that total 350,000 are Irish. They are a special case, provided for under a mutual agreement between the Irish state and the British government that dates back to the 1920s. They do not have to complete any settlement forms since they are treated as if they are UK citizens. Irish residents can, for example, vote in UK General Elections. But that means roughly 3.5 million other EU citizens were expected to complete the settlement forms. After a public outcry the Settlement Scheme £65 fee was dropped in 2018. Instead of raising money from applications, the 'hostile environment' programme actually cost the British government money and bureaucratic time.

Since the scheme started I have talked with countless EU nationals, including some from Germany, France, Italy, Lithuania, Poland, Estonia, Romania, Portugal, Sweden and Spain. Beyond the tedious tangle with the British bureaucracy they were more distressed by the way the scheme made them feel unwelcome. Many of them told me it was as if they had become a burden on the British state, allowed to stay, but their work and skills not appreciated. Some expressed their profound sense of resentment and disappointment at British government incompetence coupled with a kind of officially sanctified nastiness. This Westminster-created atmosphere was clearly intended to be hostile. It was also futile. After ten years of Conservative-led governments and the promise of a net migration cap at 100,000 a year, according to the Office for National Statistics, net migration to the UK in 2019 was 270,000.[9] In terms of the unity or otherwise of the United Kingdom the key point is that both the failed policy and nasty rhetoric were strongly rejected in Scotland, while being embraced with great vigour by English nationalist politicians at the top of the Conservative government in London. That disjunction in sentiment and policy has important consequences for the future of the UK.

*

Scotland Says No to a Hostile Environment

In their differing attitudes to migrants, the contrast between Westminster and the official Scottish government position could not be more stark. The SNP administration, as we noted, asked for the creation of 'Scotland Work Visas' to allow EU migration to continue, but England's 'hostile environment' policy meant this was rejected. The official website made the Scottish government ambitions clear:

> We want Scotland to continue to be a vibrant, diverse country that faces outwards and is a confident and responsible global citizen. That means welcoming free movement of people because it reflects the welcoming place we want to be. Not only does Scotland (and the UK) benefit enormously from the contribution made by citizens of other EU countries, but we also benefit from the opportunity that free movement gives to Scots to live and work in other EU countries. We are particularly concerned about protecting the rights of family members of EU citizens, the processes of applying for new settled status in the UK, and continued access to independent judicial redress. We will do all we can to support the 237,000 EU citizens living in Scotland through this difficult time, and we will continue to push the UK Government to do the same.[10]

This attitude is hardly surprising since it concerns around 5 per cent of the population of Scotland, and Scotland has a skilled labour shortage. There is particular difficulty attracting workers for the hospitality industry, farm work, nursing and social care. To take one example, in 2020, on arrival in a popular tourist area of the Scottish highlands, I was checked into the hotel by a Polish woman, two of the waiters were Czech and I heard Spanish spoken by other members of staff. In Edinburgh, the café at the Palace of Holyrood – like pubs and restaurants all across the Scottish capital – also depends upon workers from European Union countries. Edinburgh has had a thriving Polish community for years. The welcoming attitude to migrants is therefore ethically driven and also self-interested. In February 2018, the Scottish government published *Scotland's Population Needs and Migration Policy*. This explained in detail that migration was crucial to Scotland's prosperity and that UK policy was 'not appropriate' for Scotland. The Holyrood administration demanded 'a tailored approach to migration for Scotland'. When these findings and the demand for Scottish work visas were rejected by the Westminster government, this opened up another key area of conflict between the needs of Scotland and the political imperatives of Brexit.

Alasdair Allan, formerly Scotland's minister for international development and Europe, is in a way typical of the international outlook in Scotland which sees its interests as very different from those of the Conservative administration in London. As Mr Allan said in 2017: 'The Scottish government will oppose any changes to UK immigration rules that create barriers to business and industry accessing the talent it needs to grow.'[11] Mr Allan speaks English, Gaelic and Norwegian. The Norway model is also attractive for some in the Scottish government – a small, broadly social democratic and rich Nordic country which, although not in the EU, has a close association with it.

The Scottish government website has consistently adopted a very different tone on refugees and asylum seekers compared to that in England: 'Scotland has a long history of welcoming refugees and asylum seekers and recognizes it is a human right to be able to seek asylum in another country.' In 2019 First Minister Nicola Sturgeon went even further. Reacting to the treatment of EU27 citizens after the Brexit vote by Mrs May's government, Ms Sturgeon launched the 'Stay in Scotland' campaign. The avowed aim was to help EU citizens navigate the extremely complicated (and much resented) British Home Office EU Settlement Scheme. Whatever the opposite is of a 'hostile environment', Scotland has attempted to demonstrate it: 'Scotland is your home, you are welcome here, and you are valued. The closer we move towards the UK's exit from the European Union the more real and substantial reassurances about your rights and position in this country you need.'[12] This was the clearest possible affirmation of a benign environment for EU citizens, and with it a rejection of the Westminster and British government policy in tone and in substance.

History is full of 'hostile environments'. It is also full of evidence that this is both cruel and short-sighted. In 1492 King Ferdinand II of Aragon and Isabella I of Castile expelled all Jewish people from Spain. Many of them fled to the Ottoman empire, and in particular to Thessalonica. Sultan Bayezid II is credited with a withering response to courtiers who felt Spain had done the right thing by getting rid of people considered 'of impure blood'. Bayezid said: 'You venture to call Ferdinand a wise ruler – he who has impoverished his own country and enriched mine.' The spirit of Ferdinand and Bayezid lives on in the differences between the Westminster and the Scots/Irish approaches to migration. Whatever you think of Ms Sturgeon's statements, and Scotland's response to migrants and asylum seekers, they are not nativist; they are not anti-English or anti-foreigner. They are strongly anti-Westminster, and they find support among those, not just in Scotland, who are scunnered by the policies and the attitudes struck in the 'Mother of Parliaments'. There is a thrawn and persistent desire to set a different course, internationalist in spirit and tone, in the face of policies which appear narrowly English nationalist in character. On immigration Scotland is asserting that it is a different country. If it is to become independent – and even if it stays in the UK and wants to thrive economically – the Scottish government understands that it needs vigorously to follow the Irish example and reject the narrow nationalism in evidence in England. If Scotland does that, the prize is to reverse centuries of a brain drain of clever young men and women leaving for England, for the British empire and more recently the US and EU. A 'brain gain' of clever newcomers making Scotland more economically competitive is a political imperative. This idea is utterly at odds with the philosophy as well as the policy of Boris Johnson's English nationalist government, but there is nothing within the current political system that Scots can do about it, except complain. And when they do complain, they are 'othered'.

Othered and Scunnered

Part of the bargain of devolution was that Scotland would gain its own parliament but have reduced representation at Westminster, down from seventy-two to fifty-nine seats. Even with this loss of seats, it still takes more English voters to elect an MP than Scottish voters. But representation in a democracy is not just a matter of numbers. Democracy cannot just be majority rule. It is also a matter of listening to minority voices. SNP MPs are not exactly ingénues, but their contributions to the Mother of Parliaments are often treated with particular scorn. For several years, when the SNP Westminster leader Ian Blackford, or other articulate voices such as Joanna Cherry – a respected lawyer – made contributions, Conservative front benchers including Boris Johnson stood up and left the chamber rather than listening. In one particularly egregious example from 2019 the then Speaker John Bercow witnessed the Tory benches emptying while Joanna Cherry is reduced to saying that the video record of the proceedings shows such Conservative Party contempt for Scotland that it could be useful for SNP election broadcasts.[13] In February 2020 Scots complained that a similar lack of respect was shown to London-based journalists from Scottish newspapers and broadcasters who were kept out of a contentious meeting about post-Brexit trade plans. Aberdeen South MP Stephen Flynn, told the Commons:

> My constituency, Aberdeen, is projected to be the hardest hit city in the entire UK as a result of Brexit, yet the Westminster correspondent for the *Press and Journal* was not invited, indeed no Scottish lobby journalist was invited. Does the contempt that this government shows to Scotland now extend to our press corps too?[14]

Brexit was apparently an England-only affair. Scotland was being dragged along but not being kept informed.

Some journalists from London-based and English regional newspapers and media companies were also not allowed to attend this highly selective briefing, but the row was dismissed by Lee Cain, Downing Street director of communications: 'We are welcome to brief whoever we want, whenever we want.'[15] This is true. But that does not make it either wise or acceptable. Those excluded were also welcome to complain about the arrogance of Mr Cain as a spokesman for what is supposed to be the government of the whole United Kingdom. These various displays of contempt for less-favoured publications or less supportive parts of the country are of particular significance in Scotland. Many Scots, not just SNP politicians and the Scottish media, see such incidents as going beyond mere rudeness. They see instead a pattern of behaviour through which the concerns of 5 million people with a strong sense of national identity are marginalized by politicians and bureaucrats responsive only to the demands of England (and even then, only to part of England).

Some Scots, those with a sense of history, draw another parallel with Ireland – to the decades in the late nineteenth century during which Irish Home Rule representatives received a rough ride, were snubbed or ignored by English MPs and resorted to obstructive tactics in the Commons. Their demands were ultimately accepted within the then powerful Liberal Party, causing it to split and provoking a massive pro-Unionist campaign in Ulster. All of this did not end well. After the violence of the Easter Rising in 1916 and the repression that followed, Sinn Féin MPs set up an independent Irish parliament in Dublin in 1919. That act precipitated the Irish War of Independence. Nothing so dramatic, one can assume, is in store for Scotland now, but underlying the policy differences over immigration and Brexit, there is something even more damaging and difficult to change. Social and cultural differences between Scotland and England are widening. In the long term these will prove much more important. Scots see a cultural divide represented daily on their TV screens.

The News Where You Are

This sense of being othered and scunnered is perhaps best captured by the Scottish poet James Robertson. During the 2014 independence referendum campaign he performed a new work, 'The News Where You Are', to amused Scottish audiences. At its heart it is an exploration of 'us' and 'them', using broadcasters as an example. When the BBC1 national *Six* or *Ten O'Clock News* ends – that is, the London-based British and international news from London's New Broadcasting House – Huw Edwards or another news presenter will say, in the opening words of James Robertson's poem, 'That's all from us. Now it's time for the news where you are.' If social scientists ever want a clear example of the marginalization of the non-metropolitan parts of Britain, including the north of England, Wales and Northern Ireland, then Robertson's poem provides it. The division between 'us' and 'you' is one in which 'our' news is important while 'yours' is merely 'the news where you are'. To gain a real sense of his wit, it's worth watching Robertson himself performing the poem on YouTube.

Here is the text in full:

That's all from us.

Now it's time for the news where you are.

The news where you are comes after the news where we are.
The news where we are is the news. It comes first. The news
where you are is the news where you are. It comes after. We
do not have the news where you are. The news where you are
may be news to you but it is not news to us. The news may
be international, national or regional. The news where we
are may be international news. The news where you are is
never international news. Where you are is not international.
The news where you are comes after the international and
national news. The news where you are may be national news
or regional news. However, national news where you are is not
national news where we are. It is the news where you are. If the
news where you are is national news it is only national where
you are. The news where we are is national wherever you are.

On Saturdays, there is no news where you are after the news
where we are. In fact there is no news where you are on
Saturdays. Any news there is, is not where you are. It is where
we are. If there is news where you are but not where we
are it will wait until Sunday. After the news
where you are comes the weather.

The weather where you are is not the national weather. The
weather where you are comes after the news where you are,
and after the weather where you are comes the national
weather. Do not confuse the national weather with the
weather where you are. The weather where you are comes
first but is lesser weather than the national weather.

Extreme weather is news. However, weather that is more
extreme where you are than where we are is not news. Weather
that is extreme where we are is news, even if extreme weather
where we are is only average weather where you are. On
average, weather where you are is more extreme
than weather where we are. Tough shit. Good night.

Of course Londoners have their own regional news too, and all
across the United Kingdom regional or local news programmes are
extremely popular. But James Robertson touches on a specific Scottish exasperation with London-based media and irritations which
have resonance beyond Scotland and beyond broadcasting. The suspicion persists that not only are events in London considered more
important than similar events in other parts of the UK but also
that decisions taken in Westminster have relevance all across the
country. That is not the case, as we will see in more detail in Part
Two. In his poem, Robertson focuses on apparently minor details as
symbols of a larger sense of neglect. There is no 'news where you are'
on Saturdays because BBC Scotland did not have the resources to
cover Scottish news that day. The BBC in London refused demands
for a Scotland-based *Six O'Clock News* – the 'Scottish Six' – which

would be presented at teatime from the studios at Glasgow's Pacific Quay, although eventually the BBC did react, launching a dedicated BBC Scotland TV channel in February 2019. There is a particularly sharp observation about metropolitan or London bias in Robertson's lines: 'If the news where you are is national news it is only national where you are. The news where we are is national wherever you are.' This is the key point in the poem. It is the sense that Scots, and by extension everyone in non-metropolitan England, Wales or Northern Ireland, listening to the 'national' news, is not where 'we' are (London and Westminster), but separate, less interesting and ultimately less important – although in the case of the BBC paying exactly the same licence fee as the better-served folk in London and the south of England.

To be clear: the point here is not to second-guess BBC decisions and its use of limited resources, or those of ITV, which at times comes in for similar criticism. In some ways Scotland is super-served by the BBC. BBC Gàidhlig produces Gaelic-language programmes for BBC Alba (Scotland) and has been doing so since 1985. According to the 2011 UK census there are only 57,375 Gaelic speakers in Scotland – 1.1 per cent of the population, and only 32,400 can actually read and write the language. The number of speakers has been falling since 2001, although 'original' languages continue to play a significant role in nationalism. In Ireland, Raidió na Gaeltachta and TG4, the Irish-language channels, serve the small minority of actual speakers of Irish. Yet symbolically these minority channels are evidence of commitment to a distinct Irish culture. Irish is a remarkable survivor, refusing to die, with most Irish people retaining fragments of it, and officially it remains the primary language of the state.

In Scotland, despite the investment in services for Gaelic speakers, the BBC, for at least some licence payers, is an omnipresent British national institution which at times replicates the 'othering' of Scotland seen in parliament and other institutions of the British state. The BBC in this sense becomes a metaphor for Britishness, its strengths, burdens and increasingly its weaknesses. Everyone pays the same for a service everyone uses, a bit like paying the same taxes (according to income) for the services the government provides in the NHS, or schools or transportation or policing – except that not everyone feels satisfied they are receiving the same services as London or other more favoured areas of the country. National (that is, British) public broadcasters are caught in a vice. If they refuse to give in to demands for more localism, including from the tiny minority of Gaelic speakers, then they are deemed as not adequately serving all of Britain. That makes them London-centric and out of touch. But if they do devolve their media power in some way, as the BBC has done in creating a dedicated TV channel for Scotland and transferring its Breakfast News TV show, sport and children's programming to Manchester, with wildlife and nature shows in Bristol, then the accusation switches to one of bureaucratic duplication and wasting resources. The BBC, as we will see when we come to consider supposedly 'British' institutions in detail, has become increasingly decentralized, an example of how the United Kingdom is now federalized by stealth. This expanding and yet – for most of us, unobtrusive and unremarked – federal structure in many institutions jars with our London-centric style of government. The cracks between the two are widening.

Before we move on to consider Britain's federalization by stealth and how that may be put to work in the service of re-forming the United Kingdom for the twenty-first century, we need to examine in more detail why Ireland may provide a model for an independent Scotland, and why people in Northern Ireland – the home of Ulster unionism and those who have at times violently resisted demands for a United Ireland – may now be having second thoughts about where they stand within the UK. Jonathan Powell, a former British diplomat who became Tony Blair's chief of staff, has publicly suggested that Boris Johnson's English government may be about to deliver by its blunders what the IRA could not achieve by its bombs: 'Paradoxically, Mr Johnson and Brexit may have done more for a United Ireland than the IRA ever did,' Powell says, adding that Boris Johnson's plans may mark the end of the union of the United Kingdom, 'leaving a Little Englander government ruling a Little England.'[16] A Little Englander government ruling a Little England maybe closer than you think.

English people have often talked about 'the Irish Question'. But Ireland has historically always had an English Question: what on earth are the English playing at?

7

Ireland's English Question

'It is hereby declared that Northern Ireland… shall not
cease to be (part of the United Kingdom) without the
consent of a majority of the people of Northern Ireland
voting in a poll.'

'Good Friday Agreement', 10 April 1998

'Irish unity is now discussed across the island in a way
that I never recall in my lifetime. If you look northwards,
the unionist majority is gone. There has been a generational
turning of the wheel. Brexit was driven by the lowest common
denominator of English nationalism… you see a society
that is hopelessly divided.'

Sinn Féin Leader Mary Lou McDonald, Times, 15 February 2020

'So, as I grew from boy to man,
I bent me to that bidding
My spirit of each selfish plan
And cruel passion ridding;
For, thus I hoped some day to aid,
Oh, can such hope be vain?

When my dear country shall be made
A Nation once again!'

Thomas Davies, 'A Nation Once Again'

'History, Stephen said, is a nightmare from which
I am trying to awake.'

Ulysses, *James Joyce*

In *Ulysses*, James Joyce's hero, Stephen Dedalus, is speaking of Irish rather than British history when he talked of it as 'a nightmare from which I am trying to awake'. Although the histories of Britain and Ireland have frequently collided, at times it is as if the two sides of the Irish Sea are looking at the same events through opposite ends of binoculars. Their perspectives are not only different, but sometimes completely contradictory. For many in Ireland, the British historically were the very definition of a nightmare. Mention Oliver Cromwell or the nineteenth-century Great Famine among Irish people and you will get a flavour of what that means. When the future British home secretary Priti Patel appeared to suggest the British government could use food shortages as a weapon in Brexit negotiations with Ireland, forcing them to drop their insistence on the 'backstop' as a way of avoiding a hard border with Northern Ireland, she was condemned as 'despicable' by Irish politicians. The normally very diplomatic Irish prime minister Leo Varadkar pointedly rebuked her: 'Where I stand now in Donegal the population has still not recovered from the famine that was imposed on us. I would hope that with the passage of time she has thought better about those remarks and did not mean them to be said in that way.'

For many in England 'the Irish' historically have simply been a puzzle. Irish history is not studied in any depth in English schools, but most English people know that Ireland is a country divided by a border because for some unaccountable reason Protestants and Catholics have found it difficult to live together. They also know that even after the creation of an independent Irish state various factions began fighting a civil war. In 2020 any English person paying attention to Ireland would be surprised by the words of the leader of Sinn Féin, the party that was the political wing of the Provisional IRA. Ms McDonald claimed that Brexit was driven by 'the lowest common denominator of English nationalism... you see a society that is hopelessly divided'. The idea that the leader of a strongly Irish nationalist party which for decades had fought to end the partition – that is, the division – of Ireland while the IRA's campaign of violence increased divisions in Northern Ireland could criticize the English for being nationalistic and divided among themselves was most certainly a political innovation in the twenty-first century. It was also an accurate analysis of British political life.

What English, Scottish and Welsh schoolchildren do learn about Ireland is that there is something called 'The Irish Question'. Seen from England, this question was mostly associated with agitation for Irish Home Rule, bitter and sometimes violent sectarian divisions between Irish Protestants and Catholics and attempts by the British prime minister William Ewart Gladstone to deliver an acceptable kind of self-rule for Ireland in the 1880s. Gladstone's great rival, Benjamin Disraeli, phrased the Irish Question most succinctly. In the House of Commons in 1844 during the years of the Great Famine Disraeli put it this way:

A dense population, in extreme distress, inhabit an island where there is an Established Church, which is not their Church, and a territorial aristocracy the richest of whom live in foreign capitals. Thus you have a starving population, an absentee aristocracy, and an alien Church; and in addition the weakest executive in the world. That is the Irish Question.

Indeed it was. The catastrophe of the Great Famine eventually passed, but the Question remained, as did the absentee aristocracy, the alien church and the weak and remote executive.

The English attitude to their apparent inability to 'solve' the Irish Question in the nineteenth century was reflected in the humour of the historical satire *1066 and All That*, first published in 1930. It suggested that Gladstone 'spent his declining years trying to guess the answer to the Irish question; unfortunately, whenever he was getting warm, the Irish secretly changed the question'. Amusing though all that may be, it suggests Ireland was and is still a problem or a question for the British, more specifically the English, rather than the other way round. This pressing problem stretching back centuries could easily be rephrased as Ireland's English Question. At its heart it is this: what, after centuries of living with English or British conquerors, does Ireland have to do to find unity on the island of Ireland, domestic tranquillity and a degree of understanding from their closest neighbours and former occupiers? The answer to that question – at least for most people on the island of Ireland – was the Good Friday Agreement or Belfast Agreement of 1998. The Irish Republic no longer claims jurisdiction over Northern Ireland; unity can happen only by consent. Only Sinn Féin pursues the aim of unity as a priority, but even they accept that it must be consensual. There remain many obvious barriers to the unification of Ireland. What future awaits those from my own family background, Scots 'Planters' who settled in Ulster during 'the Plantation' as far back as the seventeenth century and who remain stubbornly Protestant and stubbornly British? How welcome in a united Ireland would such people be after years of sectarian Troubles including 3,600 dead, half of them civilians, in the most recent outburst of violence, from 1968 until 1998? And why would the increasingly prosperous and modern Irish Republic wish to take on the responsibilities and financial burdens of Northern Ireland and its sometimes recalcitrant unionist majority?

Within Ireland there are three main strains of Irish nationalism reflected in political parties with long roots and historic disagreements. The two traditional Irish democratic parties created in the 1920s are Fine Gael (in English, Tribe of the Irish) and Fianna Fáil

(Warriors of Destiny). The third party, the tribe or warriors which have agitated most strongly for it, is Sinn Féin. Just as the Scottish National Party has distanced itself from previous Anglophobic incarnations, Sinn Féin has had an even tougher job. Although they do not like being reminded of it, their former military wing killed people, accounting for the majority of the deaths during the recent Troubles. The inner core of Sinn Féin's current leadership still includes former IRA commanders with blood on their hands. Some do not admit their IRA past. Others talk of their regret at 'innocent lives' being lost, with the implication that some of those whose death they caused must have been 'guilty' of something – 'guilty' of being a police officer, or political opponent, perhaps.

The IRA (or PIRA) was the armed insurgent group that for thirty years until the Belfast Agreement was in armed conflict with British forces in Ireland. By British forces in Ireland the IRA meant – and targeted and killed – some of their neighbours in Northern Ireland, mostly Protestants but also Catholics, if they happened to be members of the security forces, the Royal Ulster Constabulary (RUC), or customs officers, prison guards, government officials or simply people who were politically active in the unionist cause. The IRA said it did not target people just because they were Protestants, but that did happen. On 5 January 1976, ten Protestant workers were selected for murder at Kingsmill in South Armagh. Five years later the IRA murdered a Methodist minister whom I happened to know, the Reverend Robert Bradford. He was also a Unionist Member of Parliament for South Belfast, which presumably was their excuse.

If the Great Famine is not forgotten, nor the Easter Rising, nor the British repression carried out by the Black and Tans, neither are the murders carried out by the IRA in a campaign supported by Sinn Féin. The killings include the Enniskillen bombing of 1987, the murders of former as well as serving members of the police, off-duty policemen murdered on their doorsteps, farmers who had joined the part-time British army regiment the Ulster Defence Regiment and countless ordinary people going about their business who happened to be in the wrong place at the wrong time. These victims were mostly

Protestant, but there were many Catholic victims too, some of whom were 'executed' because the IRA believed them to be police informers known as 'touts', some whose bodies have never been discovered, others in Catholic areas who were 'kneecapped' in punishment shootings as part of the IRA's rough justice on those who caused it offence. In England the dead include the civilian victims of the indiscriminate Birmingham, Guildford and Woolwich bombs and the Brighton bombing, which was planned as the assassination of the prime minister, Margaret Thatcher. These attacks will not be forgotten, however much Sinn Féin hopes otherwise.

Nevertheless, for more than twenty years now, Sinn Féin activists, including those I personally knew, and who were imprisoned as IRA gunmen convicted of terrorist crimes, have played an active and constructive part in bringing peace to Northern Ireland. This is not just my opinion. It is also the opinion of the British government, the Irish government, the United States government and also the opinion of unionist leaders such as the Reverend Ian Paisley, who served with Sinn Féin in the power-sharing executive in Northern Ireland. This is a remarkable if at times imperfect transformation. It may now be at risk, as a result of English rather than Irish nationalism.

'We Ourselves'

'Sinn Féin', or more correctly 'Sinn Féin Amháin', was an old slogan of Irish republicans dating back to the nineteenth century. It is usually translated as 'We Ourselves' or 'Ourselves Alone'. The phrase conveys precisely the sense of separatist and nationalistic exceptionalism that George Orwell eviscerates in his 1941 essay. Irish writers, and Sinn Féin's leader, Mary Lou McDonald, have noticed that twenty-first-century English nationalists and their 'we stood alone' narrative means that English exceptionalist rhetoric is now more Sinn Féin than Sinn Féin itself. On the island of Ireland the question of who 'we' are in the phrase 'We Ourselves' is crucial. Protestants and unionists have always felt that it does not mean them, that Sinn Féin is a narrow, extreme nationalist party. When Sinn Féin supporters yell the slogan 'Brits Out!' the message it sends to unionists is clear: they mean anyone in Northern Ireland who feels British. On an island in which the events of 1690 or 1916 are sometimes referenced as if they took place last week, change appears to come very slowly. But change has come. The genius of the Good Friday Agreement of 1998 is that it gives everyone in Northern Ireland the right be Irish as well as British. The Agreement recognizes 'the birthright of all the people of Northern Ireland to identify themselves and be accepted as Irish or British, or both, as they so choose'. That means everyone in Northern Ireland has the right to be an EU citizen and to have multiple identities if they wish.

Sinn Féin has changed too. The gun has largely gone out of Irish politics. Among those I have met from Sinn Féin in recent years are political activists who say that 'We Ourselves' in the twenty-first century signifies all residents of the island of Ireland who are prepared to accept an Irish identity, whether they are Protestant or Catholic or Jewish or Muslim or of no religion, or immigrants from the EU, or from other countries including refugees, and those who also hold British passports. Sinn Féin has positioned itself as a tolerant, democratic socialist party. The change is significant. Sinn Féin could have been the obvious vehicle for anti-immigrant, xenophobic sentiment at a time when the numbers of non-Irish people living in Ireland rose from negligible figures to over half a million in a single generation. Ireland remarkably, and almost uniquely in Europe, has no serious far-right, racist party. As a Scottish Protestant with strong Ulster Protestant and unionist roots and a British passport I should also say that for all the sometimes heated debates and discussions I have had with Sinn Féin and IRA activists over the years I have never felt threatened or treated with anything other than respect. Two personal experiences may help explain why this is significant for Ireland's future.

*

The Gibraltar Three

When three unarmed IRA members were killed in Gibraltar by British army special forces, the SAS, the bodies were returned to Northern Ireland for burial in West Belfast's Milltown cemetery. It was a moment of great tension. As we filmed the funeral of the 'Gibraltar Three' on 16 March 1988 for the BBC, a loyalist gunman and member of the paramilitary group known as the Ulster Defence Association (UDA), Michael Stone, attacked the mourners with guns and grenades, killing three people, one of whom was an IRA member. Catholic areas of West Belfast erupted in anger. Cars and buses were hijacked and set alight. After Stone ran away and my crew and I left the cemetery, I kept to an arrangement to interview a priest with strong contacts within the republican movement, Father Alec Reid, at the Clonard monastery in the heart of West Belfast. After the interview my TV crew left in their car full of BBC equipment. My producer and I chatted a little more with Father Reid – one of the architects of peace in Northern Ireland – about the horrific events in the cemetery. We then walked to our car. As I started the engine, I noticed four men at the exit point to the monastery car park, men I had reason to believe were IRA members. They stood across the exit and stopped the car. I rolled down the window.

'We are taking the car,' one of them said, stretching in and pulling the keys from the ignition before I could react, 'in the name of the Irish Republican Army.'

'Don't be daft,' I responded. 'The IRA does not hijack reporters' cars.'

'This is not a reporter's car,' the leader of the group said. 'It's a hire car. You drive a dark-blue Ford. This is a commercial vehicle, and we are taking it.'

My own car was indeed a dark-blue Ford. An argument followed, but the upshot was that the IRA 'Active Service Unit' (as they would have described themselves) opened the boot, took out my briefcase, handed it to me, apologized for the inconvenience and drove off. The point of this story is not to excuse their actions, but to point out two important facets of this most extreme form of Irish nationalism. These young men loathed the British presence in Northern Ireland and were prepared to kill – and to die – in order to remove 'the Brits'. They were part of an organization that killed members of the security forces and also murdered civilians, including those they believed were police informers, children killed in bomb attacks, pub drinkers in Birmingham and many others. However, as a Scottish Protestant reporter with (on that occasion) a Welsh producer, I experienced no direct personal animosity towards either of us. The hijacking was a businesslike transaction resulting in the expropriation of a 'commercial vehicle' expressed legalistically on behalf of the Irish Republic declared at Easter 1916. Loathing of the British state was combined with a peculiar love-hate relationship towards British people.

On another occasion I was with a leading member of the IRA at Sinn Féin headquarters on the Falls Road when we heard that a well-known English journalist was leaving Belfast. I thought I was making a joke when I said, 'and you'll be pleased because it's one less Brit in Ireland'. The IRA man was deeply offended. 'He's not a Brit,' he said. 'Don't call him that. He's a journalist doing his job. And a good one at that.'

These anecdotes are meant to begin to explain why, if the United Kingdom is indeed coming to an end, Protestants and unionists in Northern Ireland may be embraced as citizens of the modern Irish Republic, even by those with a violent past. It is however doubtful whether, given the history of the past few decades, many Ulster unionists would wish to accept an embrace from Sinn Féin. Even so, change is happening. Sinn Féin has developed as a credible left-wing democratic republican force in Ireland. In the Irish Republic's General Election in February 2020 the party polled slightly more than either Fine Gael or Fianna Fáil, and in terms of seats Sinn Féin took thirty-seven to Fine Gael's thirty-five and Fianna Fáil's thirty-eight. This was an extraordinary achievement. Abandoning the gun, pushing for social justice and developing a left-wing ideology for a united Ireland has proved successful for the republican movement in the south. Yet to adapt the title of Seán O'Casey's great play *The Shadow of a Gunman*, the gunmen may have gone, but some of the shadow remains. There will always be those in Ulster who remain sceptical of a party whose military wing once thought it could unite Ireland by blowing parts of it up and murdering some of its citizens. Moreover, a united Ireland, again according to the Belfast Agreement, 'shall be brought about only by peaceful means with the consent of the majority of the people democratically expressed in both jurisdictions in the island'. That would mean, presumably, a referendum in both Northern Ireland and the Irish Republic on Irish unity, the result of which could not be taken for granted. As they look north to Belfast, Ballymena and Portadown, some voters in the Irish Republic may themselves be as hesitant about what Irish unity might mean as unionists in Northern Ireland.

As I was writing this chapter, I consulted a friend from Derry (who happens to be Catholic). He said he would vote *against* Irish unity on the grounds that integrating Northern Ireland would be a significant blow to prosperity in the Irish Republic. Another friend from the Irish Republic countered that if it came to a vote, nationalism would triumph over economics. I tend to side with the latter view, but either way a vote on Irish unity will come. Whatever the practical difficulties, any future prime minister of Ireland would undoubtedly wish to enter the history books as the man or woman who finally brought about the peaceful creation of a truly united Ireland. For now, what is certain is that Irish people, including the most hardline nationalists, have studied England much more carefully than English people have studied Ireland. Successive British governments – with some notable exceptions – have been particularly remiss in this. English politicians posted to Northern Ireland, again with some important exceptions, have often failed to understand the complexities of either Irish nationalism or of the strong-willed Protestant group of unionism to which members of my family belonged. This lack of interest and lack of empathy goes back at least fifty years, and continues to have consequences even now.

*

'What a bloody awful country'

The usual starting point of the recent violent conflict between two nationalisms, British and Irish, which is known as the Northern Ireland Troubles is the development of civil rights agitation in 1968. In January 1969 Ulster 'loyalists' attacked a People's Democracy march at Burntollet Bridge. People's Democracy had Protestant as well as Catholic supporters, and the marchers were complaining peacefully and justifiably about religious discrimination against Catholics in housing, employment and political representation. They were inspired by the 1960s protests of African Americans against racist discrimination in the United States. The marchers were violently assaulted, in full view of television cameras and British and Irish reporters. The British government had, broadly, left Northern Ireland to its own devices since Partition in 1921. The Province, as it was called, was run by the Northern Ireland parliament at Stormont on the outskirts of Belfast. When the first prime minister of Northern Ireland, Sir James Craig, called it 'a Protestant parliament for a Protestant state' it was an accurate description. Northern Ireland was overtly sectarian from its birth.

The population of Northern Ireland in 1921 included half a million Roman Catholics, more than 40 per cent of the total. The parliament, in Craig's definition, was not for them. They were the 'other', the supposedly disloyal and possibly subversive Irish nationalist minority, and they were treated accordingly, as second-class citizens. Discrimination on sectarian lines in everything from gerrymandered electoral areas to housing and jobs festered for years within a part of the United Kingdom and without interference from Westminster. The fighting at Burntollet led to fierce rioting in Catholic areas, notably the Bogside in Derry. In London, the government was finally forced to take notice. When it became clear the Northern Ireland security forces – the Royal Ulster Constabulary and the paramilitary police known as 'B-Specials' – could not cope, the Westminster government sent units of the British Army to the Province in August 1969. They were at first welcomed by Catholics, who felt that the British were saving the Catholic minority from reprisals by the overwhelmingly Protestant RUC and their auxiliaries. Reginald Maudling, once tipped as a future British prime minister, made his first visit to Northern Ireland as Conservative home secretary in 1970 to survey the scene. After just a few hours in the Province he decided he loathed the place and swiftly departed. On his plane back to London he said, 'For God's sake, bring me a large Scotch. What a bloody awful country.' The 'bloody awful country' was and remains part (at the time of writing) of the United Kingdom, theoretically at least Mr Maudling's own 'country'. Prime Minister Margaret Thatcher took a much more robust stance in favour of the union when she famously emphasized her attachment to Northern Ireland by saying that it was as British as her own constituency of Finchley, in north London. That promise died with Boris Johnson and his acceptance of a customs border in the Irish Sea. There is no customs border round Finchley.

Ulster and the Other

My first jobs as a journalist were with the *Belfast Telegraph* newspaper and then the BBC in Belfast. Reginald Maudling's reaction to Northern Ireland was not shared by my journalist colleagues from England. Martin Bell, Jeremy Paxman, Peter Taylor and many other distinguished broadcasters spent the early parts of their careers on the streets of Ulster. Most loved Northern Ireland as much as I did. My first boss at the BBC was the novelist Bernard Cornwell, one of those Englishmen who enjoyed supping Guinness with me in illegal drinking clubs in west Belfast, and who retained a strong sentimental attachment to the place. Other incomers were, like Maudling, simply baffled by it. Unionists sometimes complained to me, often in the most striking terms, that neither the BBC nor the British government were standing up for what they considered to be British values, and that Ulster was not treated as if Fermanagh was indeed as British as Finchley (personally I could not see any resemblance). The founder and leader of the Democratic Unionist Party, the Reverend Ian Paisley, was a firebrand orator but off-camera he was much more thoughtful. He spoke with me many times of his disappointment that English government ministers rarely tried to understand his views and those of his many supporters in Protestant areas of Northern Ireland. In a mirror image of this, Irish republicans and nationalists also claimed neither incoming journalists nor British government minsters truly understood their historic grievances. There were exceptions – Mo Mowlam, the Northern Ireland secretary in the crucial years from 1997 to 1999, and earlier Jim Prior, exiled to Northern Ireland by Mrs Thatcher, and more recently Julian Smith, were all well regarded. They made friends among the various feuding groups in what was a very difficult posting. Some British ministers from the House of Lords also fitted in well, in Ulster's not-very-deferential society. But the ignorance of others, including journalists, was quite embarrassing.

During the difficult period of the IRA Hunger Strikes I heard one English TV producer ask a Catholic priest with IRA sympathies, 'What do the other Fathers think of the Hunger Strike?' He meant other priests. A newspaper photographer at an event in Armagh asked the Catholic primate of All-Ireland, Cardinal Tomás Ó Fiaich: 'Would you like your wife in the picture?' Cardinal Ó Fiaich was celibate. The lady was his housekeeper. She did not appear in the photograph. In the fifty years that have passed since Maudling's day one might have assumed that English politicians might finally have grasped some of the key characteristics, if not the subtleties, of Northern Ireland, but that is not always the case. As we noted, even as recently as 2018, when the Conservative MP Karen Bradley became Northern Ireland secretary, she openly admitted she did not understand that nationalists and unionists do not vote for each other's political parties. When I heard those comments I rather wished that the power-sharing first minister Reverend Ian Paisley or his deputy, the former IRA commander Martin McGuinness, had been alive to share the joke. After years of enmity, Paisley and McGuinness, got on so well that in a classic twist of Ulster humour the Protestant verbal incendiarist and the ex-IRA man were known as 'the Chuckle Brothers'.

Singing 'The Sash'

The unspoken English response to the Ulster Troubles from 1968 to 1998 tended to be a mixture of outrage, puzzlement and indifference. From time to time this was punctuated by bursts of unsuccessful initiatives and frustration at their failure because people in Northern Ireland were 'not being reasonable'. Ulster Protestants with their Union Jacks, marching bands and Orange Lodges, their bowler hats and triumphalist songs were, for the English political classes, reminders of a kind of Britishness – militarist, imperialist and anti-Catholic – best left to history. Yet the chorus of the most famous Protestant anthem, 'The Sash My Father Wore', or just 'The Sash', is well known outside Northern Ireland. Orange Order marches still take place in the West of Scotland, and there is a Liverpool Provincial Grand Orange Lodge, and, at least until the 1990s, there were active Orange Lodges in former colonies including Ghana, Canada and Australia. 'The Sash' is the battle cry of Orangeism, listing the victories of Protestant forces over Catholic rebels more than 300 years ago:

> It is old and it is beautiful and its colours they are fine.
> It was worn at Derry, Aughrim, Enniskillen and the Boyne.
> My father wore it as a youth in bygone days of yore,
> And on the Twelfth I love to wear the sash my father wore.

The Twelfth of July 1690 was the date of William of Orange's victory over the Catholic army of King James at the Battle of the Boyne, although the decisive battle was a year later, at Aughrim, in Galway, the bloodiest battle in Irish history. This encounter destroyed the Jacobite army and is remembered in Catholic popular memory as the final disaster for Catholic fortunes. Yet Protestants on the island of Ireland remained an uneasy and insecure minority even when they controlled the most significant levers of power. In 1912 at least a dozen members of my family signed the Ulster Covenant against Home Rule because, quite simply, they feared domination by the Catholic

Church, which was considered at best an unenlightened superstition and at worst a repressive and intolerant force. If this seems ludicrous now, it was anything but ludicrous in the early twentieth century. The last reputed witch in Ireland was burned in her cottage in Clonmel, County Tipperary as late as 15 March 1895. The body of Bridget Cleary, aged twenty-eight, was found in a shallow grave. She had been burned to death by her husband and family members who suspected her of being possessed by a fairy. The Irish Free State in the 1920s was clearly in thrall to the Catholic Church, ceding control of education, social policy and much else to the bishops. Divorce and contraception were banned. Right up into the 1980s condoms were smuggled from Belfast to Dublin. Films and books were censored if they offended Catholic Church ideas of morality.

The 1912 Ulster Protestant and unionist rebellion against Irish Home Rule had powerful supporters in England. The nineteenth-century English statesman Lord Randolph Churchill, father of an even more famous son, Winston, is said to have put the position most clearly: 'Ulster will fight. And Ulster will be right.' The Conservative prime minister Lord Salisbury said he 'would no more give democracy to the Irishman than to the Hottentot'. Conservative politicians for their own ends would 'play the Orange card' throughout the late nineteenth century and beyond. The Orange card has not entirely gone out of service. It was played by Theresa May's government from 2017 onwards. Mrs May realized that only by co-opting Ulster's Democratic Unionist Party did her hapless administration have a hope of surviving long enough to deliver a form of Brexit. It came at a price. The DUP agreed a 'supply and confidence' deal. That meant on the most important budgetary and other issues DUP MPs at Westminster would vote to keep Mrs May in power, though they did not enter a formal coalition and did not receive any posts in government. What they did receive was money, an extra £1 billion or so for their trouble, including £400 million for infrastructure development, £150 million for ultra-fast broadband and £200 million for health, plus cash to tackle deprivation and mental health issues.

In the previous financial year (2015–16), Northern Ireland had already received £26 billion of UK public spending. That's a gross figure which does not take into account revenues raised by the British Exchequer from Northern Ireland taxpayers, VAT and the like, but British newspapers, including the *Independent*, worked out that at £14,018 of public spending per head, each Northern Ireland citizen received 20 per cent more than the UK-wide average of £11,579. We will return to money matters and differences across the United Kingdom later, but the DUP's experience proved that those who can be bought can also be sold, despite their flag-waving Britishness. When Mrs May fell from power and Boris Johnson became British prime minister in 2019, his Ulster allies and their concerns proved to be of little more significance at Westminster than those of Lord Salisbury's Hottentots.

As we noted, in his October 2019 discussions with the Taoiseach Leo Varadkar, Boris Johnson suddenly conceded the principle of a customs border not as it had been on the island of Ireland between north and south, but in the Irish Sea between Britain and Ireland. To readers in England or elsewhere moving a largely invisible line from the land to an imaginary line in the sea may seem of little significance. To Ulster unionists it was an existential issue, rather as if the British government conceded that Mrs Thatcher's Finchley constituency could be treated as part of France for customs and excise purposes. The cabinet minister Michael Gove in somewhat slippery fashion tried to soften the blow by denying something which had never been on the agenda, that there would be 'any kind of international border in the Irish Sea'. But there was to be a customs border with 'expanded infrastructure' to check food and goods going from Great Britain to Northern Ireland and an increase in staff to check those goods at the ports of Larne and Belfast and elsewhere. There are no similar arrangements surrounding Finchley or indeed any other part of the UK. The Johnson–Varadkar agreement suddenly confronted the Democratic Unionist Party and their supporters with a truth that should have been obvious for years. No matter how British you claim to be by birthright, no matter how many of your young men served in the British army and died at the Somme, you will never be treated as if your concerns are as important as those of England.

We Are the Sacrifice

Leaving aside the cynicism of the 'Orange Card' and the Conservative Party's internal management problems, there used to be true believers in England and Scotland in the idea that Ulster represented something vital to British interests and Britishness itself. There may be a few such true believers today, but their voices are less apparent. In the early part of the twentieth century, Rudyard Kipling was one of the most vocal English supporters of Ulster's resistance to the British government. Signatories to the 1912 Ulster Covenant believed, in the age-old phrase, that 'Home Rule is Rome Rule'. In his stirring call to arms 'Ulster 1912', Kipling touched not just on Ulster's enemies in Ireland but what he called 'England's oldest foe' – the Catholic powers of Europe:

> The dark eleventh hour
> Draws on and sees us sold
> To every evil power
> We fought against of old.
> Rebellion, rapine hate
> Oppression, wrong and greed
> Are loosed to rule our fate,
> By England's act and deed.
>
> The Faith in which we stand,
> The laws we made and guard,
> Our honour, lives, and land
> Are given for reward
> To Murder done by night,
> To Treason taught by day,
> To folly, sloth, and spite,
> And we are thrust away.

The blood our fathers spilt,
Our love, our toils, our pains,
Are counted us for guilt,
And only bind our chains.
Before an Empire's eyes
The traitor claims his price.
What need of further lies?
We are the sacrifice.

We asked no more than leave
To reap where we had sown,
Through good and ill to cleave
To our own flag and throne.
Now England's shot and steel
Beneath that flag must show
How loyal hearts should kneel
To England's oldest foe.

We know the war prepared
On every peaceful home,
We know the hells declared
For such as serve not Rome –
The terror, threats, and dread
In market, hearth, and field –
We know, when all is said,
We perish if we yield.

Believe, we dare not boast,
Believe, we do not fear –
We stand to pay the cost
In all that men hold dear.
What answer from the North?
One Law, one Land, one Throne.
If England drive us forth
We shall not fall alone!

Within ten years of that poem being published, Ireland was partitioned, divided between a largely Catholic south and a largely Protestant north. The nine counties of historic Ulster were also divided. Six became Northern Ireland, which had its own new parliament at Stormont, a magnificent white building on a hill at the end of a great imperial driveway on the outskirts of Belfast. My family members in Northern Ireland, mostly unionists, spoke of two religious minorities on the island of Ireland, both at times fearful of the other. Protestants remained the minority on the whole island, and particularly in the Irish Republic, while Catholics were and still are (just) the minority in Northern Ireland. These distinctions have mattered in Ireland for generations, but how much do they matter now? Certainly, whatever the core of 'Britishness' may be nowadays, to most people across the UK it is no longer Protestantism or, as Kipling puts it, 'For such as serve not Rome.'

The historian Linda Colley offers a list of the kind of grievances and fears behind Protestant resistance to Irish unity:

> It had been a Catholic who had plotted to blow up James I and his parliament. A Catholic Queen Henrietta Maria, together with her interfering priests, had led Charles I astray and the whole island into war. The would-be tyrant James II had been Catholic just as those responsible for the St Bartholomew's Day massacre in 1572, or the Irish 'massacres' of 1641, or the Great Fire of London in 1666, had, they were assured, been Catholic also. That much of this Protestant version of the past was grossly inaccurate was immaterial. As Ernest Renan once remarked, 'Getting its history wrong is part of being a nation.'[1]

Yes, we all get history wrong, but the sense of grievance and fear is genuine. Yet perhaps the profound changes in the Irish Republic, the transformation of a poor country into a rich small nation in the past fifty years, and the removal of the shadow of the gunman from Irish politics may yet ensure that past grievances remain no longer politically salient. It does not mean they will be forgotten.

Changes

In the last UK census in 2011, 60 per cent of the population of the
United Kingdom – around 40 million people – identified as Christian.
That is, nominally Christian. When it comes to going to Christian worship, only a million or fewer (just over 1 per cent) said they
actually attend a church on a Sunday. Ireland's pattern of religious
observance has changed too. Church attendance among Catholics
and Protestants in Northern Ireland declined significantly in the
twenty-first century. In the Irish Republic fifty years ago almost the
entire population would have identified as Catholic. By the time of
the 2016 census that was down to three-quarters (78 per cent) of the
population, and weekly Mass attendance had fallen sharply to 35 per
cent, and below 20 per cent in Dublin. In some urban parishes it was
much lower. In an Irish-speaking pub in County Kerry, where I had
gone to watch a Munster rugby match, I found myself among a group
of men in red Munster shirts. The south-west of Ireland has a long
and proud tradition of Gaelic games, hurling and Gaelic football,
but rugby also has a strong following there. At half-time I started
chatting to one of the rugby fans. He volunteered the information
that his cousin had been one of the first men to take legal action
against the Catholic Church in Ireland for abuse he had suffered as
a boy.

'The church is dead to me and my family now,' he said.

While 35 per cent attendance at Mass is significant enough, it marks
a sharp fall in enthusiasm for church-going and brings Ireland down
to the level of Italy, where around 30 per cent of the population is
said to attend Mass every week. In the Irish Republic, the second-
largest group in the census was that of people who said they had
'No Religion', at 10 per cent. Whatever the traditional religious core
of the Irish Republic, the Roman Catholic Church has been much
damaged by the exposure of paedophile priests and other scandals.
Its influence is in decline. Abortion (except in cases of danger to the
mother's life) was always illegal in Ireland. Then as recently as 1983 it
was also made unconstitutional in a referendum. But in a profound

change, in 2018, in another referendum, two-thirds of Irish voters overturned the ban and legalized the termination of pregnancies in a way once thought unthinkable. The legalization of gay marriage, divorce, contraception and the election of the first openly gay Irish Taoiseach in Leo Varadkar show that Ireland is a modern western European nation with a strong Christian tradition but a much more complex modern reality. In this it is now just like everywhere else in Europe.

A striking example of this change is to be found a few miles outside Dublin in Maynooth. From 1795, St Patrick's College, Maynooth was a religious establishment training priests to serve their flocks all over Ireland and indeed beyond. The photographs of the priests graduating from the seminary look very different over the years. Decades ago the priests were almost all white Irishmen. More recently the photographs show many more non-European students aiming towards the priesthood. In 2019 the Association of Catholic Priests, representing a thousand or so priests in Ireland, predicted an end to 'basic sacraments' like marriages and baptisms in some smaller parishes as a result of the lack of Irishmen willing to embrace the celibate life. As Father Tim Hazelwood, ACP spokesman, put it:

> We're facing a catastrophic situation in the next ten to twenty years because there are not enough male celibate vocations to keep our parishes alive… In maybe ten, but definitely twenty years, priests in Ireland are going to be an endangered species unless things change. We're facing a really bleak future unless new measures are brought in.[2]

One thing is certain, and it could be a comfort to northern Protestants. Whatever a modern version of Irish Home Rule might look like, it certainly won't be Rome Rule.

The 'catastrophic situation' of the priesthood is yet another indicator of change in the Irish Republic, and there have been profound changes in the north as well. The Good Friday Agreement of 1998 brought (mostly) peace to Northern Ireland. European Union membership has brought (mostly) money, investment and a better economy for both parts of Ireland. Northern Ireland farmers did well out of EU grants. Northern Ireland's population makes up just 3 per cent of the United Kingdom, yet Northern Ireland farmers managed to secure 10 per cent of the farm subsidies from the EU to the UK. The agriculture sector is hugely important in Northern Ireland, and Ulster farmers may come to feel they have a greater community of interest with those in the Irish Republic than with the priorities of a London government.

Religious issues remain, but not with the profound sense of antagonism and threat that they had in the past. The same is true of the Irish border. It was once a dangerous flashpoint. During the Troubles I would frequently drive from Belfast to Dublin, and the journey could take three or four hours or more. You could never predict how long or how disrupted it might be. Customs posts were heavily fortified and often attacked by the IRA. Suspicious cars parked near the road were treated as part of a terrorist threat and blown up by the security forces. I'm not especially timid but I avoided border roads at night. It was never clear which armed group – the British army, the Royal Ulster Constabulary, the Irish army, the Irish police (Garda Síochána), the IRA, the INLA or even loyalist paramilitaries would decide to conduct their own 'security checks'. People were murdered after being stopped by terrorists wearing fake security forces uniforms. The toxic border issue, apparently solved by the Good Friday Agreement, has been raised again by Brexit. But this time, the notional customs border in the Irish Sea is the one which unionists wish would not exist. Even the imagined existence of this border has 'othered' the six counties of Northern Ireland by making them formally not-quite-British. Unionists have finally come to recognize that the English Conservative Party of the twenty-first century does not have the same attachment to their cause and interests as Rudyard Kipling – or Margaret Thatcher – clearly did. The Orange Order marches, the marching bands, sectarian songs, anti-Catholic rhetoric, the bowler hats and furled umbrellas are to many British people not part of a celebration of the Glorious Revolution and

Protestant succession, but an embarrassment, and an expensive one at that.

English Nationalism and Ireland

I visited Belfast in October 2019 a few days after Mr Johnson's volte-face on the customs border. The sense of shock was obvious. Unionists I talked to, from taxi drivers to university academics, were stunned. After thirty years of the Troubles and all the sacrifices of human life, including the victims of IRA bombings and killings in England as well as in Northern Ireland, there was considerable dismay at discovering Brexit was more important to Boris Johnson and his Conservative and 'Unionist' Party than the principle of the union itself. They should not have been so surprised. Boris Johnson is not a 'One Nation' Conservative but a 'One Notion' Conservative. His One Notion has always been to do whatever is best for Boris Johnson. After all, he is the politician who wrote two versions of his newspaper column – one for and the other against Brexit. Then he had two versions of Northern Ireland – one with a border on the island of Ireland, one with a border in the sea between Northern Ireland and Great Britain. And at least two versions of what to do about coronavirus – seeking 'herd immunity', then a lockdown and then using 'good British common sense'. Johnson is consistent only in choosing what appears best for Johnson, and certainly not best for traditional unionism in Northern Ireland. In Ulster 2020 rather than Ulster 1912, unionists may again have need to recall Kipling's words:

> The traitor claims his price.
> What need of further lies?
> We are the sacrifice.

The *Daily Telegraph* paid Mr Johnson a quarter of a million pounds a year to write for the newspaper along with his part-time jobs as mayor of London, British foreign secretary and MP for Uxbridge and South Ruislip. On the day that Mr Johnson met his Irish opposite number at the Wirral, the *Daily Telegraph* carried an op-ed piece by someone called David G. Green. Mr Green is the founder of a right-of-centre 'think tank', Civitas. The article suggested that getting shot of Northern Ireland might be no bad thing for England and significantly that Northern Ireland and its people must not be an obstacle to Brexit:

> Northern Ireland has long been a *millstone round the neck* of the rest of the UK and to *fail to take back our independence* because of it would be an historic tragedy. It is not widely known that it costs the UK more to support Northern Ireland than it does to be in the EU. In 2016–17, according to HM Treasury figures, total expenditure by the Government on Northern Ireland was £20.6 billion. HMRC reports that tax receipts from Northern Ireland in the same year came to £11.7 billion, a net payment of £8.8 billion.[3] (My italics.)

Traditionally the unionist case has been very easy to make. In Mrs Thatcher's language, Northern Ireland is part of the United Kingdom. That means Belfast is as much a British city as Birmingham; Londonderry/Derry is as British as Liverpool. It's all as British as Finchley. What is significant in this *Telegraph* article is that Mr Green has found space in a British newspaper that supports the Conservative and formerly 'Unionist' Party to make a robust English nationalist argument about abandoning his fellow British citizens. The *Telegraph* has printed the inflammatory (to unionists) suggestion that these fellow British citizens are a 'millstone round the neck' of the rest of the UK because they cost more than they bring in. Pushed to its logical conclusion, Scotland and Wales are also millstones round the neck of the English people. The overt case for English rather than British nationalism could not be put more starkly than in this newspaper whose readership is largely Conservative. Little England has found its voice.

The most obvious response to Mr Green comes from that great bulwark of Ulster unionism, Edward Carson. During the debate on the Third Home Rule Bill (1911–14), Carson asked the question which Mr Green ignores: 'What is the object of the United Kingdom?' Carson then went on to give his answer:

> As I understand it, it is that all parts of that Kingdom should be worked together as one whole; under one system, and with the object that the poorer may be helped by the richer, and the richer may be the stronger by the co-operation of the poorer. If you were to take certain counties in England at the present moment – I shall not name any, as it might seem invidious – and work out what their contribution to the United Kingdom is, you will find that many of them do not pay for their upkeep. Is that a reason that they should be deprived of that upkeep? No; and I say this further, that a worse, a more foolish, and a more impossible policy it would be impossible to inaugurate than to suggest that either Ireland, or any other part of the United Kingdom, whether large or small, should be allowed to go back in the race of progress, and civilisation, and not to be kept up to the same standard as you yourselves, or as near thereto as possible. The whole of this argument is based upon a fallacy, because the moment you make a common Exchequer you have no right to segregate any unit paying into that Exchequer towards local or Imperial upkeep. As Ireland pays exactly the same taxes as Great Britain pays, you have no right whatsoever to segregate her.[4]

Carson, in the early twentieth century, thought deeply about the reasons why a union is a union. Mr Green in the *Telegraph* in the twenty-first century is merely an example of the shallow lack of thinking of English nationalism which is bringing our present union to an end. But who or what is this vehicle being given publicity by the *Daily Telegraph*, something called Civitas? It is possibly just one man and his English nationalist obsessions, one of a number of libertarian right-wing organizations based together at an address just round the corner from the House of Commons, at 55 Tufton Street. These Tufton Street libertarians include the so-called 'Taxpayers' Alliance', the grandly named 'Institute of Economic Affairs', the Adam Smith Institute, Leave Means Leave, the Global Warming Policy Foundation, Brexit Central and the Centre for Policy Studies. Despite some of the engaging names, the Tufton Street address is home to a carnival of right-wing agitprop groups whose funding generally remains opaque, although they are suspected to have links to American groups of a similar ideological persuasion. When they put up spokesmen and -women – as they do frequently – for talking-head news programmes on TV, they tend to know the answers to just about every political question except one: who funds you? For some reason their generous donors are embarrassed to admit the work they do. It is not clear why.

The so-called Taxpayers' Alliance is particularly reticent on this point. It does not seem to be a widely based alliance of taxpayers. I have never met any 'taxpayer' who has joined this 'alliance'. Civitas, according to Who Funds You?, pulls in around £760,000 a year in donations and is a registered charity – which presumably means it is able to reduce its own tax through essentially a subsidy from other taxpayers. Civitas also fails to make public who gives it money and how much each donor gives, or even if there is more than one donor. Who Funds You? gives Civitas the lowest possible transparency rating of 'E', which is a Failing Grade. Nevertheless the 'thinking' it does, from the evidence of Mr Green's *Daily Telegraph* article, is significant if only in defining how unthinking English nationalism is happy to advocate the destruction of the United Kingdom as currently constituted.

The Civitas self-pity for the Englishman's Burden and the 'millstone' of Northern Ireland strikes a chord with others too. One is the *Monty Python* and *Fawlty Towers* comedian John Cleese, who offered his own insight in a Tweet:[5]

And now that Eire is no longer a theocracy, the English will be absolutely delighted if you'll take Northern Ireland back and unite Ireland and good luck to the Emerald Isle and all who sail in her, especially the ones who tell me that 'they love a little bit of mischief'.

Among the many responses to John Cleese were some pointing out that the name of the country is the 'Irish Republic' or Ireland and in Irish it is 'Éire' whereas 'Eire' (written without an accent on the first letter) isn't correct. Others politely reminded Mr Cleese that Her Majesty the Queen is both head of state and the head of the Church of England, which could justify a belief that technically Ireland is less of a theocracy than England. The phrase 'the English will be absolutely delighted if you'll take Northern Ireland back' as well as the tone of arch condescension towards 'the Emerald Isle' will also strike a chord with many people on the island of Ireland who are used to the Stage Irishman, Top O' The Morning, Begorrah style beloved of English music halls in days gone by. But there is a serious point here. During the 2019 European elections I debated with the lead Brexit Party candidate in London, Ben Habib, at a hustings organized at the Irish Centre in Hammersmith. Mr Habib suggested the Irish border and the Irish question were not problems at all because a country he called 'Ire' would inevitably bow to the wishes of Britain. He was corrected by a member of the audience on the name for Ireland – and that 'ire' meant anger. He was also schooled on his characterization of the border as a non-problem. Mr Habib was subsequently elected as a Member of the European Parliament by London voters.

Ignorance about Irish and Northern Ireland sensitivities is no barrier to success in English politics. It extends throughout English culture. Some examples are fairly innocent and even amusing. The charity the MS Society, publicizing a good cause, multiple sclerosis, promised in February 2020 that their fundraising walk would 'turn the streets of Belfast orange'. Orange is the colour, obviously, of the Orange Order, whose hugely controversial marches through the streets are often the cause of tension and sometimes violence. The MS Society was however in good company. In the 1990s a leading phone provider had to rethink its marketing in Northern Ireland after using the slogan 'the future's bright; the future's Orange'.

The Stage Irishman so beloved of the English for decades, a stereotypical good-natured but impoverished drunk, has given way to the Stage Englishman – an arrogant, condescending Brit who actually knows nothing yet knows it with supreme confidence. Add to these comments the findings of Lord Ashcroft's opinion poll suggesting that a slim majority of Northern Ireland people – especially younger voters – are warming to the idea of a United Ireland, along with anger within the Democratic Unionist Party at being 'betrayed' by Boris Johnson, and the decision in January 2020 of the Northern Ireland Assembly to withhold consent on the Westminster parliament's Brexit bill, then Northern Ireland is weathering a perfect storm of insecurity about its future. To repeat the obvious – these conditions are not brought about by Irish nationalism or Ulster loyalist agitation. They are brought about by English nationalism, a constant source of disruption at a time when British–Irish relationships, thanks to the Good Friday Agreement, had since 1998 seemed stable and amicable. When I have talked with Irish politicians since the Brexit vote there is a genuine sadness about this. In Brussels one Irish MEP told me that relations between Britain and Ireland had 'never been better' than in the decade leading up to the Brexit referendum, but the sour atmosphere of the Brexit negotiations put this warm relationship in jeopardy.

Fintan O'Toole predicted these difficulties in a prophetic *Irish Times* column back in 2016. Reflecting on the idea that the Irish had 'changed the (Irish) question' for Gladstone, O'Toole insisted that as a result of Brexit:

> it is the British who have changed the question. Just when relations between Ireland and Britain had reached an unprecedented equilibrium, Brexit makes everything deeply unsettled again. When James Joyce's alter ego Stephen Dedalus claims in *Ulysses* that 'History… is a nightmare from which I am trying to awake', it is surely Irish history he has in mind. But now the Irish

have to awake to the living nightmare of British – perhaps we should say English – history.[6]

Sinn Féin's leader, Mary Lou McDonald, seemed filled with a renewed optimism about the reunification of Ireland. She said 'Irish unity is now discussed across the island in a way that I never recall in my lifetime. If you look northwards, the unionist majority is gone. There has been a generational turning of the wheel.' Ms McDonald went on:

People in the North of Ireland didn't consent to Brexit. It is not their democratic wish. They are being coerced into this position, so I think what he (Boris Johnson) has done and what Brexit has done is to write up in the starkest terms the undemocratic nature of the partition of our island. It leaves the population, the economy, the provision of services entirely at the whim of a Tory government and the Tories have no support in Ireland. The polling data demonstrates the trend is only in one direction. What we need to do now collectively is to start making the preparations for a referendum… it could happen in three years. If you said to them (the English) why is there a border on the island of Ireland I imagine the vast majority of them would not know. This is a place apart.[7]

The slow end of the UK's sense of Britishness has brought about an unlikely series of convergences. Jonathan Powell, who as Tony Blair's adviser played a key role in the Good Friday Agreement, was never a fan of Sinn Féin or the IRA, and yet, to repeat his words: 'Paradoxically, Mr Johnson and Brexit may have done more for a United Ireland than the IRA ever did', because Boris Johnson's plans may mark the end of the union of the United Kingdom 'leaving a Little Englander government ruling a Little England'. But there's more to the 'othering' of Ireland than the political events of the past few years and a few daft comments in English newspapers. Rather as with Scotland, the cultural differences are now embedded, and politics will eventually catch up. Once more Shakespeare is a good starting point.

'Who talks of my nation?'

In *Henry V*, Act 3, Scene 2, Shakespeare's only definitively Irish character, Macmorris, muses on his identity in an exchange with a Welsh officer, Fluellen:

> *Fluellen:* Captain Macmorris, I think, look you, under your correction, there is not many of your nation—
>
> *Macmorris:* Of my nation! What ish my nation? Ish a villain, and a bastard, and a knave, and a rascal. What ish my nation? Who talks of my nation?

One of the most acute insights into the twenty-first-century Irish Question and the 'othering' of Ireland in English literary and cultural studies comes from a leading American Shakespeare scholar. Writing in *The Irish Times*, Columbia University Professor James Shapiro admitted:

> In the late 1980s, when I began research on what turned into my book *1599: A Year in the Life of William Shakespeare*, I had never heard of the Irish leader Hugh O'Neill. I had no idea that England had been caught up in a bitter nine-year war to crush an Irish revolt, knew nothing of the difference between the 'New' and 'Old' English then living in Ireland, and didn't know that Queen Elizabeth's popular courtier the earl of Essex had marched out of London leading an army 16,000 strong to resolve England's Irish problem once and for all. I didn't even know that Edmund Spenser, so admired for his Elizabethan epic *The Faerie Queene*, had also written a tract arguing for the brutal suppression of the Irish, if necessary by starvation.

I think it fair to claim that in all this I was representative of most Shakespeare scholars.[8]

Professor Shapiro, in other words, humbly accepts what had been his ignorance towards some of the realities of Ireland just as clearly as John Cleese, Boris Johnson, Karen Bradley, Louis de Bernières and others merely demonstrate theirs. But the most revealing phrase in Shapiro's article is his belief that 'in all this I was representative of most Shakespeare scholars'. Those immersed in the English tradition of Shakespeare scholarship, Shapiro suggests, some of the best and brightest English scholars, had shown little interest in or knowledge of some of the biggest national upheavals in Shakespeare's day, including the Earl of Essex's campaign, Spenser's advocacy of what we would now call ethnic cleansing in Ireland and what would become in Shakespeare's lifetime the Plantation of Ulster under James I.

By the twentieth century, Irish or Anglo-Irish contemporaries of Rudyard Kipling were able to poke fun at and distance themselves from this English ignorance. As we have seen, in George Bernard Shaw's only full-blooded meditation on Irish nationalism, *John Bull's Other Island*, his decent English central character, Tom Broadbent, wants to run for parliament to give Home Rule to Ireland. But throughout the play Shaw makes his Englishman a figure of fun to the Irish. Broadbent appears to believe that all Irishmen play cricket and will happily accept a new Irish Home Rule flag with the Union Jack in one corner. By Act IV Broadbent says, with the supreme confidence of a Boris Johnson, that 'as a reasonable man, yes, I see no evils in the world... that cannot be remedied by freedom, self-government and English institutions. I think so not because I am an Englishman but as a matter of common sense... we'll take Ireland in hand and by straightforward business habits teach it efficiency.'

That other great Anglo-Irish writer, William Butler Yeats, like Shaw, also lived for a time in England. Yeats's home as a boy from 1867 to 1874 was in London's Primrose Hill. His attitude to England's greatest human catastrophe of the twentieth century, the First World War, is revealing. It simply was not his concern. He did not write about it at all, except in an extraordinary short poem filled with a kind of cold artistry. Shaw creates in Broadbent a stage Englishman, increasingly ludicrous in Irish eyes. Yeats treats England's titanic struggle with utter indifference by flying above it, literally and metaphorically in 'An Irish Airman Foresees His Death':

> I know that I shall meet my fate
> Somewhere among the clouds above;
> Those that I fight I do not hate,
> Those that I guard I do not love;
> My country is Kiltartan Cross,
> My countrymen Kiltartan's poor,
> No likely end could bring them loss
> Or leave them happier than before.

Yeats's indifference to Britain, in what was seen as an existential struggle in the trenches below his airman, is even more devastating as a critique of English narrowness than Shaw's ridicule of Broadbent making a fool of himself.

Consequences

Some English political writers, such as the former Conservative MP and *Times* columnist Matthew Parris, have recently raised the question of the reunification of Ireland in positive terms. Parris says reunification, handled with care, could benefit Ireland, Northern Ireland and also England. The existence of Northern Ireland as a part of the United Kingdom can no longer be taken for granted, Parris writes:

> When the expected border with the rest of the UK is established in the Irish Sea the case for reuniting north with south will get its biggest boost since Partition in 1921... The province has been a bottomless pit. At around £12 billion net per annum Northern

Ireland costs the (British) taxpayer slightly more than our net payments to the EU. We pay more to keep the province in the Union than we'll get back by leaving the EU.[9]

Parris's figures are slightly different from those of David G. Green, and he does not use the language of millstones round the neck, but the argument is broadly the same. The prize of the biggest political change for Ireland since the foundation of the Free State in 1921 is waiting for any Irish politician who successfully makes the case for reunification. Since the Ashcroft poll showed only Northern Ireland voters over the age of sixty-five were resolutely opposed to a united Ireland, such a wish may be expressed publicly before too long. It is a wish that, once granted, will utterly change the political geometry of these islands.

Scots, as we saw in Chapter 6, have noticed what is going on. In conversations with Scottish friends, and not merely those convinced of the case for independence, I am struck by how often Northern Ireland and the Irish Republic are discussed in very different terms from those used by Englishmen like Louis de Bernières, John Cleese, David Green and Boris Johnson. To many Scots Northern Ireland is not a burden or a millstone, and the Irish Republic is not some kind of irritant. Northern Ireland folk are kith and kin; and the Irish Republic is potentially an example Scotland could emulate. One Scottish friend (traditionally of unionist convictions) told me that the way in which the European Union had stood up for the 5 million people of Ireland against the almost 70 million people of the United Kingdom was instructive. It meant, he said, that it was unlikely the EU would fail to stand up for the 5 million people of Scotland in similar circumstances. By February 2020 Scotland's first minister, Nicola Sturgeon, was already urging the EU to 'leave a light on for Scotland' with a promise that 'Scotland will return to the heart of Europe as an independent country'.

There were clear signs that the mood within the EU had changed too. In 2014, during the Scottish independence referendum, EU sources suggested that if Scotland broke away from an EU member state – the United Kingdom – then Spain might veto an independent

Scotland joining the EU club. Spain fears its own separatist move-ments, most notably in Catalonia. But the fact that Britain has left the EU is an obvious 'material change' in circumstances. This has been reflected in some of the more recent comments from EU leaders and former leaders. The former European Council president Donald Tusk said he 'felt like I'm Scottish especially after Brexit'. He then said of an independent Scotland being welcomed back into the EU that 'emotionally I have no doubt that everyone will be enthusiastic here in Brussels, and more generally in Europe. If you ask me about our emotions, you will witness I think always empathy.' By 2020 the EU's chief Brexit negotiator Michel Barnier said simply, 'We will see,' rather than the much more negative mood in Brussels towards an independent Scotland in 2014. And Latvia's foreign minister, Edgars Rinkēvičs, suggested a significant change of tone while retaining a degree of diplomatic non-commitment to the outcome: 'Whenever somebody in the UK decides to apply Article 49, we would be the staunchest supporters of [the] Article 49 process.'

Whither Wales?

One piece of the United Kingdom political jigsaw, however, has not been so vocal about its future status: Wales. The Principality voted in favour of Leave in 2016, even though the Cardiff administration later voted against Boris Johnson's plans on how precisely to do so. If the United Kingdom is moving slowly towards reconfiguring itself, with potentially an independent Scotland and a united or reunited Ireland, where does Wales stand in all this? YesCymru, which began in 2016, is one of the groups agitating for a referendum on Welsh independence, but the take-up has been modest. YesCymru was looking for 10,000 Welsh people to sign up to commit to voting Yes in a referendum. By August 2020 the number of signatures was almost 12,000 and they are now aiming for 25,000, although a change.org petition for a Welsh referendum attracted just 854 signatures. The YesCymru campaign website says:

Our aim is to gain independence for Wales, in order to improve the way our country is governed. We believe in an inclusive citizenship, which embraces and celebrates the fact that everyone who chooses to make Wales their home – regardless of their background – are full citizens of the new Wales. Our group will promote independence for Wales through a range of activities, to make the case that Wales, like so many other nations throughout the world, would be better running its own affairs, as part of a wider European and international family. Our organisation is open to all who believe in independence for Wales.[10]

Support for independence, especially in South Wales, has never been high on the political agenda, although Brexit and English nationalism mean that the phrase 'Indy Curious' has entered the popular vocabulary in Welsh politics. Carwyn Jones, Labour's former first minister, was one of those who publicly suggested the union was not working for Wales. But Wales has always been told it is too weak, too poor, too small and too divided between Welsh-speaking areas, especially in the north and west, and the bigger population centres in the south to make independence work. Carwyn Jones spoke of Wales being regarded as 'subsidy junkies' during the rise of English nationalism.[11]

In the *Atlantic* magazine of December 2019, Helen Lewis wondered aloud why cultural nationalism in Wales – love of the Welsh language and culture – did not translate into the strong political nationalism in evidence in Scotland. She called it 'the dragon that never roared', with support for independence only at 28 per cent, and Wales narrowly voting in favour of Brexit alongside England. One reason the Welsh dragon has failed to stir may be economic insecurity. Most Welsh jobs are in towns within thirty miles of the English border, including the capital, Cardiff. Wales is also divided by geography – North Wales is better connected to Liverpool than to Cardiff in the south. Getting from Anglesey to the Welsh capital is more convenient via England. Politically, the Welsh nationalist party, Plaid Cymru, is, despite its efforts, at times regarded as an exponent of Welsh language and culture rather than a voice for all of Wales, and, unlike in Scotland, a charismatic leader for Welsh nationalism has not emerged.

But – as we will consider at greater length in Part Two – the event which caught countries around the world unprepared, the coronavirus pandemic, on the face of it should have brought nations together. We all want the same things, to stop the spread of the virus, stay healthy, find a cure and keep the economy moving. But the rules set by the government of the United Kingdom in London have at times been dismissively rejected by the administrations in Wales, Northern Ireland, Scotland and even in some local authority areas of England. Boris Johnson's 'Four Nations' approach was rejected very clearly by the Welsh first minister, Mark Drakeford. He said Welsh police would patrol the border to 'advise and explain' to holidaymakers arriving from England that they should go home. Wales, along with Scotland and Northern Ireland, also rejected the changing messaging on the virus chosen by Boris Johnson. Mr Johnson said the UK should 'Stay Alert', while Wales joined Scotland and Northern Ireland in insisting a clearer message was that we should instead 'Stay Home'. By the end of June 2020 the Scottish newspaper *The National* carried a front-page headline, announcing 'ENGLISH BORDER BIGGEST RISK TO BEATING VIRUS'. Edinburgh University professor Devi Sridhar, one of the Scottish government advisers on the pandemic, suggested Scotland could with patience and hard work be Covid-free by the end of the summer, and officials in Scotland, Wales and Northern Ireland implied that England could be the weakest link in the Covid response. When it came to operating quarantine measures for holidaymakers coming home to the UK from abroad, England, Scotland, Northern Ireland and Wales again all acted differently. Johnson's plea that we should 'pull together as a United Kingdom' simply did not work in practice.

The remaining chapters of this book examine in more detail the creeping federalism already evident in the British system of government.

The intention is to expand existing federal structures to offer possible solutions to the problems of our competing nationalisms. What follows is the exploration of two main points, and two intractable problems.

First, many supposedly British institutions are not very 'British' in the way they operate. They are devolved, and that is a good thing. This existing federal structure could be built upon to address the 'democratic deficit' felt in all parts of the United Kingdom. One possibility would be to update the model that was first suggested in the late nineteenth century and almost came to pass by 1914, when devolution was interrupted by the First World War. As we noted, that model was described as 'Home Rule for All Nations'. Reinvigorating this old idea would require devolving more powers to Scotland, Wales and Northern Ireland, plus rethinking the relationship between the regions of England and Westminster.

Second, and even more important, recognizing and building upon an existing federal structure would require bringing to an end the outdated and unfair Westminster voting system. If the United Kingdom is to stay broadly as four nations in one state – and that is by no means certain – then power has to be devolved more effectively across the country. That will require a written and properly codified constitution. In England in particular the idea of formalizing and writing down in words most people can understand some kind of constitution has been resisted for centuries. Nowadays, especially in conservative and right-wing Conservative circles, it has become an English nationalist fetish. 'The glories' of an unwritten constitution are, as we will see, constantly referenced without ever really being available for inspection. Devolution, even as currently constructed, cannot forever survive the inevitable conflicts within an increasingly complex polity without some kind of agreed rules which only a codified constitution can provide.

Boris Johnson's government was elected to 'Get Brexit Done', erroneously suggesting that Brexit is some kind of event rather than a long-drawn-out process. Brexit, and the way in which this, the biggest decision taken by the people of the United Kingdom since the Second

World War, is pulling us apart, suggests that for some nationalists, especially in Scotland, it may be too late to reform the creaking edifice of Britain. But in federalism there is, at least, a template, a thought-provoking model demanding action before it is too late.

PART TWO

Institutions and Solutions

'A lack of political trust contributed to the Brexit vote, providing fertile ground for anti-establishment rhetoric and divisive politics. The further people are geographically from Westminster, the further they feel emotionally and ideologically.'

UK in a Changing Europe *report, November 2019*

'We cannot simply be dragged along on decisions we have no knowledge of, that we don't understand the basis of and might be wrong for our circumstances.'

Scotland's first minister, Nicola Sturgeon, commenting on the coronavirus response from Boris Johnson's government and in particular his decision to allow travellers from selected EU countries to avoid fourteen-day quarantine rules, 30 June 2020

8

Do 'British' Institutions Exist?

'People who do not enjoy the political freedoms and
economic opportunities we all take for granted look to
the UK as an exemplar, a template for the kind of fair,
stable and open society they want for themselves and
their communities… Our institutions exemplify our
values, although… what exactly "British values" are
remains disputed.'

'Harnessing the soft power of British institutions', July 2017

'We have a bizarre system of government in this country,
don't we? A remote, London-centric operation that
doesn't trust local government, doesn't invest in it,
doesn't believe in it.'

*Andy Burnham, Mayor of Greater Manchester,
quoted in Guardian, 12 October 2020*

On 'Brexit Day' Boris Johnson promised, as leaders always do, to bring the United Kingdom together. Like Lincoln after the Civil War he would bind up the nation's wounds. After a series of self-imposed and unachievable deadlines, Britain formally left the European Union on 31 January 2020, while agreeing to spend the rest of 2020 acting as if nothing had changed. The UK said it would obey all the EU rules until the end of December that year, although the British government would have no future part in making those rules. Never short of a mixed metaphor, Mr Johnson celebrated the occasion in characteristically bloviating style. He said this was 'the moment when the dawn breaks and the curtain goes up on a new act', at a 'moment of real national renewal and change', which was also 'the dawn of a new era in which we no longer accept that your life chances – your family's life chances – should depend on which part of the country you grow up in'.[1]

But when coronavirus struck it was obvious that those chances were indeed dependent on some very familiar factors. War or external threats traditionally were part of what helped keep the United Kingdom together and solidified the idea of Britishness. Coronavirus might have seemed similar – a foreign invasion which we all wanted to repel. It was an opportunity for a competent British leader truly to confirm the unity of the people of the United Kingdom in preventing the spread of the virus, healing the sick and aiding the search for a cure. It hasn't worked out like that. Your 'family's life chances' depended on many things, including 'which part of the country you grow up in' as well as your age and existing state of health, and also your wealth, race, and the kind of work you did. This was hardly a 'new act' or 'the dawn of a new era'. It was verbal porridge, celebrating the same old Britain.

Coronavirus proved to be anything but an equal-opportunity killer. As we noted, in England's poorest areas people died from the virus at twice the rate of people in the richest areas. People of colour, notably those who were health workers, died at a much greater rate than white people in the same jobs. Newham – a relatively deprived area of London with a large ethnic minority population – reported

144.3 deaths per 100,000. The richest areas of London had a death toll of 25 per 100,000. Liverpool, Birmingham, Wolverhampton and Middlesbrough also had a high death rate. In February 2020 a report by Professor Sir Michael Marmot, one of Britain's leading experts on health inequalities, had revealed that for the first time in a century life expectancy in England had stalled over the previous decade. Coincidentally or otherwise, this was a decade of Conservative governments and austerity policies, with deep cuts in public spending, growing inequalities in wealth and income, 'reorganization' of the National Health Service, at least in England, and severe reductions on local authority budgets.

Boris Johnson told the British people, repeatedly, that his government's actions would always be based on 'the science'. This was misleading. There is no such thing as 'the science', since science is an endless inquiry into the unknown coupled with honest admissions of fallibility from scientists who, like the rest of us, disagree and test out ideas which may in practice turn out to be wrong. Science is also a constant argument between people with expertise who make differing judgements in good faith. Politicians then have to decide which version of the best available scientific advice should be acted upon. It is often difficult to know what is right, although it can be easier to decide what is wrong, at least from an ethical rather than scientific standpoint.

When the pandemic hit the United Kingdom, Boris Johnson's advisers talked about achieving 'herd immunity', meaning that if enough of us caught the disease the general population would be immune thereafter unless the virus mutated quickly. The suggestion was that millions of us would develop natural immunity while scientists would have a breathing space to figure out a cure or vaccine. This strategy quickly unravelled. It was politically and morally unacceptable. Letting vast numbers of people die seemed obscene: herd immunity is fine unless you are among the weakest of the herd and are sacrificed so that others may live, and no one could predict how many would die from coronavirus. Estimates went from a few thousand to half a million deaths.

Despite the 'island race' rhetoric of those who led Britain towards

Brexit, including Mr Johnson, and the influence of the president of the United States, obsessed with America First and building a 'big, beautiful wall', most of the problems we need to worry about in the twenty-first century turn out to be a bit like coronavirus. They do not recognize borders. They are global rather than national and include HIV, cancer, other potentially more lethal viruses that will leap from animals to humans, global warming, mass migration, extreme weather events, trade policies, a massive run on stock markets, poverty, war, terrorism, drug trafficking, money laundering and the explosion of fakery on social media. Since the 'herd' affected by all these phenomena is global rather than national, what one national government does – even in a relatively rich and prosperous country like Britain – only works if there is coordination with neighbours. The threat from a new disease in any one place turns out to be a threat everywhere. John Donne's often quoted observation that 'no man is an island entire of itself; every man is a piece of the continent, a part of the main' has never seemed more apt than in a world where popular culture, the economy, technology, social media, disease, terrorism and crime are interlinked phenomena worldwide.

In the case of coronavirus, writers and historians drew comparisons with the so-called Spanish flu epidemic of 1918–19. Spanish flu was not 'Spanish', and not just because viruses have no nationality. Spanish flu is thought to have originated in Kansas, in the United States. It was referred to as 'Spanish' only because Spain was where it was first reported. Spain was not a combatant in the First World War and therefore did not have wartime newspaper censorship and could report the disease freely. Attempts by Donald Trump and his acolytes to brand the 2020 pandemic as 'Chinese' coronavirus appealed to a section of American voters in a presidential election year, those for whom the words 'foreign' and 'threats' are naturally linked. Piers Morgan, a British television presenter, taking his cue from President Trump, Tweeted in March 2020: 'Seeing a lot of liberals & media getting very agitated by President Trump calling it the "Chinese Virus". Yet everyone calls the last similar global pandemic "Spanish Flu". What's the difference?' The difference was about 100 years, and a few important but overlooked scientific facts, as Piers Morgan eventually recognized, although Donald Trump did not.

The global health emergency prompted different national solutions, although most nations listened to advice from the World Health Organization and cooperated with neighbouring countries. But in the United Kingdom the pandemic once more raised serious questions about our multinational state. Boris Johnson, as prime minister, had a leadership role, but many British institutions including the National Health Service are devolved to the nations that make up the UK. They are administered differently in different parts of the country. There is a common ethos and central funding, but they have different structures and priorities.

To take an obvious example, there are four chief medical officers in the United Kingdom, one each for England, Scotland, Northern Ireland and Wales. The English and Scottish CMOs go back to Victorian times; the Northern Ireland CMO to the 1920s and Partition, and the Welsh CMO to 1969. They coordinate their work with the CMO for England acting as the adviser to the United Kingdom government (there being no devolved English assembly). The existence of the four CMOs points to a strength of the union of the United Kingdom, but also a weakness. The strength is that the UK has enabled considerable diversity within the four nations of the British state so that what works best in one region can be copied elsewhere. There is often no one-size-fits-all policy, in health and other matters, for all of the UK's regions and nations. The weakness is the way in which deepening disagreements now occur between individual parts of the United Kingdom without a clear mechanism to resolve those differences. We are sliding at a glacial pace into a constitutional crisis.

Union of Unequals

In March and April 2020, the UK government's approval ratings at first rose considerably. Mr Johnson told the country again and again that 'we will get through this together', just as his predecessor David

Cameron had used the same rhetoric of being 'all in it together' during the difficult years of austerity. Under Mr Cameron, the divisions between rich and poor widened; with coronavirus at first it appeared that the UK was indeed working together, truly a United Kingdom. There was considerable goodwill towards Mr Johnson, especially when he himself took sick with the virus. There was also a great deal of coordination between London, Edinburgh, Cardiff and Belfast, and even talk of the wisdom of forming a government of national unity or of bringing together an advisory group, perhaps of former prime ministers. But that was not part of Mr Johnson's definition of getting through things 'together'.

By mid-May 2020, the 42 per cent approval rating for the Johnson government turned to net minus 3 per cent. The death toll continued to rise, and by the end of June the UK had the third-highest number of deaths from coronavirus in the world, exceeded only by the USA and Brazil, countries with much larger populations. The performance of the UK government was painfully slow, at times incompetent and confused, and measurably less effective than many other countries. The prime minister himself appeared to be – in the words of the former Conservative cabinet minister Michael Portillo[2] – not a leader but a spectator as the greatest health-care crisis in living memory hit the people of Britain.[3]

On 10 May, Mr Johnson made an address to the nation watched by 27 million viewers, during which he appeared confused about his plans to ease the lockdown. The speech was mocked in newspapers and social media and comedians delivered their own satirically chaotic renditions of the prime ministerial performance. This was followed by blustering performances at Prime Minister's Questions in the House of Commons, where Mr Johnson simply denied facts which were then immediately presented to him with documentary evidence by the leader of the Opposition, Sir Keir Starmer, an experienced trial lawyer, whose weekly eviscerations of the prime minister became compelling viewing. But what was interesting was how rapidly the man who held the title of prime minister of the United Kingdom of Great Britain and Northern Ireland rapidly shrank to becoming the prime minister of England only, and even then at times only speaking for parts of England.

Primary schools, Mr Johnson said, were to be allowed to open from 1 June. More exercise was to be permitted, as were limited meetings with people beyond those sharing the same house. London had been affected by the initial spread of coronavirus earlier than other areas, and was ready earlier than other nations and regions to move out of lockdown. The R rate (the virus's reproduction rate) had fallen below 1 in the capital, but in areas of the north-east and north-west of England the R rate was still more than 1, which meant that an exponential increase in infections was still possible.

In Cardiff the Welsh government immediately made clear that they would not be following Mr Johnson's easing of the lockdown, nor did they accept his new slogan, that the public should merely 'Stay Alert'. Existing rules continued to apply in Wales. English tourists would be discouraged from visiting Welsh lakes, beaches and mountains or their holiday homes; Welsh schools would not be reopening on Mr Johnson's timetable; Wales would retain the simple message 'Stay Home'. Mr Johnson's advice that people must 'Stay Alert' was mercilessly lampooned as at best vague and at worst daft when faced with the invisible threat of a virus. Plaid Cymru's leader, Adam Price – an advocate of Welsh independence – was blunt about the consequences of this division between the Welsh and English stance on the virus: 'Let's not beat about the bush. If you drove into Wales from England at the moment without a legitimate excuse you would get arrested. Many people would not have thought that it was even possible, but that is the reality on the ground.'[4]

It is worth taking a moment to reflect on the significance of this. Despite the prime minister of the United Kingdom insisting that the lockdown was being eased, English drivers who crossed an ancient border into Wales were risking arrest for crossing from one part of the UK to another. Snowdonia, one of the UK's biggest tourist attractions, was working to Welsh, not English, rules, turning away those who chose to visit. Police issued fines to those who did not comply with the rules.

In Scotland First Minister Nicola Sturgeon assured Scots that her message had not changed either – 'Stay at Home'. She said she had no idea what 'Stay Alert' meant and that 'if you are coming into Scotland for reasons that are not covered by those essential purposes then you potentially would be breaking the law'.[5] Scottish schools would not reopen on England's timetable. Northern Ireland, separated by a sea and also separated by smouldering Unionist anger at Mr Johnson's division of the United Kingdom by conceding the customs border in the Irish Sea, also went its own way. The first minister, Arlene Foster, began to relax some lockdown rules but at a different speed to Mr Johnson's announcement, and she also rejected Mr Johnson's change of slogan. Notably, schools in Northern Ireland were not going to reopen until September – in line with the decisions taken by the Dublin government, out of step with the decisions taken by the government in Westminster.

All this, you might say, was reasonably predictable for devolved administrations, even if the Democratic Unionist first minister in Northern Ireland aligning with the Irish Republic would in normal times be considered highly unusual. What was less predictable was the rebellion in England. Teachers' unions immediately objected to the prime minister's ideas of leading England (and by now only England) out of lockdown. They said they had not been properly consulted and that their members might be put at risk, a risk shared by the children gathered in their classes. The Johnson plan was to limit the opening of state primary schools at first to the youngest and oldest pupils only, reception, year one, and year six. English private schools however, including Eton, which Mr Johnson had attended, were not reopening until September. Amid unconfirmed reports that no member of Mr Johnson's Cabinet had children at state schools, it appeared that other people's children were to be affected by the government decision to reopen English primary schools in June.

Then English councils began to go their own way. Hartlepool council, in the north-east of England, issued a statement noting that 'coronavirus cases locally continue to rise' and in consultation with local schools the council 'agreed they will not reopen on Monday

1 June'. Newcastle and Gateshead councils refused to adopt the new government message and continued to urge local people to 'Stay at Home'. Martin Gannon, the leader of Gateshead council, noted pockets of deprivation in his area which put people more at risk from the virus. He said the R rate in Gateshead was too high: 'We locked down too late; this unlock down strategy is premature... the R rate isn't low enough. They're doing this too soon. It means a second wave will happen.'[6] The Labour mayor of Greater Manchester Andy Burnham wrote a scathing op-ed piece in the *Observer*[7] saying the biggest towns and cities in England had no notice of the decision to allow people back to work if they could not work from home 'even though that would clearly put more cars on roads and people on trams, no one in government thought it important to tell the cities who'd have to cope with that'. Councils immediately joining those in opposition to the Johnson government represented more than 1,500 primary schools including those in Birmingham, Bury, Calderdale in Yorkshire and Conservative-controlled Solihull. Other councils delayed making decisions and still others suggested that the decisions should be taken by headteachers and governors. Referring to the prime minister's chief adviser, Dominic Cummings, Mr Burnham dismissed the ensuing confusion as 'another exercise in Cummings chaos theory'.

Whatever the theory, it was certainly chaotic in practice. Explaining the new rules to an increasingly sceptical British public was made even more difficult when Dominic Cummings himself was forced to admit that he broke the rules he had helped create. Mr Cummings said that while he and his wife were suffering from coronavirus symptoms they drove to stay at Mr Cummings's parents' farm in Durham, along with their child. They then went on a day-trip on his wife's birthday to the beautifully scenic spot of Barnard Castle. He claimed that this 50-mile round trip was in order to check that his eyesight was good enough to drive.

The prime minister, the health secretary, Matt Hancock, and other members of the cabinet publicly supported Mr Cummings remaining as Mr Johnson's chief adviser. As the rows continued, Mr Hancock, apparently without irony, told the media that his message to the

British public was that they should 'do their civic duty'. Among the causes of deep divisions in the United Kingdom, the most damaging is the idea that a privileged few make rules that others must obey, but members of the ruling class do not feel the need to obey those rules themselves. The front page of the *Metro* newspaper showed a picture of Mr Cummings with the headline 'STAY ELITE'.

This creaking system – of Westminster imposing rules based on a timetable that accorded only with the infection R-rate in and around London – proved unworkable.

By the end of June an outbreak in Leicester led to a reimposition of lockdown-type conditions for the city and the surrounding areas, while Mr Johnson's decision first to impose fourteen-day restrictions on visitors coming from abroad, then to relax them, led to further confusion. First Minister Nicola Sturgeon was blunt: 'We cannot simply be dragged along on decisions we have no knowledge of, that we don't understand the basis of and might be wrong for our circumstances.'[8]

Tony Travers, a local government expert at the London School of Economics, noted that 'federally structured nations like Germany seem to have been more flexible than the somewhat monolithic approach in Britain'.[9] Travers also noted that a devolved, locally centred response in England was made much more difficult because English local government resources had been cut by 40 per cent since the Conservatives, and their Liberal Democrat partners, began their policy of austerity in 2010. Damian Green, a thoughtful and prominent Conservative MP who speaks for the 100-member 'One Nation' centrist group among Conservatives in parliament, suggested that devolution in England might be the answer to these serious shortcomings. He said there was now a need to discuss 'spreading power out from the centre to local people'. Indeed there is.

For years politicians and some scholars in the United Kingdom have fetishized the supposed 'glory' of an 'unwritten' constitution. However if a written constitution were to exist, such a document might conceivably offer clearer guidance on the powers of the prime minister and the differing roles of local councils and devolved governments. We will dive into the nature of this glory in the next few chapters. Unlike an American citizen, or indeed a citizen of almost any other democracy anywhere, you cannot go into a British bookstore or government department or go online and read the text of the principles and rules by which our country is governed. The vagueness and the vagaries of this constitution have significant implications for relations between London and the rest of England, between England and the rest of the UK, and also for institutions within England itself – in particular the monarchy, central government, parliament, local government and the courts.

More positively, the way in which dealing with coronavirus managed to be both centralized at Westminster and yet also devolved in Scotland, Wales and Northern Ireland is a gateway into understanding just how 'British' supposedly British institutions really are. They are not as British as you might think. From the very start of the coronavirus outbreak there were signs of a nascent federalism, similar to that praised by Tony Travers in Germany. Northern Ireland was, yet again, in a special position. When the first coronavirus cases were reported, on the other side of the Irish border the Irish Republic immediately took much more radical measures than those of the UK government. Leo Varadkar announced the closing of all schools and pubs and even the cancellation of that great national occasion, the St Patrick's Day parade. In Belfast Arlene Foster and the Northern Ireland Executive initially chose the more relaxed approach of Boris Johnson in London. The nationalists of Sinn Féin loudly complained and demanded that schools in Northern Ireland follow the line of the government in Dublin, not the line from London. Under pressure to act, Boris Johnson eventually did announce that schools in England were to close. Important examinations, including those for university entrance – GCSEs and A levels – were cancelled, and Northern Ireland then fell into line with the Westminster government. In Scotland the Holyrood administration made their own rules. At first they said they had not immediately reached a decision on postponing the Scottish 'Highers', the Scottish examinations used for university entrance, although they did postpone them eventually.

The point here is not to quibble about details of who was right and who was wrong, although by international standards Boris Johnson's UK government was judged to have performed poorly, one of the worst among the rich countries of the world. But different administrations all acted in good faith, and broadly took the same decisions although not at the same time. It is surely a strength of British democracy that we do not all have to march in lockstep. But the key point is perhaps best expressed by a Northern Ireland-born but London-based journalist, Andrea Catherwood. She reported on Twitter an exchange with her children:

Son 1: Our cousins in Ireland are all off school for at least two weeks.
Son 2: No, only the Dublin cousins, the Belfast ones are still at school.
Son 1: Why? Does coronavirus know there's a border?

A global pandemic was addressed with different national strategies, and that included the nations of the United Kingdom. The biggest and most densely populated part of the UK, London, had its own peculiar difficulties. The mayor of London, Sadiq Khan, contemplated London-specific measures, working out what to do about crowded Underground trains and the safety of bus drivers. Skye had different priorities from Southall, and it is, one might think, a symbol of good government in very testing times that we did have a kind of informal federal approach to a common problem, recognizing that one size does not fit all. But that is also surprisingly true of other parts of British public life. We have federalized the United Kingdom by stealth. We could build on the advantages of federalization, but only if we strengthen it and codify who does what, by setting down some clear rules.

*

Think Global, Act National, Live Local

The phrase 'think global, act local' is credited to a Scottish town planner, Sir Patrick Geddes. In 1915 he published *Cities in Evolution*, in which he argued that while we all love the 'local character' of the places in which we live, that character depends upon 'the whole environment, and in active sympathy with the essential and characteristic life of the place concerned'. Sir Patrick's work inspired the environmental movement and others, but the phrase 'think global, act local' is never adapted to read 'think global, organize national, act local'. Yet the nation-state is precisely where we regulate our activities when faced with enormous global issues, and that may not always be for the best. When in March 2020 Boris Johnson addressed the nation – in this case, the entire UK – about coronavirus, he admitted he was concerned about limiting the liberties of people. At one point he said: 'We're taking away the ancient, inalienable right of free-born people of the United Kingdom to go to the pub, and I can understand how people feel about that… To repeat, I know how difficult this is, how it seems to go against the freedom-loving instincts of the British people.' Interestingly, when Mr Johnson's words were picked up by the *Sun* newspaper, they misquoted him in a way that indicated he was (once more) pretending to speak of the United Kingdom and of the British people, but he was actually only speaking for and about England. The *Sun* report said: 'Mr Johnson said he realised it went against what he called the inalienable right of people "in England" to go to the pub.' As Fintan O'Toole pointed out in the *The Irish Times*, in the *Sun*'s version, the freedom to go to the pub was conferred by genetics and history, not on the 'people of the United Kingdom' or 'the British people', but on 'people born in England'. It does not apply 'to Scots, Welsh or Northern Irish people and certainly not to the 9.4 million people living in the UK who were born abroad. It is a particular Anglo-Saxon privilege.'

British politicians, as we have seen, regularly speak of, to and for Britain but in reality refer only to England. There are plenty of examples of this elision in other British institutions too, some of them apparently trivial, but all pointing to the gap between the words used to describe our United Kingdom and the reality of the state. To take another apparently minor example, the Scottish businessman and SNP adviser Andrew Wilson posted a screen grab on Twitter of an ITN news broadcast he captured while watching the Scottish television channel STV. It showed a map of England and Wales, with Scotland cut off. The graphic was headlined 'Critical Care Capacity'. The cities of Cardiff, Liverpool, London, Manchester and Bristol all featured. Glasgow, Edinburgh, Dundee and other Scottish cities did not, since Scotland was not shown on the map at all. Wilson's post was directed at the ITN political editor Robert Peston: 'Come on @peston make an effort you are broadcasting to the whole UK… @STVNews.'[10] For Andrew Wilson and other residents of Scotland this was not 'the news where you are', and that's the point. Even in the struggle against a global pandemic, and despite coordination between scientists, public health workers and others across the UK, British 'national' institutions often fail to reflect a sense of Britishness.

Broadcasting organizations present themselves as British national institutions. Yet they, and most of the institutions which are important in our daily lives, are administered very differently in Scotland, Northern Ireland and Wales, and there are also differences between parts of England. ITV – independent television – and ITN, independent television news – are indeed British national institutions, but STV broadcasts only in Scotland. The differences in health-care administration and the kind of differences Andrew Wilson complained about seeing on our TV screens are inevitably reflections of the different needs and interests in different parts of the UK. But they are also just two of the more obvious ways in which Britain has become federalized.

When we ask ourselves which British institutions bind us together and are definitively British, the monarchy and the armed forces spring immediately to mind. Perhaps we might add the Coastguard, RNLI, Border Agency, the National Lottery and the National Grid. Some of these British institutions have their headquarters and centre of gravity in London, yet they do also reflect the wider UK. The

Coastguard National Maritime Operations Centre is in Fareham; RNLI HQ is in Poole; and National Lottery HQ is in Watford. The more you examine how 'national' institutions are organized, the more federal our organizational structure already appears to be.

What follows are further examples that make two broader points. First, Federal Britain exists already. Scotland, Northern Ireland, Wales and to an extent London are places where residents understand they are different from other parts of the country not just in how they feel about their identities but in the public institutions and services which are a part of their lives. Yorkshire, Lancashire, Greater Manchester, the West Country and East Anglia may all have a strong sense of local identity, but in England that identity is often not validated by having clearly devolved public institutions with the significance of those in Scotland, Wales and Northern Ireland. That's because England-outside-London is not allowed to have them, and because local authorities in England have been weakened by years of austerity cutting their resources.

Second, federalization of our 'British' institutions is a good thing. The question for the future is whether that devolutionary impulse can be built upon to be made more coherent while maintaining the idea of a United Kingdom where the central government has diminishing powers – or whether formalizing a federal structure comes too late, and we need to go our separate ways.

How 'British' is the National Health Service?

The NHS generally tops the list of 'things that makes us most proud to be British', according to the pollsters Ipsos Mori. Technically it is an NDPB – a 'non-departmental public body' of the UK government Department of Health and Social Care. That means its centre of gravity is in London, and yet if you Google 'where are the headquarters of the NHS?' you do not get a simple answer. In practice the NHS is one of the most devolved and decentralized of our institutions, and this goes way beyond having four separate chief medical officers.

The NHS Scotland website is clear where power lies: in Scotland: 'Responsibility for the National Health Services in Scotland is a devolved matter and therefore rests with the Scottish Government.' Legislation affecting the NHS is made by the Scottish parliament. The Scottish cabinet secretary for health and wellbeing – note the emphasis on 'wellbeing' – has ministerial responsibility. Scotland traditionally has had a problem with excessive drinking. In response, Scotland became the first country in the world to introduce minimum pricing for alcohol at 50p per unit. Prices went up above those in the rest of the UK even for the cheapest booze. The encouragement of locally effective innovation is one of the advantages of devolution or – though in the UK we tend not to use these words – a federalized structure. The Scottish government also decides what resources are to be devoted to the NHS. Of approximately £34.7 billion controlled by the Scottish government, around a third, £11.9 billion, is spent on health (2019).

In Northern Ireland the organizational health provider is formally called HSC rather than the NHS. HSC brings together – sensibly – health and social care. As the website says: 'This is your gateway to Health & Social Care Services in Northern Ireland, containing links to the Hospital and Community services provided by the 6 Health Trusts, General Practices, Health and Social Care Board and other HSC Agencies.'

NHS Wales is also now a devolved responsibility directed by the Welsh government in Cardiff.

The NHS in England is directly the responsibility of the UK Department of Health and Social Care, although the integration of social care and the health service has proved to be what English civil servants euphemistically call 'a challenge'. The structure of the NHS in England was 'reformed' by Conservative health secretary Andrew Lansley in 2012. An adviser to English politicians at that time told me Lansley's organizational chart looked like badly arranged spaghetti, with the creation of Public Health England on April Fools' Day 2013. This was described as 'the world's biggest quango' by some critics, an unwieldy bureaucratic system which no other nation has copied, and which – despite the extraordinary efforts of NHS frontline staff – has been beset by repeated winter bed shortages and bottlenecks in Accident and Emergency. Public Health England and the messy structure of the NHS more widely in England will be the subject of much debate when formal inquiries into the handling of coronavirus are eventually conducted. In the midst of the coronavirus crisis on 18 August 2020, the government announced that Public Health England was to be abolished and replaced by a 'National Institute for Health Protection'.

A 'British' Education?

How about a British school system? There isn't one. Or a British university system? No, that doesn't exist either. There are, of course, British schools and universities but no truly British education system, no British national curriculum, no British examination system, and no British university system. When the history of these islands is taught to our children, it is taught – as I can testify from my schooldays in Edinburgh – very differently in different parts of the United Kingdom. There is no reason why children in a Welsh-speaking school in North Wales and children in Newcastle or Paisley or Ballymena should necessarily have exactly the same curriculum. In Northern Ireland there are 'mixed' schools, that is schools which teach Protestants and Catholics together, although traditionally many Catholic children are taught in Catholic church schools, and Northern Ireland state schools cater mostly for Protestant children. A friend who taught history in a Northern Ireland state school in County Antrim told me that when she was teaching the Reformation one of the children in her class baulked at her presentation. The boy understood that Protestantism was a break from the Roman Catholic Church, but he was furious at the suggestion that before the Reformation his relatives must by definition have been Catholics.

'We have no Catholics in my family, miss,' he said, firmly, 'and never had.'

The 'British' Exam System

Differences in the curriculum are relatively minor compared to differences in educational structure. The English education system is based on GCSEs and A Levels. These typically lead to a slew of GCSE examinations at sixteen, with students specializing in perhaps three A level subjects for examinations they sit at eighteen, followed by three-year courses for undergraduates at English universities. English universities charge fees. Scottish universities do not charge fees to Scottish students. Scotland, going back to the parish school system that existed before the Union of the Crowns in 1603, always maintained a very different education system to England. For university entrance, Scottish pupils mostly sit 'Highers'. The standard is less advanced for 'Highers' than A levels but the advantage is that in Scotland these examinations lead to a school curriculum for seventeen- and eighteen-year-olds which is broader than the narrow concentration on three A level subjects. In England students who plan to go to university typically have to choose at around age sixteen to focus on science or arts subjects. This choice is a fork in the career path and can define a student's future. In Scotland when I was seventeen, I sat seven 'Highers': three arts subjects, three sciences and maths. This was useful because at sixteen I wanted to study medicine at Edinburgh University while by the time I was eighteen I had changed my mind and was studying English and then postgraduate Irish literature at two universities in England. I was able to switch because, like most Scots, as a seventeen-year-old, I could keep up arts as well as sciences.

The differences between these various systems in the UK are not always understood. Scottish academics tend to be familiar with applications from English A level students, but when at seventeen I went for an interview at a leading English university, having passed my 'Highers', the professor looked at my application and seemed puzzled. His first question was: 'When are you taking A levels?' My answer was 'Never.' The professor appeared to be stunned by this response. I was equally stunned by his question. As a result of increased competition between universities, nowadays even the most traditional English establishments have become more adept at dealing with a variety of international student qualifications, including those from as far away as Edinburgh. Scotland, incidentally, was quicker than much of England in recognizing the value of universities. The oldest universities in the UK are both English – Oxford (1096) and Cambridge (1209). But the next tranche were all Scottish – St Andrews (1410), Glasgow (1451), Aberdeen (1495), and Edinburgh (1583). After these six, no other universities were founded anywhere in the UK for 250 years until Manchester (1824) and University College London (1826).

The British Monarchy (1): Defender of the 'British' Faith?

Britain may consider itself to be a Christian country, but there is no British church or British national faith. If you pull a pound coin from your pocket you will see it says 'Elizabeth II D.G. REG. F.D', meaning Elizabeth by the Grace of God (Deo Gratia) Queen Defender of the Faith (Fidei Defensor). In England – England only – the title of Defender of the Faith was first conferred on Henry VIII in 1521 because he rejected the Protestant teaching of Martin Luther at the start of the Reformation. Henry had published a pamphlet under his own name, reinforcing his position as a Catholic monarch – *Assertio septem sacramentorum adversus Martinum Lutherum* ('Declaration of the Seven Sacraments Against Martin Luther'). When Henry's priorities changed, his faith changed too, and he proved a faithless defender of Roman Catholicism. The Fidei Defensor title was removed by Rome. But it was restored, to signify that he was a defender of the Protestant faith, by the English parliament in 1544, and it has been used on coins since the reign of George I. Their shared Protestant convictions ensured the Union of the Crowns of England and Scotland, the triumph of William of Orange and the Glorious Revolution of 1690, binding the United Kingdom together against the Catholic powers of Europe. But as the historian Linda Colley notes 'some of

the incitements to Britishness that operated powerfully in the past –
Protestantism, empire, recurrent successful wars, and a complacent
sense of superior constitutional freedoms – has faded'.[11] We will
consider the complacent sense of superior constitutional freedoms
in a moment. But if the idea of Protestantism as a kind of glue of
Britishness has weakened considerably, the organizational structure
of the Protestant religion in the United Kingdom has always been
fissiparous rather than binding.

Even though we all have the same monarch, Scotland, Northern
Ireland, England and Wales are, in terms of the role of the monarchy
and religion, very different. The royal website (royal.uk) treads dip-
lomatically here:

> As Sovereign, The Queen has important and distinct constitu-
> tional relationships with the Established Churches of England
> and Scotland, dating back to the sixteenth and seventeenth cen-
> turies. As Head of the Nation and Head of the Commonwealth,
> Her Majesty also recognises and celebrates other faiths in the
> UK and throughout the Commonwealth.

Prince Charles once speculated that the monarch should in fact be
titled 'Defender of the Faiths' but has since apparently changed his
mind. It is possible that when he becomes king the idea may be revived.
In England, the monarchy's website tells us, 'the Sovereign holds the
title "Defender of the Faith and Supreme Governor of the Church of
England".' That means in practice that 'the Queen's relationship with
the Church of England was symbolised at the Coronation in 1953
when Her Majesty was anointed by the Archbishop of Canterbury
and took an oath to "maintain and preserve inviolably the settlement
of the Church of England, and the doctrine worship, discipline, and
government thereof, *as by law established in England*"' (my italics). On
the advice of the prime minister, the sovereign also appoints senior
clergy in the Church of England.

In Scotland, meanwhile, the royal website tells us 'the duty to
"preserve the settlement of the true Protestant religion as established

by the laws made in Scotland" was affirmed in the 1707 Act of Union between England and Scotland'. There is one big theological difference with England: 'The Church of Scotland is a Presbyterian church and recognises only Jesus Christ as "King and Head of the Church". The queen therefore does not hold the title "Supreme Governor" of the Church of Scotland; when attending Church services in Scotland Her Majesty does so as an ordinary member.' The Scottish church is much less hierarchical – the queen is indeed 'an ordinary member' in the eyes of the Scottish church. The slightly comic Scottish phrase is 'we are all Jock Tamson's bairns', meaning we are all – Her Majesty included – the children of God.

The attempted imposition of bishops and archbishops on 'the Kirk' has over the years been met with theological disagreements, rioting and worse. Attempts to force Scotland to accept an Episcopal Book of Common Prayer in 1637 famously led to an Edinburgh market trader, Jenny Geddes, hitting the church minister over the head with a prayer stool in Edinburgh's St Giles Cathedral. She is reputed to have yelled at him 'De'il gie you colic, the wame o' ye, fause thief; daur ye say Mass in my lug?' which translates roughly from Lowland Scots dialect (Lallans) as 'May the Devil give you colic in your belly, you false thief: how dare you say the (Catholic) Mass in my ear?' In practical terms the Church of Scotland, which played such a big part in Scottish parish school and university life, has always been distinct from the English church model, sometimes violently so. Presbyterian religious activists known as Covenanters who refused to swear oaths of loyalty were (in the words of the Duke of Rothes) choosing to 'glorify God in the Grassmarket'. He meant that in maintaining their separate Presbyterian faith they knew they were deliberately choosing to be hanged in the area of central Edinburgh where criminals and religious dissidents were executed.

There are therefore no bishops or archbishops in the Kirk. The Church of Scotland 'leader' is the moderator of the General Assembly. That title says it all. He is a spokesman rather than a boss, the temporary chairman of the annual meeting of the church in Edinburgh – not a figure who claims infallibility on matters of dogma when speaking ex cathedra, nor part of a hierarchy which, in England, places bishops into the House of Lords. The moderator is generally held in high regard in Scotland and acts as the figurehead for the church at many public events and ethical debates.

Church attendance and religious differences at first may seem a matter of little importance, although that in part is the point. Protestantism is no longer one of the pillars of Britishness in the way it once was. Membership of the Church of Scotland has been falling for years and was put at 325,695 in 2018. The fall in numbers, reflected in Christian churches across western Europe, led to a strategic review that spoke of the Scottish church 'missing generations in congregations... Not only do we have very few children compared to 10 years ago, or similarly young people (under 25s), the number of folks in their 30s and 40s is also very small'.* But even as church attendance declines, the cultural distinctions between England and Scotland rooted in religion remain significant. Protestantism may be one of the crumbling pillars of Britishness, but the Church of Scotland still remains a symbol for most Scots of an independence of thought that they respect and cherish.

So This Is British Justice?

When I left university, on my way to becoming a reporter on the *Belfast Telegraph* newspaper, I was sent on a six-month journalism training course in Cardiff. The course, run by Thompson Newspapers, involved practical work, shorthand, typing, plus a lot of theory about public administration in Britain and the law. While the course was excellent, the book on public administration in Britain was, for anyone working in Northern Ireland or Scotland, baffling. The textbook, and much of the course, was based solely on the parliament at Westminster and the workings of English local government. In Belfast

* 'Worshipping God, Inspiring Faith, Connecting People', Church of Scotland Strategic Plan, 2018–28.

at the time there was a very different administration – Direct Rule from Westminster by British government ministers that no one in Northern Ireland had voted for. There were also repeated attempts to revive the local parliament at Stormont, but Stormont was an alphabet soup of fragmented political parties – OUP, DUP, UPNI, Vanguard, SDLP, the Workers Party, the Alliance Party, Sinn Féin, and plenty more. The province's government had very different structures from England and a different set of public service institutions.

Then there was the law textbook *Essential Law for Journalists*. While the principles of the law in Northern Ireland or Scotland were theoretically similar to those in England and Wales – the right to a jury trial, the law of libel or defamation, contempt of court and so on – the practical administration of justice was completely different. The most newsworthy trials I covered in Northern Ireland were for terrorist crimes. These were conducted in 'Diplock Courts', no-jury courts operating under very strict security, in which the judiciary had somewhat different views on what constituted 'contempt of court'.

Contempt of court is a criminal offence. It means journalists have to be very careful about reporting matters which could sway a jury if those matters have not been heard and accepted as evidence in open court. Later in my career with BBC *Newsnight* a distinguished English barrister was called in to 'legal' one of my reports about Northern Ireland. He objected to part of my script on the grounds that it was potentially in contempt of court. I pointed out that it involved a terrorist trial in a Diplock court without a jury. The barrister laughed and said he agreed that no judge was likely to admit to being influenced by a newspaper article or a 'mere bit of reporting on television'. He let the script pass, saying that of course he had forgotten the 'peculiar practices' of Northern Ireland.

Other aspects of the law were very different too, including the law on abortion, although that more recently has changed. *Essential Law for Journalists* was essential for some of my colleagues when they were trainees, but not for me and not for journalists in Scotland either. One of my predecessors on the course, Denis Murray, later

BBC Northern Ireland political editor, scrawled on the copy of the book I inherited: 'SO THIS IS BRITISH JUSTICE!' The joke had a point, in the era of no-jury trials. But there really is no such thing as 'British' justice, even if the phrase is commonly used. And that means there is no British legal system.

The Scottish legal system is one of three legal systems in the United Kingdom, along with those in England and Wales, and Northern Ireland. In Scotland the system is based on Roman law. New laws applying in Scotland can be passed by the Scottish parliament, the Westminster parliament, or (until Brexit) by the European Union. In Scotland since 1532 top lawyers are members of the Faculty of Advocates. The Faculty is an independent body of lawyers who have been admitted to practice as advocates before the courts of Scotland, especially the Court of Session and the High Court of Justiciary. It is based in Edinburgh. The English equivalent is the Bar Council.

For Scottish solicitors, the Law Society of Scotland is the professional governing body. The Law Society of England and Wales is the professional association that represents and governs solicitors for (obviously) the jurisdiction of England and Wales. And as their website puts it 'the Incorporated Law Society of Northern Ireland, commonly known as the Law Society of Northern Ireland, is a professional body established by Royal Charter granted on 10 July 1922', immediately after Partition. On matters of justice and public administration there are forty-three police forces in England and Wales, along with the British Transport Police and some specialist forces plus separate unified police forces in Scotland (Police Scotland) and Northern Ireland (PSNI – Police Service of Northern Ireland). The existence of forty-three separate police forces in England and Wales with their separate headquarters, their own chief constables and separate bureaucracies is a reminder that the balance between devolution, local accountability and efficiency is not always easy to strike. The balance where policing is concerned is rarely in favour of efficiency.

*

The Supreme Court (1)

Since 2009 the United Kingdom has had a Supreme Court. In contradiction of the peculiar Brussels speech of the British Brexit negotiator David Frost, quoted at length earlier, the creation of a UK Supreme Court is only one of many examples of how British institutions have not – as he so complacently put it – 'just evolved'. The Supreme Court was a very deliberate creation of the then Labour government. It was, and remains, controversial, with potentially significant implications for Britain's 'unwritten' or uncodified constitution. The Supreme Court is definitely a British institution – well, sort of. Here's what it says about itself on its website: 'The Supreme Court is the final court of appeal in the UK for civil cases, and for criminal cases from England, Wales and Northern Ireland. It hears cases of the greatest public or constitutional importance affecting the whole population.' It appears it is therefore not the final court of appeal for criminal cases from Scotland.

But even that is not entirely clear. On the Scottish government website you find this:

> The UK's Supreme Court (established by the Constitutional Reform Act 2005) is the highest court in the UK. It took over the functions of the Appellate Committee of the House of Lords and the Judicial Committee of the Privy Council in October 2009. Whilst it is the final court of appeal for Scottish civil cases, the High Court (in Edinburgh) is *generally* the final court of appeal for Scottish criminal cases. However, the Supreme Court *can become involved* in Scottish criminal cases. This possibility arises from its role as a court of appeal in relation to both compatibility and devolution issues. (My italics.)

Is that clear? Not really. This is not to denigrate the work of courts anywhere in the United Kingdom, but merely to point out that taking for granted the 'British' nature of British institutions, and even deciding which institution plays a leadership role at any given time, is often not easy and sometimes impossible. Different types of authority are not explicitly defined, and are not spelled out in coherent language written down in a Constitution of the United Kingdom of Great Britain and Northern Ireland.

The Supreme Court is staffed by some of the best legal brains in Britain and its members can discuss with courts in Scotland the most sensible way to proceed in sensitive cases. Such flexibility at the margins is an advantage, but only provided that we can rely upon goodwill and the idea that reasonable people will try to do their best for all concerned. This rather optimistic view of the human condition has been called, by the English political historian Peter Hennessy, the 'Good Chap' theory of government in the United Kingdom, something we will consider in more depth in Chapter 9. Professor Hennessy means that civil servants, MPs, government ministers, senior judges and so on all know the limits of their power or authority and – since they are all 'Good Chaps' (they are indeed mostly 'chaps') – they cooperate and do not push things beyond their generally unclear or unwritten mandates. The problem, as Hennessy and others observe, is that in the twenty-first century the general public's faith in Good Chaps has disintegrated. There is a growing concern – shared by Hennessy – that a Good Chap theory of government may be ruined by a few Bad Chaps getting to the top. In any event, it is absurd to rely on the better angels of our nature to triumph in a complex modern democracy, especially when political disagreements about what we mean by our 'nation' can be so profound and bitter.

The Supreme Court (2): When 'Good Chaps' Disagree

Ever since its creation, the existence of the United Kingdom Supreme Court has provoked a wide debate about the UK's unwritten constitution. All democracies with a federal system of government, and most other democracies too, have some kind of document or series of documents outlining and limiting the powers of various branches of government and related institutions. A constitution determines who does what, and – when conflicts inevitably arise – which institution is the ultimate arbiter of right and wrong.

In the United States the 'separation of powers' doctrine divides responsibilities between Congress, which makes all laws, the president, who may propose laws and budgets but whose executive power is nevertheless limited, and the Supreme Court, which is the ultimate arbiter on the legality of political decisions. American schoolchildren are taught that when it comes to the US national budget, 'the president proposes but Congress disposes'. The downside is that partisanship means many US presidents find their budgets dead on arrival on Capitol Hill, immediately disposed of by a hostile Congress dumping them into the waste bin of history.

In Britain our federalization-by-stealth system means that it remains unclear who is the ultimate arbiter when profound conflicts and disagreements arise. That causes problems on highly charged political matters, most recently and notably in respect of the 2019 ruling by the UK Supreme Court that the prorogation of parliament by Prime Minister Boris Johnson was illegal. This is a complex saga but it gets to the heart of constitutional questions that sooner or later Britain will have to face, since it brings together the monarchy, the prime minister, the government, parliament and different courts in Scotland and England leading all the way – controversially – to the UK Supreme Court itself on the most sensitive political matter of recent years.

The Supreme Court (3): Who Decides What?

In September 2019 Boris Johnson asked the Queen to prorogue (suspend) parliament for five weeks until the scheduled formal state opening and the Queen's speech in October. That meant the country's deliberative and democratic assemblies would be silenced until just seventeen days before the UK (in one of its many self-imposed deadlines) was due to leave the European Union. Mr Johnson unconvincingly claimed the move had nothing to do with Brexit; he wanted to get on with his 'fantastic' domestic agenda of helping the NHS and other matters. Opposition MPs were outraged at what they said was the prime minister's undemocratic silencing of debate. Some 70 per cent of respondents told the Ipsos Mori pollsters they did not believe Mr Johnson. The Court of Session in Edinburgh was asked to rule, and found Boris Johnson's prorogation unlawful. The Scottish court did so a few days after the High Court in London dismissed a challenge against prorogation as a 'political' issue, saying that was not for the court to decide. So: one court in England says the matter is outside its jurisdiction while the Scottish Court of Session suggests that the prime minister of the United Kingdom had lied to the Queen. The UK Supreme Court was forced to consider the prorogation and – while it did not rule specifically on whether Mr Johnson had lied – it did find that prorogation was unlawful. Parliament went back to work, and back to arguing about Brexit.

All this is important for a number of reasons. The first is that Mr Johnson obeyed the court ruling. What if he had not done so? Britain would have plunged into its most serious constitutional crisis in modern times, but how would the matter have been resolved? Second, these events showed that the institutions of government, and indeed different courts, may reasonably come to different conclusions on matters which, as the Ipsos Mori poll demonstrated, clearly engaged the public. Third, the Supreme Court ruling was politically very embarrassing for the government, although some Conservatives called it an expression of 'judicial activism'. They meant that judges were going beyond their powers and creating rather than merely interpreting the law. Creating the law is parliament's business, not that of the courts. These disputes are hugely important matters at the core of what British democracy means, how it functions and where it is weak.

The loud and angry row following the Supreme Court judgement still rumbles on, and its echoes will affect politics for a long time to come. Conservatives renewed calls for 'reform' of the judiciary. By 'reform', one senior judge told me at the time, he and his colleagues assumed 'they want to neuter us'. He meant that there would be revenge, since the Supreme Court judgement had proved politically awkward. There was a nasty undertone to this debate. Some on the right suggested the introduction of what are known in the United States as political 'litmus tests' for judges. One wonders whether those Conservatives who were pushing this kind of argument would have done so had Jeremy Corbyn become prime minister and introduced his own political test for the judiciary. Boris Johnson hinted that US-style confirmation hearings for Supreme Court justices would ensure that they could be subject to 'some form of accountability'. Whether Mr Johnson truly approves of the packing of courts with ideologically reliable figures is not known. Perhaps he does not know himself, since he often shoots from the lip and nothing substantive follows his words. But part of this discussion had a very unpleasant undertone. Back in 2016, the *Daily Mail* put pictures of judges on their front page with the headline, 'Enemies of the People', an echo of the Nazi *Gleichschaltung* in the 1930s, when politically suspect judges were removed and the legal system was 'coordinated' by the Nazi Party.

A great deal of overheated rhetoric was vented in this debate. There is however a reasoned case to be made that some judges were meddling in politics. On Radio 4's *Today* programme the former Conservative leader and barrister Michael Howard called for reform of the judiciary. He claimed that judges:

> increasingly substituted their own view of what is right for the view of parliament and of ministers… The question is who should make the law by which we are ruled. Should it be made by elected accountable politicians answerable to their constituents and vulnerable to summary dismissal at elections. What we've seen in recent years is a very considerable increase in the power of the judiciary, partly as a result of the expansion of judicial review.[12]

But in what could be regarded as a contradiction of his own argument, Mr Howard went on to suggest that judges were invited by parliament under the Human Rights Act to 'enter the political arena', including considering whether 'measures that parliament had taken to deal with a particular problem were proportionate to the objectives they wanted to achieve', leading to 'a significant increase in the power

of the judges at the expense of parliament and indeed government...
Sometimes in order to reach the result they want to achieve, they... distort the meaning of the act of parliament which they are interpreting.'

This is chopped logic. If judges are 'invited by parliament' to do
something, how can they be entering the political arena, except by
the will of parliament – in other words doing what parliament told
the judges to do? Nevertheless, Mr Howard implicitly criticized the
outgoing UK Supreme Court president Lady Hale for saying that
because prorogation was not a decision of parliament but of the
prime minister, it did not amount to a proceeding in parliament.
If it were a proceeding in parliament the Supreme Court could not
state the view that it was unlawful. Mr Howard argued: 'Prorogation
was clearly, on any ordinary view of the language, a proceeding in
parliament' and that 'judges have increasingly substituted their own
view of what is right for the view of parliament and of ministers'.

Again, this is a deeply flawed argument about the use of prepositions
rather than principles. Prorogation was not undertaken by parliament
itself, and certainly not considered and voted upon after a democratic
debate. It was a decision of the prime minister alone, an attempt to
silence parliament and curtail discussions by executive fiat. For her
part Lady Hale robustly defended her colleagues and warned against
any attempt to 'politicize' the judiciary. On BBC Radio 4[13] she said:

> We have an independent, merit-based appointments system
> which most of us are extremely comfortable with. We don't
> want to be politicized, we don't decide political questions, we
> decide legal questions. In any event, parliament always has the
> last word. We are not politically motivated. I do not know the
> political opinions of my colleagues and they do not know mine,
> and long may it remain so.

This is a complex and politically fraught discussion, and Mr
Howard is entitled to make his arguments in a reasoned way – and so
is Lady Hale. The point is that the United Kingdom's 'unwritten' or
uncodified constitution ensures that no one knows for sure where to

draw the line. The Good Chap theory of government – common sense among decent people and everyone knowing their limits – does not help us here. It has failed. This is a debate which continues and which will have particular importance as the strains generated by competing nationalisms increase when Brexit starts to become a reality. The dispute about judicial authority is far from over, especially since Boris Johnson went on to order a review of the role of judges in line with the 2019 Conservative manifesto which stated: 'We will ensure that judicial review is available to protect the rights of the individuals against an overbearing state, *while ensuring that it is not abused to conduct politics by another means* or to create needless delays' (my italics). To judges this sounds ominous, and begs the obvious question of how to prevent supposed 'reform' of the judiciary being used as cover for a political witch-hunt to remove uncooperative figures from the bench.

The vague nature of what passes for a British constitution, then, does not suitably describe or define the power relationships within these islands. This now has serious consequences for the unity of the United Kingdom. What is urgently needed is not so much a review of the role of judges as a review of the entire constitutional relationship between the courts, parliament, the executive at Westminster and the devolved administrations to clarify the roles of each in the name of a robust and healthy democracy. But that's a problem too. One further obvious sign of the federalization of Britain by stealth is the simple fact that there is no one thing called British democracy. Thankfully, various versions of British democracy do actually exist, although the most powerful of them – the Westminster parliament – is also the most flawed.

Why British Democracy Does Not Exist

The United Kingdom has four democratic systems. All are different, and each is capable of producing results that create conflict about what British democracy means in practice.

The four UK voting systems are the system used for electing the

Westminster government and the distinct voting systems for the Scottish parliament, the Northern Ireland Assembly and the Welsh parliament. Added to that is the recent constitutional innovation of holding referendums on Europe and Scottish independence, and until the UK left the European Union there was yet another method of electing representatives, in this case for the European parliament, known as the D'Hondt system.

The Westminster 'first past the post' (FPTP) system is the best known and the most unfair. In elections held under this system a candidate with a plurality of the votes can win, even if that candidate takes only, say, 35 per cent of the votes and all her opponents together take 65 per cent. This means an MP can be rejected by two-thirds of the voters in her constituency and still claim a 'mandate'. Scotland is a good example of how unfair the Westminster system can be. In the 2019 Westminster election the SNP won an overwhelming forty-eight out of fifty-nine seats, or 80 per cent of the available seats – but with just 45 per cent of the votes.

The Scottish parliament meanwhile is elected on a much fairer voting system, the Additional Member System. Under AMS, in the 2016 Scottish parliament elections the SNP won 46.5 per cent of the vote, securing more or less that percentage of the seats. The SNP fell just short of a majority of seats and in government was forced to work with other parties, more fairly reflecting the different opinions of the people of Scotland and requiring the governing party to reach a consensus with others to solve problems and create policies.

In Northern Ireland the system in Stormont elections is called STV, the Single Transferable Vote. This system was invented in Britain, even if it is not used for UK elections. But STV is used successfully in Ireland, Malta, Australia and other nations. It has many advantages, since it retains a degree of connection with a constituency or local area, while avoiding the unfairness of FPTP. The Electoral Reform Society explains how STV works:

Rather than one person representing everyone in a small area, bigger areas elect a small team of representatives. These representatives reflect the diversity of opinions in the area. On election day, voters number a list of candidates. Their favourite as number one, their second-favourite number two, and so on. Voters can put numbers next to as many or as few candidates as they like. Parties will often stand more than one candidate in each area. The numbers tell the people counting to move your vote if your favourite candidate has enough votes already or stands no chance of winning.

Personally, I think this system has many advantages since it both reflects the diversity of views within an area but also ensures that politicians have clear responsibilities to a particular constituency.

In Wales, there is a hybrid system. For the Welsh assembly, voters have not one but two votes. One vote goes to the forty Assembly Members (AMs) elected by a Westminster-style FPTP system; the other vote goes to a further twenty AMs elected by the Regional Top-Up system. Senedd Cymru, the Welsh parliament, explains how the two-vote system works:

> The first vote is for a local constituency Member. A Member is elected for each of the 40 constituencies in Wales by the 'first past the post' system, the system by which MPs are elected to the House of Commons – i.e. the candidate with the greatest number of votes wins the seat. The second vote is to elect a regional Member. Regional Members are elected by a form of proportional representation known as the 'Additional Member System', and voters vote for a political party. Each party must supply a list of candidates for the Additional Member seats in rank order. Wales has five electoral regions, and four Members are elected to serve each region. The electoral regions are based on the European Parliamentary Constituencies created in 1994.

All three of these systems have their defects, but any one of them is better at reflecting the genuine differences in public opinion than that used to elect the United Kingdom government. The unfairness of the Westminster system is even more pronounced when considering Boris Johnson's 'landslide' victory in the 2019 General Election. He 'triumphed' with a majority of eighty seats – and just 43 per cent of the vote. His 'triumph' was therefore based on the fact that 57 per cent of voters rejected him as prime minister. The advantage of the Westminster system is that it does often make for strong majorities in parliament, but being dependent on a minority of the voters for a supposedly 'strong' majority means the strength of the political mandate is always open to question. This would not matter so much if Mr Johnson's mandate was spread evenly across the country, but it is not. Two nations with a strong sense of identity – Scotland and Northern Ireland – hardly contributed at all to the Conservative victory, although they have by custom tolerated it. London, similarly a place with a strong sense of identity, rejected Johnson's programme decisively. Wales and most big English cities were no more enthusiastic. The vagaries of FPTP mean that Boris Johnson is the prime minister of the United Kingdom based largely on the votes of England-outside-London.

In terms of fairness, then, the worst and least democratic system is undeniably that of the Westminster parliament. Unlike the NHS, which has a clearly defined overall ethos even if it is managed differently in different areas, there is no strength in diversity for the United Kingdom in having four different systems to elect four different legislatures with four different mandates and in which the biggest player is the least democratic. Even within England, the Westminster government is often considered to be out of touch and particularly unresponsive to the needs of northern England. We may casually talk about 'British democracy' and call Westminster the 'Mother of Parliaments', but the patchwork quilt of devolution means that none of the children of the Mother of Parliaments experiences much maternal love.

*

British Media. Seriously?

We've already touched on the differences between watching the BBC or ITV in Scotland, Northern Ireland, England and Wales, but there are differences in printed media too. If you buy the *Sun* newspaper in Scotland you will find it a very different beast from the *Sun* in England. In September 2019 the English version of Rupert Murdoch's leading newspaper carried a picture of a chicken with Jeremy Corbyn's face stuck on it. 'Is THIS the most dangerous chicken in Britain?' the *Sun* asked English readers, with the tagline 'Corbyn clucks up Brexit'. All very entertaining. On the same day the Scottish edition of the same paper had an unflattering photograph not of Mr Corbyn but of Boris Johnson. The Scottish *Sun* headline was 'Floppy Johnson can't get an election'. It added 'Boz booted again'. During the 2015 General Election, the *Sun* front page in Scotland showed Nicola Sturgeon carrying a light sabre with the headline 'STUR WARS' and urged readers to vote for the SNP. The English version on the same day had a picture of David Cameron as a baby in swaddling clothes with the headline 'It's a Tory' and offered reasons to vote Conservative including to 'Stop the SNP running the country'. The two editions of the same newspaper were clearly talking to two different countries, two different markets, two very different incarnations of the *Sun* reader.

This split personality is a feature of other newspapers too. *The Times*, another Murdoch paper, has its own Scottish edition. The *Daily Mail* makes similar concessions to readers in Scotland and Ireland. All this is justified by saying that different audiences have different interests and requirements. It is not generally justified by the real reason, which is that sales and profits would collapse if the *Sun* in England supported Nicola Sturgeon or if the *Sun* in Scotland supported an Eton- and Oxford-educated English Tory prime minister. As Ralph Waldo Emerson wrote, 'A foolish consistency is the hobgoblin of little minds.' It is certainly foolish to be consistent in the newspaper business when sales and profits are at stake.

How 'British' is British Broadcasting?

There are few dafter phrases in British journalism than the idea of a 'postcode lottery'. People with a postcode in Newport in Wales will undoubtedly have slightly different needs and interests from those in Newham in London or Newcastle or Nairn in Scotland. And it's not a lottery – nobody pulls a number out of a hat to decide where they live, and the services they receive. Nevertheless, when a supposedly national institution like the government, the NHS or the BBC treats people differently, or when the patients or viewers have different priorities, it can become a focus of resentment. And if a national institution treats diverse communities as if they are all the same, that too can become the focus of resentment. When Scots tune in to the BBC, as the Scottish author Iain Macwhirter puts it:

> there is also the perennial problem of the BBC's network news bulletins featuring stories about health and education that are not relevant in Scotland because of devolution – a problem that could have been remedied fifteen years ago by the creation of a Scotland *Six O'Clock News*. The BBC's own *King Report* in 2008 identified a metropolitan bias in its news and current affairs.[14]

As we saw with the example of Andrew Wilson complaining that *ITV News* did not mention coronavirus figures for Scotland in its report, the BBC is not alone in trying to solve this dilemma. Broadcast reports about English schools or hospitals or even coronavirus figures really do have limited relevance in Scotland, Wales and Northern Ireland. It is simply a fact that the parts of our lives that citizens hold most dear – the schools for our children, whether we can see our GP easily, social care for our grandparents, divorce law for our marriages – are all devolved. In that sense, reports from London on English institutions can sound a bit like foreign news.

*

Lords Spiritual 'Birkies' (Berks)

In Scotland there is a degree of pride that many 'British' institutions have a tartan twist. But at the same time there remains the continuing irritation that other British institutions are ultimately run by and for England only. Behind all this lies an aspect of Scotland's own exceptionalism – a sense of social democratic meritocracy and communitarianism different from what Scots see as a more hierarchical class system in England. We have already encountered one example, the Queen in Scotland being seen both as the respected monarch and also as an ordinary worshipper in the Church of Scotland. The office of moderator of the Church of Scotland is significant in also not appearing to be part of a hierarchical system. It is unthinkable that prominent clergy in the Scottish church should wear fancy robes and automatically be members of the House of Lords, whereas it is taken for granted in England. England has forty-two diocesan bishops, of whom twenty-six are 'Lords Spiritual', sitting by right in the House of Lords. Beyond tradition, it is not clear why this influence remains necessary for the church after years of decline. In 1920 the Church of Wales established its independence from the Church of England and does not send bishops to the Lords. The Church of Ireland (a Protestant Episcopalian church, which ceased to be the established church of Ireland in 1869) also does not send bishops to the House of Lords. Scots believe, with some reason, that they are culturally resistant to such hierarchies. One of Scotland's most popular poems, Robbie Burns's 'A Man's a Man For a' That', sums up that sentiment:

> The honest man, tho' e'er sae poor,
> Is king o' men for a' that.
> Ye see yon birkie ca'd a lord,
> Wha struts, an' stares, an' a' that,
> Tho' hundreds worship at his word,
> He's but a coof for a' that...
> For a' that, an' a' that,

It's comin yet for a' that,
That Man to Man the warld o'er
Shall brithers be for a' that.

A 'coof', by the way, is a dolt or idiot. It is not surprising that with such sentiments Burns's poetry is popular in Russia, while largely unknown except by reputation in England – presumably as a result of unfamiliarity with the idioms of the Lowland Scots dialect, Lallans. The tone of the poem is humanist and anti-hierarchical, with the concluding sentiment the idea of the Brotherhood of Man, that all the world 'shall brithers be for a' that'. Burns has written a hymn to Enlightenment values of truth and honesty with common sense and good conduct prized over the rank, money and privilege of 'yon birkie' (in English, a berk or idiot) called a lord, whether Lords Temporal or Lords Spiritual from an established church. Burns vigorously captures that side of Scotland which remains suspicious of hierarchies. And yet – interestingly – the SNP and independence supporters have been very careful to insist that an independent Scotland would still retain one of the longest-lasting and most obviously hierarchical British institutions of all, the institution which brought about the Union of the Crowns in 1603 – the monarchy.

The British Monarchy (2) and Britain's 'Unwritten' Constitution

Ask any foreigner and most British people about the ultimate symbol of Britishness and they will settle on the Queen, although, as we noted, since 1603 monarchs of the United Kingdom were not 'true-born' English. The English have been ruled by immigrants for centuries. ('They come over here, take our crowns and palaces...') From the arrival of the Scot James I in London after the Union of the Crowns, through the troublesome Stuarts to the Dutch William of Orange to the German Hanoverians, the British have not always been enthusiastic about the person on the throne, but generally enthusiastic about the institution of monarchy. (Charles I and James II were exceptions.) For a sense of the United Kingdom as an 'imagined community', it is worth remembering that for the first three years of her life that great symbol of the British empire, Queen Victoria, spoke only German. Her governess was German, Baroness Lehzen. Her mother was Victoria of Saxe-Coburg-Saalfeld. Her consort was Prince Albert of Saxe-Coburg and Gotha. Today's royal family changed their name during the First World War by royal proclamation on 17 July 1917 from Saxe-Coburg-Gotha to the more suitably English designation of Windsor. The genius of the British monarchy has been that in times of difficulty it has been willing to adapt to circumstances and has always attempted to represent continuity. Prime ministers and governments may come and go, but the monarchy continues without pause, as in the phrase 'The king is dead. Long live the king.' Or, as Philip Larkin wrote in 1978, to commemorate the Queen's Silver Jubilee:

In times when nothing stood
But worsened, or grew strange
There was one constant good:
She did not change.

Queen Elizabeth II has worked hard at her job. During her long reign she has gone to great lengths to ensure that all parts of the United Kingdom feel they are in some way enveloped in royal inclusiveness. That means the Queen leads a gipsy existence. She moves with precision between Buckingham Palace and Windsor Castle and spends Christmas at Sandringham in Norfolk and summers in Scotland at Balmoral. The family – nicknamed 'the Firm' – not only dropped its German name, it rebranded different parts of the Firm to emphasize a sense of British inclusion – the Duke of Edinburgh, the Prince of Wales, the Duchy of Cornwall, the Duke of Sussex, the Duke of York, and so on. But inclusivity can bring with it other problems.

When Princess Diana died in 1997 the Queen was reluctant to leave her Scottish retreat at Balmoral and return to London. At the time courtiers told me that Her Majesty was 'at home' in her realm in Scotland just as she is at home in England. She was not 'away' or 'abroad'. But the Blair government and popular newspapers insisted she should return to London. It was a serious dilemma, brilliantly captured in the 2006 film *The Queen*. The row developed to such an extent that the Queen eventually conceded the point and came back to Buckingham Palace. London, again, proved the centre of gravity for the nation.

The key role of the monarchy is the representation of continuity and national – that is British – coherence. When Britain lost its empire after the Second World War and endured various crises from Suez to the miners' strike, the Queen symbolized a Britain which was changing profoundly yet enduring and familiar. In 1977 she celebrated her Silver Jubilee, twenty-five years on the throne, at a time when devolution to Scotland and Wales was being seriously debated, and when Northern Ireland's violent conflict seemed interminable. Nationalists from Scotland, Wales and Northern Ireland had for the first time since the Irish nationalist surge in 1918 secured significant representation at Westminster. Her Majesty said she noted the 'awareness of historic national identities on these islands' and offered a personal reflection: 'I number Kings and Queens of England and Scotland and Princes of Wales among my ancestors and I can readily understand these aspirations.' But then in a highly unusual and blunt foray into political matters, she went on: 'I cannot forget that I was crowned Queen of the United Kingdom of Great Britain and Northern Ireland.' The message on independence or separatism could not have been clearer.[15]

But is that message likely to outlive the Queen herself? Prince Charles will face significant challenges when he becomes king. Some commentators – bizarrely given that the monarchical system is entirely dependent on the hereditary principle – wish the monarchy would 'skip a generation' and enthrone Prince William instead of Prince Charles. Constitutional experts and royal advisers say this absolutely will not happen. Indeed, it would make a mockery of the hereditary principle itself. But controversies and scandals, from the sex allegations involving Prince Andrew to the role of Prince Harry since his marriage to Meghan Markle, have shown how far the monarchy has shifted from being focused on the monarch to a wider lens on 'the royal family'. This has not been an untrammelled success. As the former Labour home secretary and historian Roy Jenkins once put it, 'the concept of an extended reigning family has not prospered',[16] although it certainly does sell tabloid newspapers even if gossip about royal celebrities has done little to advance the principle of monarchy itself. It is one of the most extraordinary features of life in England that ordinary folk who have never met any member of the royal family often have trenchant opinions about the supposed conduct of dukes and duchesses they hear about through tabloid newspapers.

But there is also a distinction to be made between the monarchy as a symbol of continuity and as a symbol of institutional fossilization. It would be possible for the monarchy to retain the affection of the British people while also changing for changed times. The number of royal households and those employed by them could be cut without losing a sense of majesty. The British honours system with its British 'Empire' medals of various types, the arcane orders, titles and practices, are beloved by some but are emblems of a nation enthralled by nostalgia. This is not to denigrate the idea of a state recognizing the service of its citizens, although the services provided by ladies of the bedchamber, the lord steward, the lord chamberlain, the master of the horse and numerous equerries and masters of households may remain a mystery to the taxpayers who pay for them. I know personally recipients of significant awards presented by the Queen who felt simultaneously deeply honoured, grateful and respectful of Her Majesty yet also uncomfortable in receiving an honour referencing a long dead 'empire' with, in the case of those whose families were formerly subjects of that empire, a difficult and controversial history. Some recipients of awards have agonized over whether it is appropriate to accept an honour or rude to turn it down. Commentators, especially on the left, have written extensively about this archaizing aspect of the British state, as if the UK accepts the Ruritanian glamour of titles which to outsiders appear simply ludicrous.

One of my 'neighbours' on the Kent coast is the 'warden of the Cinque Ports' based at Walmer Castle. The castle is a magnificent example of England at its best, built in the time of Henry VIII and now run by English Heritage. It is the place where the Duke of Wellington breathed his last. His death mask and a pair of 'Wellington boots' are on display, and the gardens are open to visitors from around the world. The current warden of the Cinque Ports is the distinguished former admiral of the fleet Sir Michael Boyce, who undoubtedly deserves our respect for his service to our country, and is very much liked locally. But do we really require to celebrate good deeds in the twenty-first century with ceremonial titles, favours and distinctions dating back, in this case, to Edward the Confessor? The contrast with that other devotedly monarchist state, the Netherlands, is very striking: no minor noble uses the title *jonkheer* or *jonkvrouw* or baron in ordinary life, nor do they expect to be addressed as such. The Dutch state stopped elevating people to such titles soon after the Second World War, though they still award royal decorations (various Orders of Oranje-Nassau) to deserving citizens. The royal family retains the affection of the people of the Netherlands without the archaisms and the cost of its British counterparts.

Detailed thoughts about the modernization of the House of Windsor are beyond the scope of this book, although the accession of Prince Charles to the throne will bring changes in style and – one hopes – in substance too. He has had a long time to rehearse for the role. Any changes which do materialize will not please those who describe themselves as traditionalists – even if they fail to recognize that the 'traditions' they venerate were themselves at one time invented, in the case of the Cinque Ports, by a monarch 1,000 years ago. But there is one part of the monarchy that is especially problematic. It is the notion of 'the Crown in Parliament', which, as we will see in depth in the next chapter, forms part of the unwritten constitution of the United Kingdom yet has not substantively adapted to reflect the changing nature of the union.

The Scottish National Party has in the past been clear that they would wish the Queen to remain head of an independent Scottish state, should one come into existence, although what that would mean in practice is not clear. Sixteen members of the Commonwealth retain the Queen as head of state – Antigua and Barbuda, Australia, Belize, Barbados, Canada, Grenada, Jamaica, New Zealand, Papua New Guinea, St Kitts and Nevis, St Lucia, St Vincent and the Grenadines, Solomon Islands, the Bahamas and Tuvalu. Presumably an independent Scotland could join this list. Barbados, however, has decided to remove the British monarch as head of state, and other nations, including Australia, continue to debate the issue. But even if the United Kingdom retains its present structure, without independence for Scotland, the 'unwritten' British constitution will become increasingly problematic as different parts of the UK assert their right to be more distinct. For all but learned constitutional scholars the existing concept of the fusion of powers implicit in the notion of the Crown in Parliament is particularly murky. It means in theory that in the governance of the United Kingdom the monarch is the ultimate authority in whom sovereignty rests, but in practice this sovereignty is delegated to elected officials (notably the prime minister), with each part of this system supposed to recognize the limits of their powers. This is the ultimate expression of the Good Chap theory of government, which, as we will see, has become a bedraggled remnant of a Britain which is no longer in existence.

For now it is worth noting that in occasional dealings with Buckingham Palace officials I have been struck by their professionalism and humour and that courtiers generally are the epitome of 'Good Chaps' (and women). Shortly after the attacks on the United States on 9/11, I was at an event in Buckingham Palace talking with one of Her Majesty's key advisers and also in the company of a well-known English writer. On 13 September 2001, as the world still reeled with shock from the terrorist attacks, the Changing of the Guard ceremony at the Palace broke with tradition. The band of the Coldstream Guards played the US national anthem. I mentioned to the royal adviser that I had been very moved by this gesture and that an American friend of mine, a journalist who had been in war zones round the world, had burst into tears at this symbol of the United Kingdom's sympathy with America's loss. The British writer turned to the royal adviser and asked, 'Was playing "The Star-Spangled Banner" Her Majesty's idea?'

'Of course,' was the reply.

The writer then left our company. The royal adviser turned to me and whispered, 'When something goes well, it is always Her Majesty's idea.' The point of this witty aside is simply to dispense with the idea that royal courtiers are bumbling, even if the system in which they operate is archaic. The courtiers take the blame for mistakes, because that is their job. But they are generally high-flyers from the civil service or senior military officers, who understand very well the shortcomings of the institution that they serve, and the limitations of some of the individuals within the royal family. They are engaged in a process of constant reinvention of the monarchy as a continuing symbol of Britishness, and for years have prepared for the royal succession and the transition to the United Kingdom's next head of state. But in his assessment of the institutions of Britain two decades ago, Anthony Sampson concluded that the monarchy had already become 'the fading fairyland'.[17] In particular Sampson pointed out that the role of the monarch in our unwritten constitution remains unclear, vague and prone to argument. That is hardly surprising. The uncodified constitution is far from clear on many more things than the role of the monarch. If the United Kingdom is to survive, a degree of clarity about what holds us together is now required, how institutions operate and how to settle disputes between them. If the UK is destined not to survive we also need a degree of clarity about what we mean by our 'unwritten' constitution, how to disentangle its archaisms and why it has – despite its increasingly obvious failings – become an English national fetish.

9

Muddle England

'You will see here the origin of our excellent constitution where
the prerogatives of the Crown and the privileges of the subject
are so heavily proportioned that the King and the People
are inseparably united in the same interests and views…
in the reigns where this union was cultivated, the kingdom
flourished… On the contrary, when by an arbitrary disposition
of evil counsels it was interrupted, the constitution languished,
mutual confidence vanished, distrust, jealousy, discord arose;
and when entirely broken … confusion and civil wars ensued.'

*Nicolas Tindal 1687–1744, historian and Anglican clergyman,
writing about the form of government in England*[1]

'He would go still further, and say, that if at the present moment
he had imposed upon him the duty of forming a legislature for
any country… he did not mean to assert that he could form
such a legislature as they possessed now, for the nature of
man was incapable of reaching such excellence at once.'

*The Duke of Wellington extolling the virtues of the British
constitution while opposing the First Reform Bill, 1830*

> 'The world has traditionally looked enviously at the solidity of UK institutions: a politically impartial civil service, an effective parliament, an independent judiciary, a pragmatic constitutional settlement and ultimately the United Kingdom itself. But for how much longer?'

> *Jill Rutter, 'How Brexit Has Battered Britain's Reputation for Good Government',* Guardian, *27 December 2019*

In 1855 the British jurist and constitutional theorist A. V. Dicey asked a deceptively simple question. The manner in which the British state actually worked in practice was a bit of a mystery. It still is. Dicey wondered: 'How is it, again, that all the understandings which are supposed to regulate the personal relation of the crown to the actual work of government are marked by the utmost vagueness and uncertainty?'[2]

There have been many attempts to answer this question since the Victorian era, but the 'utmost vagueness and uncertainty' persists. Traditionally this has been viewed as a good thing, although more recently the mystery has lost its charm. The coronavirus pandemic was a modern threat that reopened some of the old questions raised by Dicey and others. Even if coronavirus had never happened, devolution and Brexit by themselves would have demanded some answers – who is actually in charge of what? Which powers do those in charge have and where are the limits set? How does this unwritten constitution actually work? For an increasing number of citizens the answer to that last question can be summed up in one word: badly.

Governing in the Subjunctive

In 2006, after questions about whether he should fire the US defence secretary, Donald Rumsfeld, President George W. Bush put an end to the speculation with one sentence: 'I'm the decider, and I decide what's best.' What's best, he decided, was to keep his friend, mentor and defence secretary in post. In Britain, the prime minister is the decider. But what happens when he is taken ill? Who decides who the decider should be? This question arose when Boris Johnson was taken to hospital in April 2020 and then into intensive care with breathing problems caused by his coronavirus infection. The answer was a very English muddle. The foreign secretary, Dominic Raab, was nominated by Mr Johnson to fill in for the prime minister 'where necessary'. But even then it wasn't clear what 'where necessary' meant, what the limits of his powers might be, whether Raab was 'the decider' or merely one of a group of 'deciders' and what would happen if Mr Johnson were to become incapacitated for months.

On BBC Radio 4's *Today* programme a constitutional expert was asked to run through the powers that Mr Raab would now enjoy and those that remained with the prime minister on his sick-bed. The constitutional expert laughed and said that was a bit tricky to answer directly as a result of what he called the 'glories' of the United Kingdom's 'unwritten constitution'. Mr Raab was 'first secretary of state' and Mr Johnson's 'designated survivor' but, the BBC's political editor Laura Kuennsberg said, that did not mean he had all the powers of a prime minister.[3] Britain would in some way no doubt just muddle through. Fingers crossed. Muddling through has been an English national pastime, although Winston Churchill had a more colourful phrase for it – KBO, Keep Buggering On.

Lord Kerslake, the former head of the civil service, offered some expert KBO guidance on what might happen to Mr Johnson's substitute: 'Raab will step into the key functions such as chairing Cobra [security] meetings and chairing cabinet. There will also have been general plans that would have been refined over the last few days since the prime minister's illness became clear.' The seriousness of the illness did indeed become clear, but the constitutional position remained undiagnosed. The idea that Mr Raab was Mr Johnson's 'designated survivor' suggested an accidental plane crash rather more than a seamless change in political decision-making in a mature democracy.

The BBC website tried to explain how it might work: 'The formal rules for what should happen if such situation arises are unclear – a consequence of the UK's unwritten constitution.' It went on to suggest some dos and don'ts for Mr Raab:

> He could make recommendations to the Queen on appointments to the senior judiciary and to high-ranking positions in the Church of England. But it is harder to imagine him conducting a reshuffle – even though, formally, it seems he ought to have that power. And things seem to get even less likely as we get to the more significant prerogative powers. In practice any major decisions would probably be taken by Mr Raab in consultation with the cabinet or, where appropriate, the cabinet secretary and other senior officials. A tricky example would be the authorising of military action. In an urgent situation he might have to do that – but presumably it would be agreed first by other senior cabinet ministers. Another difficult question would be the letters of last resort that the prime minister writes for the nuclear submarines, giving the commanding officers instructions about what to do in the event of a deadly attack on the UK. It is hard to see that Mr Raab would be asked to write them unless Mr Johnson was going to be incapacitated for a long time – and maybe not unless he actually stepped down as prime minister.

This is government in the subjunctive mood. Everything is in doubt. The heavily qualified tentative phraseology gives the game away – 'he could…', 'it seems he ought to have…', 'probably…', 'where appropriate', a 'tricky example' (as if the other examples are all clear cut), 'presumably…', 'another difficult question…' and 'maybe not unless…' Nobody knows. For a nation facing what in health and economic terms looked like the most difficult set of decisions since 1945 and with predictions of the biggest economic slowdown since 1709, we had made the leap in just a few hours from sympathy for a sick prime minister to considering who could, in theory at least, initiate a nuclear war. And no one – no one – could tell us the answers to these questions with any confidence.

For *The Times* it was at least clear that Mr Raab was first secretary of state, meaning that he was 'first among equals', except that he did not have the powers of a prime minister – so it was not really clear at all. The prime minister has sometimes been referred to as 'primus inter pares', the Latin phrase that literally means first among equals. The prime minister is also first lord of the Treasury. The assumption, indeed the practice, of prime ministers of the UK in recent years has been that they are much more than 'primus inter pares', although if the entire cabinet threatened to resign the prime minister would find his or her position untenable. Mr Raab was expected to take major decisions only with the consent of cabinet colleagues.

Fortunately for all concerned, the interregnum was short, and Mr Johnson recovered. But listening to these wise constitutional experts explaining the inexplicable reminded me of a Calvinist minister explaining the theodicy question, the question of why an all-powerful and infinitely good God nevertheless permitted the existence of evil. The answer – to the constitutional as well as the theological question – all seemed to end with the injunction 'just believe'. But when the believing stops, the questions remain.

Why KBO is NBG

Whatever the supposed 'glories' of not having a written or formally codified constitution, in practical terms the way in which the United Kingdom is governed is, to quote Winston Churchill (in a different context), 'a riddle wrapped in a mystery inside an enigma'. British governments are expected to work under a set of rules that no one finds easy to explain. That probably does not matter if everything is going well. The United Kingdom managed over four centuries to bring together four separate nations on these islands while expanding aggressively overseas and repelling foreign enemies. The result was the largest empire the world had ever seen. A superpower is less inclined to worry about the niceties of whatever methods it uses in order to succeed. But the United Kingdom in the first half of the twentieth century was forced to contract, losing most of Ireland and then the empire. It did so, remarkably, with minimal suffering, at least within the core of the United Kingdom itself.

The domestic political management of the contraction of an empire is arguably an even more extraordinary achievement than its expansion, given that it was the successful management of failure. When the Ottoman and Russian empires collapsed, the result was not merely loss of territories, but a period of revolution and disruption that has continued ever since, especially in the Middle East and the borderlands of Russia. The British imperial legacy resulted in conflicts all over the globe, including partition in Ireland, the partition of India and the chaotic consequences of borders arbitrarily drawn in the Middle East and Africa for the convenience of the imperial power rather than local citizens. From Kashmir to Iraq to west Africa and west Belfast, the Middle East to Cyprus, deep divisions remain between neighbours from the former British empire who even now are still engaged in trying to find a way to live together, and who glare at each other over walls, peace lines and lines of control. And yet compared to other European countries over the past century, Britain has been blessed with great domestic tranquillity. Constitutional vagueness and uncertainty may not work in theory, but it seemed to work in practice.

But now? In the second decade of the twenty-first century, would four independent nations of England, Scotland, Northern Ireland and Wales sign up on current terms to a United Kingdom? The answer would be no. Then ask if those four independent nations would sign up to membership of a European Union. England – probably not, although that may change. But at least two of the other three nations of the United Kingdom would say yes. Part of the argument in what follows, then, is that the current structure of the United Kingdom is increasingly unworkable. It does not reflect the way we live now. It can't cope with the federalization by stealth that has transformed its inner workings. It does not give due weight to competing nationalisms, nor does it appear to demonstrate the effortless competence that so impressed English historians and commentators in the past. In Boris Johnson's case, his time as prime minister may indeed be remarkable due to its lack of obvious effort, but competence has at least so far been more difficult to discern.

Above all, the structure of the United Kingdom does not reflect the needs and feelings of large numbers of people in England, whose English nationalism has become the most destabilizing force in the UK. The vague structure of our governance makes it impossible to manage the often contradictory aspirations within the different nations of the UK. Brexit, to repeat the point, is a symptom of this rather than a cause, but the cause cannot be addressed without considering how to amend the uncertain system under which we are governed. We need to explore the possible future relationships on these islands. Before we get to that, we also need to understand in more detail why we are now in such a muddle.

Muddle England and the End of Britain

For centuries English people have accepted Dicey's categorization of constitutional uncertainty, apparently believing it had positive advantages. Rather like monolingual worshippers in the medieval Catholic Church listening to the Latin Mass without understanding a word of it, we have been conditioned to worship the impenetrable constitutional mumbo jumbo of precedents and customs. The unwritten constitution, as we have noted, is in reality written but uncodified. That means it is embodied in arcane bits and inaccessible pieces of past judgements, traditions and precedents without a coherent sense of which bits are most important. There is no precision about who decides what when disputes occur.

If you want to read the United States Constitution, you can follow this link right now: constitutionus.com. If you want to see an original document, you can visit the upper level of the excellent US National Archives Museum. There you can find the Rotunda for the

Charters of Freedom, which is the permanent home of the original Declaration of Independence, the Constitution of the United States and the Bill of Rights. But for a British citizen seeking to understand the uncodified constitution, he or she has to rely on various experts who can translate it into the vernacular, rather like medieval peasants in pre-Reformation Europe going to the priest for guidance on what the Bible actually says. They then discover that the priest claims that it means the peasants have to do what the church authorities order them to do, including paying tithes to build the Sistine Chapel in faraway Rome. Perhaps a more apt religious simile is that in Britain the constitution is like the Holy Trinity. It has several parts, one-in-three and three-in-one, and it is difficult to grasp any of them with absolute clarity.

The uncodified constitution regulates the relationship between the British crown and United Kingdom government, parliament and the courts, as well as the web of relationships between the central government in Westminster and the devolved administrations in Belfast, Cardiff and Edinburgh. All these administrations do their own 'actual work of government', to use Dicey's phrase, but they do it in different ways and from different political perspectives. The danger is obvious. Muddling through no longer works. If the United Kingdom is to continue to exist, some kind of reinvention is necessary or else the great experiment of the past 400 years is destined to come to an end. And in that case, we will need to negotiate a divorce deal to divide up assets and liabilities as part of a future constructive relationship.

There are two main reasons why it seems likely that Britain may end. The first, as we have explored at length already, is that culturally as well as politically the nations of the United Kingdom have drifted apart. We have no clear unifying core, no credible political leaders arguing for a British identity, no strong unionist impulse, except in Northern Ireland, no road map for the way ahead. Even the Conservative and Unionist Party is 'unionist' in name only. Under such circumstances, competing nationalisms, as expressed in the Brexit vote, will, unless challenged by a convincing centripetal political force, pull the United Kingdom apart. The second reason that Britain may soon end is even more brutal. It can be summed up in Peter Hennessy's phrase: the Good Chap theory of government.

With 'Good Chaps' (or good women) at the helm, if one of the 'chaps' steps out of line or becomes a Bad Chap, the others 'have a quiet word'. Self-regulation means that no one pushes things to the limits. Bad Chaps resign before they can be fired. The Greek poet Hesiod expressed the aspiration towards balance in public life that has characterized English political commentary for centuries: 'Observe due measures; moderation is best in all things.' Peter Hennessy characterizes his 'Good Chap' theory in similar terms: 'The British constitution is a state of mind. It requires a sense of restraint all round to make it work.'[4] But as Hennessy himself wondered more recently, what happens if we run out of Good Chaps and a few Bad Chaps, men and women who do not show restraint, take over? Or, less dramatically, what happens if the British people have lost so much trust in the political system that they have begun wondering if its vagueness and uncertainty is really able to protect them from abuse by those in power? Trust in the British system of government is at an all-time low.

A constitution that is 'a state of mind', as Hennessy suggested, does not make for clarity. It is inevitably dependent on which 'minds' are in charge, and whether those minds truly recognize 'a sense of restraint all round'. Some do. Lord Carrington is an example. As Margaret Thatcher's highly regarded foreign secretary, Carrington resigned following Argentina's seizure of the Falkland Islands on 2 April 1982. After a moment of national humiliation, resignation was a matter of honour for Carrington – although the Franks inquiry published a year or so after the Falklands War found that no blame attached either to him personally or to the Foreign Office under his supervision. Peter Carrington may have been one of the last of the Good Chaps, if by that we mean a politician imbued with the idea that government ministers should resign as a result of failure, even if he or she is not directly responsible. This idea has not survived. Indeed, a number of ministers have shown, in the words of the old joke, that they possess all the political virtues, except resignation. One of those is Chris Grayling.

How Do You Become Chris Grayling?

Chris Grayling is not by anyone's definition a Bad Chap. But he has been a serial failure as a government minister for years. And yet he has survived, even, one might say, thrived. At public meetings, I have been repeatedly asked why really good and capable people are often turned off from politics and public life. I always argue against that idea. The majority of MPs, MEPs and government ministers I have met, male and female, from various political parties, would easily fit into the 'Good Chap' definition. Sure, they make mistakes, but they are generally clever, dedicated and hard-working. My heartfelt response was, and is, that most politicians I have come to know are not useless, venal or corrupt, and many are among the brightest and most engaging people I have ever met – Margaret Thatcher, William Hague, Ed and David Miliband, Michael Gove, Ed Balls, Shirley Williams, Gordon Brown, Nicola Sturgeon, John Hume, Menzies Campbell, Tony Blair, and many others. My personal list includes politicians that many British people may never have heard of – Stephen Gethins, Kit Malthouse, Molly Scott Cato, Wera Hobhouse, Rosie Duffield, Seamus Mallon and many others. But then, inevitably after such a response, someone in the meeting says, 'But how do you become Chris Grayling?' I have asked myself that same question for many years.

Mr Grayling was secretary of state for justice from 2012 until 2015 and secretary of state for transport from 2016 until 2019. He also held other ministerial jobs. As justice secretary he introduced a ban on sending books to prisoners. It appeared he had given up on the idea of rehabilitation in prisons, although he did not say so. After a legal challenge the ban was overturned as unlawful in a judgement of the High Court in December 2014. It was undoubtedly one of the most clearly indefensible ideas in recent governmental history. Mr Grayling also supervised the privatization of the probation service, which was a truly abysmal failure. According to a study in the journal *Work, Employment and Society*, 'The privatisation of probation is unprecedented in terms of its scale and scope and it has proven to be something of an unmitigated disaster for professionals.'[5]

Surviving apparently unscathed from yet another disaster, Mr Grayling went on to become transport secretary during Britain's Brexit preparations. Here his impact was even more notable at home and noticed even abroad. The *New York Times* ran numerous articles about Britain's loss of competence in managing its own affairs, including one focusing on 'Failing Grayling'. They outlined his history of masterminding projects that ended in embarrassment. One was a £13 million contract with a company called Seaborne Freight to provide cross-Channel ferries in the event of having to secure emergency supplies if Britain crashed out of the EU without a trade deal. Seaborne Freight did not actually have any ferries and had no directly relevant experience. The contract was scrapped, but the manner in which it was negotiated led to Mr Grayling's department paying compensation of £33 million of taxpayers' money to Eurotunnel. This is the company that runs the under-sea train route to France, and Eurotunnel claimed they should have had a chance to bid for the business given to Seaborne Freight. Then yet another transport company, P&O (which does have actual ferries), began its own litigation, claiming that it too had been put at a commercial disadvantage by the incompetence of Mr Grayling's department.

The Labour Party opposition calculated that Mr Grayling's serial mistakes cost the British taxpayer £2.7 billion in total, and no ferries were, in the end, required. Britain did not leave the EU on one of several occasions when we were promised it would. Mr Grayling's department also prepared for Brexit by trying to figure out how to handle a long queue of lorries at the key port of Dover. One of the trial preparations involved placing miles of traffic cones on the M20 motorway, well in advance of the date we were supposed to leave, causing disruption at the same time as work commenced on a new roundabout system. Another exercise involved paying lorry drivers to create a phoney traffic jam on a Kent airfield. One of those drivers told me he was paid £500 for the day. He said that Mr Grayling was one of those politicians who 'couldn't even create a traffic jam' and that the government could have saved money by just halting the operation of Dover port for half an hour, which would immediately create a real-life traffic problem.

Now, Chris Grayling is not an evil person. But he was a puzzle to many British people, somehow surviving and even rising in government despite being a laughing stock in the UK and beyond. He failed upwards. By the summer of 2020 he was tipped for another new job, pushed by Boris Johnson to chair parliament's Intelligence and Security Committee, despite having no experience in either intelligence or security matters. But the committee members resisted. They voted for another Conservative MP Julian Lewis to become chairman instead. Mr Grayling, it was said, was unable even to win a rigged election. He later resigned from the committee. Chris Grayling is emblematic of a system in which failure is rewarded provided that it is backed up by party loyalty. And that is the key. The two-party system which thrives under Westminster electoral rules means that a donkey with a red or a blue rosette will, if selected by Labour or the Conservatives, continue to win positions in parliament, and a loyal minister or adviser can be retained by the whim of a prime minister despite public scandal. Many talented politicians of an independent cast of mind, or people outside politics who wish they could help steer the United Kingdom in a better direction, are sidelined by a system that favours time-servers, hacks and bores who can secure advancement by sucking up to the leader and endorsing an ideologically 'sound', even if practically idiotic, position.

'Flaws That Require Urgent Attention'

By November 2019 Peter Hennessy and his co-author, Andrew Blick, worried that something much worse than lack of competence might cause profound problems for the United Kingdom. What if, they wondered, our 'vague and uncertain' system were to fall under the spell of a populist leader, someone who did not take seriously the unwritten checks and balances and sense of restraint inherent in the Good Chap system? Might we be entering Trumpland – a Trumpland without a clear constitution to limit the powers of a leader who pretended he or she wanted to Make Britain Great Again?

Hennessy and Blick produced a report for the Constitution Society called 'Good Chaps No More'. In part they were thinking of the conflict between Boris Johnson and the UK Supreme Court over the prorogation of parliament, the role of Her Majesty the Queen and the devolved governments. Hennessy and Blick argued that following the Brexit vote:

> recent turbulence affecting the British system of government has revealed flaws that require urgent attention. The period since the European Union referendum of June 2016 has seen a series of disputes about whether or not constitutional abuses have taken place. They have touched upon many of the main governmental organs: the Cabinet, the Civil Service, Parliament, the judiciary, the devolved institutions, and even the monarchy. Collectively they serve to demonstrate potential weaknesses in the traditional model of constitutional regulation. If general standards of good behaviour among senior UK politicians can no longer be taken for granted, then neither can the sustenance of key constitutional principles.[6]

The wording is careful but the meaning, especially of that last sentence, is explosive. Two of the most thoughtful constitutional experts in Britain are warning that the British uncodified constitution is potentially dangerous rather than glorious, and no one can guarantee that it can be sustained in the long term. It depends upon 'general standards of good behaviour' – a shaky foundation in modern politics. The arrival of a Trump, an Orbán, a Salvini or a Le Pen at the top of British politics would expose 'potential weaknesses' in Muddle England. In very calm language Hennessy and Blick are warning about potential disasters ahead, the end of Britain in a different sense –

the end of supposedly British values; the death of the last Good Chap. The authors called for:

> the incoming Speaker of the House of Commons to make a major contribution in this area. He could convene a Speaker's Conference of the type that paved the way for the Representation of the People Act 1918, that expanded the parliamentary franchise to women of 30 and over and previously excluded men. Other options could include the formation of a Royal Commission or a special parliamentary select committee. There is also scope to work with a Citizens' Convention comprising a representative sample of members of the public chosen at random.

All or some of the Hennessy-Blick ideas could be implemented, but why would they be? If 'general standards of good behaviour' among politicians are now being questioned, why would those demonstrating a lack of good behaviour want to thwart their own ambitions? Why would the fox wish to change the lax system in the henhouse before eating his fill? Hennessy's co-author, Dr Andrew Blick, is director for the Centre for British Politics and Government at King's College London. He went further in a reflection on the turbulence of twenty-first-century political life by concluding, in effect, that the last good chap may indeed have perished and implying that the optimism of those who believed in the British genius for moderation may be misplaced. Blick's views are disturbing and worth quoting at length:

> The UK constitution relies heavily on self-regulation. Here lies the core of possible concerns about the viability of the UK system under pressure… One component of this school of thought is the so-called 'good chap' theory. It holds that people who come to positions of political authority in the UK have an almost innate knowledge of what are appropriate forms of conduct and where the boundaries lie; and that they also have a desire to act in accordance with such protocols. A second aspect to this

theory of constitutional stability is the observation that in the UK, partly thanks to its parliamentary electoral system, there is a strong tendency towards dominance by two parties that tend to converge on the political centre, thereby eschewing more extreme programmes. Present circumstances should cause us to revisit these precepts. As David Klemperer has shown in his recent Constitution Society report on the subject, there is a strong case to be made that, lately, the so-called 'First-Past-the-Post' system used for Westminster elections is having a polarising impact upon the two main parties. Furthermore, in a related development, the current political climate seems to be conducive to the ascendancy of politicians who are not only characterised by a lack of regard for the more traditional conventions of the political system, but make a positive virtue out of this disdain...

Whatever the precise motives, it is now appropriate to discuss the possibility of a self-consciously 'anti-system' politician, at the head of a similarly inclined party, becoming Prime Minister. The over-used label 'populist' might at this point be apt... Examples from around the world in different time periods suggest that, while such leaders might not immediately seek to supplant the democratic system in its entirety, it is none-theless intrinsic to their approach that they behave in ways that are democratically problematic. Their ideology is founded in the idea of powerful, privileged and embedded enemies, whose rules and authority are illegitimate, and whose treachery must be exposed and eradicated. In rejecting sections of the social elite, populist governments may also need to cultivate power bases elsewhere. In a UK context, this perspective could lead to a number of possible activities, which would tend to have constitutional implications. They might include heavy politicisation of public appointments; the targeting of the rights of unpopular minority groups; the creation and deployment of excessively broad delegated executive powers; legislative ouster clauses restricting the potential for judicial review of those powers; attempts to bypass standards of propriety involving the use of public money to the benefit of political allies; misuse of emergency powers; and efforts to curb unfavourable media coverage (perhaps focused on public broadcasters). Individual cases of many of these kinds of activities have taken place in the past in the UK. The sign of a more clearly populist government would be its pursuance of such approaches in a more concerted, comprehensive fashion. Indeed, they could be central to the programme of an administration that actively presents some of them as a good. At this point, both the 'good chap' principle and the supposed tendency towards moderation in the party system will have failed the UK. With these protective devices circumvented, what barriers would remain, and how effective might they prove?[7]

We will return to the idea that we are witnessing 'the ascendancy of politicians who are not only characterised by a lack of regard for the more traditional conventions of the political system, but make a positive virtue out of this disdain' in a moment. But first we should reflect on how many of these possibilities, even if they have not entirely come to pass, have at least been mooted publicly. British 'government sources', 'Number 10 sources' and their friends in sections of the media have floated various ideas to 'crack down' on judges, public service broadcasters (most especially the BBC) and to begin considering the political leanings of people in public appointments. They have also targeted 'the rights of unpopular minority groups', especially migrants, and there have been 'attempts to bypass standards of propriety involving the use of public money to the benefit of political allies', among other matters. Turning a blind eye to the rule-breaking of Dominic Cummings's road trip to Durham while instructing other citizens to comply with the rules was merely the most obvious example of the declining health of the last Good Chap. Another recent example involved the housing secretary Robert Jenrick and his decision to push through a planning application by the former owner of the *Daily Express* Richard Desmond, who wished to develop a site in east London for housing. Mr Jenrick's involvement saved Mr Desmond millions of pounds, which otherwise would have gone to the local council in a relatively impoverished borough. Mr Desmond donated £12,000 to the Conservative Party. Everything which occurred was legal. Whether it was politically wise, and by-passed standards of propriety, is another matter.

The significance of these examples – and countless others, including the purging of top officials within the civil service, and the elevation of cronies and political party donors to the House of Lords – is that they shed light on the British sense of complacency about Good Chaps running the United Kingdom. This has eroded Britain's reputation for good governance. The illusion of virtue has evaporated, and the real practical problem is how anyone can run a constitutional monarchy when no one is especially clear what the rules are. From Churchill's KBO, Keep Buggering On, we are now in the era of KBU – governments which Keep Buggering Up.

Constitutional Monarchy Without a Written Constitution

At the time Dicey was writing his great work on constitutional theory, the heyday of British imperial power, England was thought to be useless at public ceremonials and celebrations. The Victorian-era prime minister and Dicey's contemporary Lord Salisbury, after observing the Queen opening parliament in 1860, believed that:

> some nations have a gift for ceremonial… In England the case is exactly the reverse. We can afford to be more splendid than most nations but some malignant spell broods over our most solemn ceremonials and inserts into them some feature which makes them all ridiculous… something always breaks down, somebody contrives to escape doing his part…[8]

The historian David Cannadine argues that when Britain lost power and influence in the world, we actually became very good at celebrations. Once the British empire had gone, British public rituals and ceremonies – royal weddings, jubilees and the 2012 Olympic Games opening ceremony – all suggested that our staging skills were not just improving but world-beating. Cannadine noted that our appetite for royal celebrations and pomp increased as the United Kingdom's hard power diminished. Such occasions became what he called 'the premiere of the cavalcade of impotence'. By the twenty-first century Britain was very different from the height of empire and the Victorian age with its 'certainty of power and the assured confidence of success' which 'meant that there was no need to show off.' We showed off because we had much less to boast about, and the 'cavalcade of impotence' became also a cavalcade of nostalgia.[9] In the twentieth and twenty-first centuries the United Kingdom continued to resurrect Victorian-era horse-drawn state coaches and to show off the Household Cavalry – their day job is working as an armoured reconnaissance unit – resplendent in their shining early nineteenth-century-style breastplates and swords. In 1997 the army confirmed that the breastplates would in future be made of polymer, inviting newspaper headlines about 'plastic armour'. All this involved the pretence, as Harold Nicolson put it in his biography of George V, that 'our own monarchy, unimpaired in dignity had survived for more than a thousand years'.[10]

The idea of the British monarchy, in Cannadine's phrase, as a 'secular religion' is a recent invention. After the death of Prince Albert and for a considerable period of her reign, Queen Victoria was unpopular. She largely withdrew from public life, while successive British governments asserted their growing confidence through imperial acquisitions and annexations and left the monarch to mourn in peace. The result was that half the area of world maps became a fetching colour of pink. Britannia really did rule the waves with the world's most powerful navy, and pomp and circumstance were not highly regarded. Whereas, Cannadine notes, 'today in England, the situation is the exact reverse. With the possible exception of the papacy no head of state is surrounded by more popular ritual than Queen Elizabeth II.'[11] Cannadine does not add – because he does not need to do so – that the world is no longer pink.

One of the monarch's most popular modern rituals is that of the broadcast to the nation and Commonwealth. It is usually confined to Christmas Day. In April 2020, the Queen made a highly unusual broadcast to the country as the coronavirus epidemic took hold. Government ministers and the prime minister himself appeared in daily briefings on television and radio, but their contributions were often dismissed in newspapers and news broadcasts as at best wishful thinking and at worst somewhat phoney, fact-free and at times even comic. Promises about testing for the virus, pledges about the provision of masks and PPE (Personal Protective Equipment) were repeatedly exposed as worthless. Government statistics on the number of tests for coronavirus carried out were massaged by adding in the number of tests sent out rather than completed. RAF aircraft were sent to Turkey on an emergency mission to pick up PPE, without anyone in government checking whether the protection equipment they had purchased from a tee-shirt manufacturer was of a suitable standard. (It wasn't.) At a time of great peril the British people earnestly wanted to trust someone, but leading politicians were shown not to be aware of basic facts. In the case of the home secretary, Priti Patel, one of the most senior ministers of the crown proved unable to read a prepared statement because it contained some rather large numbers which clearly left her baffled.

And then amidst all the fear, chaos and incompetence there came the intervention of the 93-year-old monarch. Her short, simple and moving broadcast from Windsor Castle received universal plaudits at the same time as politicians in government were drowning in a slurry of criticism. As a historian wrote in 1970, 'while people can see the gloved hand waving from the golden coach they feel assured that all is well with the nation, whatever its true state'.[12] Fifty years later, the Queen's coronavirus address was most assuredly the successful waving of the gloved hand, an effective encouragement to the entire British nation to buck up.

Unlike politicians, some of whom recycled direct references to the shared sacrifice of the Second World War and the Blitz spirit, Her Majesty – who actually lived through the Blitz as a young princess –

offered a cleverly worded reference to British stoicism. She nodded towards Dame Vera Lynn's most famous wartime song 'We'll Meet Again' by saying that 'we should take comfort that while we may have more still to endure, better days will return: we will be with our friends again; we will be with our families again; we will meet again.' Although the institution of monarchy is replete with nostalgic references, the Queen was very careful not to fall into the trap of English nostalgic pessimism and declinism. She was no John of Gaunt or Roger Scruton lamenting that the current generation was much less capable of dealing with a crisis than those of the past. On the contrary, the Queen assured us that we are as good today as we ever were, and so it must be true: 'And those who come after us will say the Britons of this generation were as strong as any. That the attributes of self-discipline, of quiet good-humoured resolve and of fellow-feeling still characterise this country. The pride in who we are is not a part of our past, it defines our present and our future.'

It was stirring, forward-looking and inspiring from a monarch who, as Dicey noted, is a key part of Britain's constitutional jigsaw. Making the different parts work together for the common good can be difficult, although, as the Queen implied, when it comes to a pandemic, the attack from a common enemy, working together should be easier. But the challenge of Brexit and our competing nationalisms is very different from a worldwide health crisis. The Queen could hardly make a broadcast admonishing us to Get Brexit Done without alienating half the state of which she is head. When in September 2014, just before the Scottish independence referendum vote, she cautioned voters in Scotland to 'think carefully', even such anodyne words were taken as evidence of Her Majesty siding against independence. That's because Brexit and nationalism are not reducible to Us against Them, a common existential threat from pestilence, death or war. Brexit and nationalism are Us against Us. And that's where the clarity of a constitution is not just desirable but essential.

★

The Cavalcade of Incompetence

Pride in Britain, its monarchy, society and culture is one thing. But competence and honesty are required to turn pride into reality, and promises into real achievements for real people. Since 2014, the people of Britain have endured many exercises of our democracy (or rather, democracies). We have had the opportunity to vote in the 2014 Scottish independence referendum, three UK General Elections, the Brexit referendum of 2016, elections for the Welsh National Assembly, also in 2016, and two European parliament elections. During these years the people of Britain were promised – as is usual in political rhetoric – that things would get better. In 2016 it was the 'sunlit uplands'. After Brexit the UK would become 'Singapore on Thames' – a revealing geographical metaphor. But by 2019 even that odd comparison to a successful but tiny Asian city-state had declined into the dismal but effective slogan that in some unspecified way we had to 'Get Brexit Done', still without having decided exactly what Brexit actually meant.

Getting something done is not an answer in itself, as Macbeth found out to his cost. As he put it, before murdering Duncan, 'if 'twere done when 'tis done, 'twere well it were done quickly'. Brexit, like the murder of Duncan, was not 'done' quickly and not 'done' at all, in the sense of being over and done with. In the play the murder of Duncan is not the end but the beginning of Macbeth's woes. Brexit is a problem that will take years to solve. That's why by the time Boris Johnson's various self-imposed deadlines eventually led to the formal departure of the UK from the EU on 31 January 2020, celebratory enthusiasm for the project was not much in evidence. Lord Salisbury's 'malignant spell' was cast once more.

Brexit Day, for all but a minority of the English population and a few tabloid newspapers, had all the pent-up excitement of the removal of a verruca. It was a relief rather than a victory. The campaign to ring the bells of Big Ben to celebrate Britain's departure was a case in point. The bell-ringing idea went all the way to the prime minister, who demonstrated simultaneously his flair for alliteration and his lack of flair for completing his populist-sounding promises with a real achievement. As Mr Johnson said: 'We're working up a plan so people can bung a bob for a Big Ben bong, because there are some people who want to.' Certainly 'working up a plan' for 'some people who want to' has been a Johnson characteristic for a very long time, although implementing a plan successfully has not been so obvious either when he was London mayor or foreign secretary or indeed as prime minister. His phrasing was another bit of nostalgia, more at home in a 1950s Just William story or the *Boy's Own* comic. Yet this is one reason for Boris Johnson's political success. Johnson represents nostalgic optimism in an English culture steeped in nostalgic pessimism. He cheers people up because he sounds like the England of seventy years ago which was – inevitably yet ahistorically – 'better' than the England of today.

The 'bob' for Big Ben was a throwback to the British currency which was decimalized in 1971 when Boris Johnson was seven years old. He may – just – have paid for something with a 'bob' – 12 old pence – but nobody under the age of fifty has had that pleasure. And in 2020, no matter how many happy people wanted to offer a 'bob' to ring a bell for Brexit (a bob is now worth 5p), a single phone call from Mr Johnson to House of Commons staff or engineers would have alerted the prime minister to the temporarily un-bongy nature of Big Ben, due to costly repairs. The bells remained silent. In what could be an epitaph on Johnson's career, Lord Salisbury acidly commented in 1860, 'some bye-motive is suffered to intervene and ruin it all'. In the case of the Johnson government the bye-motive is generally something called 'reality'.

Brexit Bells Toll for Britain

Brexit ceremonials, such as they were, did seem to bear out Lord Salisbury's gloomy characterization of British misadventures with pomp and ceremony. There was an attempt to coerce the Church of England to ring out all the church bells on the occasion of the formal departure on 31 January 2020 – again, an English-only celebration of a supposedly British event. A phone call to the Archbishop of Canterbury's office at Lambeth Palace would have established that this was unlikely to happen. Brexit might involve a leap of faith, but it was not a religious occasion. Then there was the minting of special 50p coins, which patriotic Britons could buy, if they so wished, for many more times than their face value. Some were selling for £4.50. A 'Festival of Brexit Britain and Northern Ireland' was promised – not an especially catchy title for a series of unspecified 'British' concerts and spectacles, which are also unlikely to happen.

Lord Salisbury's 'malignant spell' manages to make contemporary political celebrations seem ridiculous, and yet in his day – despite his scepticism – Victorian-era Britain could, when necessary, put on a good show. One example was the Great Exhibition of the Works of Industry of All Nations. It opened in the summer of 1851, organized in part by Queen Victoria's consort Prince Albert and more popularly known as the 'Crystal Palace' exhibition. It attracted everyone who was anyone, from European royalty and Charles Dickens to an obscure German refugee living in Highgate in north London, Karl Marx. For the man or woman taking an omnibus through Knights-bridge, the Great Exhibition was extraordinary, a palace made of glass, so large that trees grew inside part of the structure. The entire exhibition displayed 100,000 objects, with more than 15,000 con-tributors. Britain and its empire – of course – occupied half the available space rather as the British empire occupied half the world. The displays included adding machines, Axminster carpets, steam hammers, a 'stiletto or defensive umbrella' and other extraordinary representations of British manufacturing genius. All this was a public display of how Britain was admired, and sometimes feared, for our extraordinary problem-solving abilities in everything from technology, transport and military might to our democratic form of government, our literature and our wider culture – hard power to soft power. We didn't need circuses and other showy celebrations, although we could put them on if necessary. The stability and com-petence of Britain's governance was at least symbolically behind the display of technological and manufacturing genius. Prince Albert was able to write to his cousin King William of Prussia that 'we have no fear here either of an uprising or an assassination', unlike many a royal house across the rest of Europe.[13]

Britain's soft power is still a force in the world, even as the UK's hard power has declined, but Brexit and Boris Johnson's mishandling of the coronavirus pandemic have affected our reputation for competence in government at home and our image abroad. Britain, in that well-worn phrase, used to punch above its weight. The history of stable and competent governments, the Enlightenment values of our scientists, schools and universities, meant that foreign leaders from Pakistan's Benazir Bhutto to Iran's President Rouhani and America's Bill Clinton all studied in Britain. German Chancellor Angela Merkel once told me that she learned English in part by listening to the BBC World Service under her bed covers as a child in the former East Germany. The British reputation has been a nation not of shopkeepers, but of practical people who fix things, make things and create things. But since the Brexit vote, in particular, other countries have witnessed a pattern of British government behaviour that suggests our missteps are not merely the occasional blunders that great nations may make from time to time. With Brexit we are enduring systemic failure and almost comic incompetence caused by reverence for a system of governance mired in the Victorian past and incapable of dealing with the structural failures that English nationalism and Brexit have exposed. This systemic failure has been noticed by those who fret about the United Kingdom's reputation in the world.

In November 2017, Simon Fraser, the former permanent secretary at the UK Foreign Office, said in a speech: 'It is hard to call to mind a major foreign policy matter on which we (in Britain) have had a decisive influence since the referendum.'[14]

Tony Blair's chief of staff Jonathan Powell wrote in *The Guardian* newspaper: 'To put it even more cruelly: we have rendered ourselves irrelevant by Brexit.'[15]

Jürgen Maier, chief executive of Siemens in the UK, spoke sorrowfully when he observed that 'the world is watching, and where the UK used to be [a] beacon for stability, we are now becoming a laughing stock.'[16]

The *New York Times* journalist Steven Erlanger appeared to echo the words of Dean Acheson from his 1962 West Point speech, regretting that Britain had lost an empire and failed to find a role. In a long and sad dissection of British decline, Erlanger wrote:

Many Britons see their country as a brave galleon, banners waving, cannons firing, trumpets blaring. That is how the country's voluble foreign secretary, Boris Johnson, likes to describe it. But Britain is now but a modest-size ship on the global ocean. Having voted to leave the European Union, it is unmoored, heading to nowhere, while on deck, fire has broken out and the captain – poor Theresa May – is lashed to the mast, without the authority to decide whether to turn to port or to starboard, let alone do what one imagines she knows would be best, which is to turn around and head back to shore. I've lived and worked for nine years in Britain, first during the Thatcher years and then again for the last four politically chaotic ones. While much poorer in the 1980s, Britain mattered internationally. Now, with Brexit, it seems to be embracing an introverted irrelevance. The ambitious Mr Johnson was crucial to the victory of Brexit in the June 2016 referendum. But for many, the blusterings of Boris have lost their charm. The 'great ship' he loves to cite is a nationalist fantasy, a remnant of Britain's persistent post-imperial confusion about its proper place in the world, hanging on to expensive symbols like a nuclear deterrent while its once glorious navy is often incapable of patrolling its own coastline... Britain is undergoing a full-blown identity crisis.'[17]

Nevertheless, Boris Johnson is sure-footed when capturing the zeitgeist of the nostalgic heart of England with his antique vocabulary, while he looks optimistically to the future in a series of grand sales pitches. For him, all will be a 'fantastic success' with lashings of ginger beer and plenty of cake for tea, and yet unfortunately things never quite turn out as promised. His 'world leading' coronavirus test and trace system and 'oven ready' Brexit deal simply did not exist. Even so, Johnson's nostalgic optimism hits exactly the note that chimes with the nostalgic pessimists of English nationalism. Nostalgic pessimists do not truly expect things to get better, and therefore they can rarely be disappointed by Johnson's failures. They do not even expect the truth, especially from politicians, but they are willing to be entertained, and Mr Johnson is the nation's crooner and stand-up comedian at the top of the bill. Voters were well aware that the Johnson promise on the Brexit bus that the £350 million a week supposedly given to the EU would instead be given to 'our NHS instead' was probably nonsense. Sir David Norgrove of the UK Statistics Authority publicly rebuked Johnson for a gross misuse of statistics. Economists, journalists and fact-checkers did the same. But none of it mattered. It was the right optimistic tone for a world in which we're about to have our cake and eat it as we prepared for the easiest trade deal in history because we held all the cards, and of course we would 'Take Our Country Back'.

Mr Johnson, like Richmal Crompton's Just William, was the scruffy boy in a timeless English village where the clocks stopped about 1930, always getting into scrapes but gifted with a peculiar charm. As Boris Johnson himself put it, he has only one serious conviction – for speeding. Mr Johnson's ambition, he told his fellows at Eton, was never to do something; it was to be something – 'World King'. As we noted, even on the most divisive issue of our times, Brexit itself, he had no fixed opinion. He famously produced two versions of his weekly column for the *Telegraph* newspaper, one in favour, one against, and at the last moment decided he was in favour of leaving the EU. His political career has been built on merry japes and orotund oratory. He spent around £53 million – most of it public money – on a Garden Bridge for London, a bridge that will never be built but which he described as 'a wonderful environment for a crafty cigarette or a romantic assignation'.[18] He suggested that an airport be built in the waters of the Thames estuary in similarly folksy terms. He backed the idea of a bridge between Northern Ireland and Dumfries and Galloway in Scotland (yes, another bridge too far, which will also never be built). As Mayor of London he did achieve something by purchasing German riot control water cannon. Unfortunately, Mr Johnson didn't check whether it would be possible to use them. They were sold for scrap. Mr Johnson is, as friends delicately put it, 'not a details person'.

In *Watching the English*, Kate Fox suggests an apt phrase to sum up Johnson's political success – 'the importance of not being earnest'.[19] She argues that English people adore eccentrics and gifted amateurs and take against those who try too hard, the kind of people Mr Johnson dismisses as 'girly swots'. The English, in this reading of national character, if such a thing is possible, have to wear their learning lightly and with humour, although Mr Johnson's humour is that of a seedy, nudge-nudge, wink-wink, double entendre-addicted Englishman of the kind parodied so well by Eric Idle or Terry-Thomas. This is tempered with the ability to quote a dead language, Latin, and a shambolic appearance. It is worth noting that this shambolic appearance is carefully crafted. Numerous TV make-up assistants have told me that prior to appearances on television they powder and fix the Johnson visage and coiffeur immaculately and watch as he looks in the mirror and deliberately ruffles his hair and makes sure his tie is not quite straight. It is, of course, an act, a style rather than an ideology. The political performance art known as 'Boris Johnson' somehow works in an England which not only tolerates muddling through, but has elevated it from a means of travel into a final destination.

The Catch: Muddling Through and 'Good Chap' Theory Doesn't Work

Space does not permit a full account of Mr Johnson's lies, misstatements and uncorrected falsehoods, although Martin Fletcher writing in the *New Statesman* in 2016 has a summary,[20] and Heathcote Williams's *Boris Johnson: The Beast of Brexit* (also 2016) gives a flavour of his behaviour. In March 2020, fewer than two in five voters (36 per cent) said they trusted what Mr Johnson said on the subject of coronavirus, while 59 per cent trusted health officials. These figures changed once Mr Johnson was himself incapacitated by the virus, when he received a great deal of understandable sympathy, but they fell again as Johnson recovered and the performance of the government did not. The constitutional question is not about policy or popularity. It is whether a prime minister – any prime minis- ter – can be held to account for falsehoods and incompetence, and if so how, and whether a vaguely articulated system of government can cope with a leader who is 'economical with the truth' on an industrial scale.

The answer is, as always, unclear. What is clear is that Mr Johnson rose to the top of British politics despite his reputation as a liar, despite being fired twice for lying, despite not being candid about how many children he has fathered, despite being recorded on a tele- phone call to a friend apparently conspiring in the beating-up of a journalist, despite a peculiar relationship with an American busi- nesswoman, Jennifer Arcuri, who apparently received public money while offering Mr Johnson 'technical support' at her home in the afternoons and despite his various impossible schemes and bridges to nowhere. Or perhaps his success is not 'despite' this catalogue of failures, which would have doomed lesser men, but because of all his frailties and peccadilloes, enabling Mr Johnson to connect with the voters of England as a 'bit of a character', a lovable chap with all-too-human flaws. We tell ourselves he is not vanilla, not 'just like all the rest', not boring, the life and soul of the party. He is, after all, a living tautology – 'Boris being Boris' ideally suited for an age in which Theresa May's response to any evidence of difficulty about Britain's departure from Europe was to offer the incantation that 'Brexit means Brexit'.

There was even a short-lived hope expressed eloquently after Mr Johnson's illness by the veteran Conservative MP Nicholas Soames that Boris Johnson would use his near-death experience in intensive care to reflect upon his life, and, like Candide at the end of Voltaire's novel, that he might embrace hard work and the detailed problems of governing. It did not come to pass. Unfortunately, unwritten constitutions and the mechanism of good governance need more than uncertain hopes. The Good Chap theory of government fails not as a result of defective policies but as a result of politicians with defective characters.

The populist style is not a problem the United Kingdom faces alone, but the UK is alone of the major developed nations in not having – and refusing to contemplate – a codified constitution. We live in an age of the normalization of lying in public life, where crowd-pleasing but essentially vacuous slogans connect with millions of citizens. Italy, France, Germany, Hungary, Poland and other countries have all experienced this problem. The United States exhibits these same characteristics of nationalistic, nostalgic pessimism, brilliantly captured by another nostalgic optimist, Donald Trump. His slogan 'Make America Great Again' implicitly reflects a sense of America's decline, and his promise to make America the way it once was captures the American zeitgeist for many in the deindustrialized heartlands.

The US impeachment process demonstrated that even with a seriously flawed leader and a much-revered constitution, lying in public life may nevertheless proceed without any penalty beyond reputational risk. And reputational risk is only problematic for those with a positive reputation to lose. In this the example of Trump is instructive. Donald Trump tells so many lies that the *Washington Post* publishes a tally of them every three months. In the summer of 2020 the paper's Fact Checker noted that 'it took President Trump 827 days to top 10,000 false and misleading claims … an average of 12 claims a day. But on July 9, just 440 days later, the president crossed the 20,000 mark – an average of 23 claims a day over a 14-month period.' It is an extraordinarily productive record for falsehoods, almost one every hour, every day. In the coronavirus category alone Mr Trump managed 350 misleading statements in a couple of months, including proposed cures which had no basis in medical fact and the suggestion that injecting disinfectant might kill the virus.

The Trump impeachment process inevitably failed in January 2020. The barrier to Congress removing a president elected by the American people is – rightly – set very high by the US constitution. But even if impeachment has never in US history actually removed a sitting president, the constitution at least enshrines the separation of powers in ways that limit presidential actions, and the threat of impeachment may indeed act as a brake on some unwise presidential actions.

America's separation of powers is very different to the eliding of powers implicit in the British notion of the Crown in Parliament. When it comes to fixing Britain's divisions over Brexit and English nationalism, therefore, the glue of Britishness has gone, the Good Chap theory continues to run into impossible difficulties, and we have to consider what we are left with. Political scientists describe the British system as 'executive dominance', meaning that the prime minister is subject to far fewer checks and balances than a US president. In his 1976 Richard Dimbleby lecture, the former lord chancellor Lord Hailsham used a different phrase. He called the British system 'an elective dictatorship'. This was not meant merely as a joke, but also as a warning about complacency. The warning has been forgotten; the complacency persists.

The Way We Were – Or the Way We Like to Think We Were

Ben Jonson's great country-house poem 'To Penshurst' (1616) captures how in some ways the British and more especially the English liked to be seen – and indeed were seen for centuries. They did not show off because it was vulgar, and because they did not have to:

> Thou art not, Penshurst, built to envious show,
> Of touch or marble; nor canst boast a row
> Of polished pillars, or a roof of gold…

No 'envious show' meant Penshurst, Robert Sidney's (the Earl of

Leicester's) great house in Kent, like much of English life, was just naturally good, without too much obvious effort and definitely without having to boast – although Jonson's poem goes on to boast quite a bit in the lines that follow. 'To Penshurst' is in essence a seventeenth-century humble-brag. The same false modesty was true of commentaries on the British system of governance, and is even true today. In her otherwise informative study *Watching the English*, the English anthropologist Kate Fox writes: 'The English are not usually given to patriotic boasting.'[21] This, frankly, is laughable, and is a humble-brag of Jonsonian (and indeed Johnsonian) proportions. But it does reinforce the idea that the English like to think that they have a special quiet genius for making government work. Part of the boast is to pretend that it is all utterly effortless. The British way of governance was magically intuitive and natural, the constitutional version of Boris Johnson's hair or Penshurst's quiet glory. Everyone in England understood all this as easily as they breathed. The humble-brag of Britain's EU negotiator David Frost in his Brussels speech quoted earlier is in this long line of English enthusiasm for our 'natural' political genius, 'where institutions just evolved and where governance is pretty deep-rooted in historical precedent'. Lord Frost is in distinguished company. For three centuries English history has been replete with similarly faux-humble yet staggeringly boastful constitutional eulogists.

The clergyman and historian Nicolas Tindal is one of those who considered at length the British genius for good governance. Tindal believed it was rooted in the 'excellent constitution where the prerogatives of the Crown and privileges of the subject are so heavily proportioned that the King and the People are inseparably united in the same interests and views'.[22] This was achieved not by a written constitution – heavens forfend! A written constitution would be a construction 'created by design' and built 'to envious show'. The English genius was much better than mere words in a legal document. It was rooted in what Boris Johnson calls 'good British common sense', a type of common sense unknown in less fortunate corners of the world. The Reverend Tindal was less clear on some of the details in defining exactly how everything was 'heavily proportioned', nor was he precise about how kings, lords and commons were all 'inseparably united in the same interests and views', when English history was even in his day littered with evidence of profound differences in interests. Tindal did accept that the British genius was not entirely infallible. It could go wrong 'when by an arbitrary disposition of evil counsels it was interrupted, the constitution languished, mutual confidence vanished, distrust, jealousy, discord arose; and when entirely broken… confusion and civil wars ensued'.[23]

Assuming the avoidance of 'evil counsels', by 1744, when Tindal died, the misery of the previous century, the overthrow of the monarchy and Cromwell's Protectorate, had been replaced by a form of government which did run, so Tindal appeared to think, like clockwork. Even as a schoolboy I found this notion very puzzling. In school we learned of the supposed glories of this unwritten constitution as outlined by Tindal in the 1740s, and yet a mere three decades later, in 1776, a bunch of upstart, nominally British people, the colonists of North America, hated the 'excellent constitution' so much that they rebelled and went out of their way to throw it into the dustbin of history, at least in the 'New World'. In doing so they demonstrated that the king and people were far from being 'inseparably united'. They created that great republic known as the United States of America. My history teacher at the time, the estimable Mr Hogg, pointed out to us the strange paradox that the British way of governance was regarded as so successful that nobody else in the entire world wanted to copy it, not even those formerly British Yankee rebels who met in Philadelphia and came up with a very different set of rules for governing themselves.

The House of Lords: Ourselves Alone – Again

The American Constitution, written by people who were rooted in British culture, accepted some British philosophical and practical values. Those Americans in Philadelphia told the world that they loved liberty (though that included their liberty to own slaves). They were in favour of democracy (except for women and the lower classes, including indentured labour). And famously they knew that they did not accept 'taxation without representation'. The US division of president, Senate and House of Representatives mirrors the British design of monarch, Lords and Commons, but with two significant differences. The first is that all three of those parts of the US system of government are elected, whereas two out of three parts of the British system – the monarchy and House of Lords – are not democratic and are based on hereditary principles. Reforms of the House of Lords have changed its composition, but even now it is still not an elected house of parliament. The British people take this anachronism for granted and yet it is symbolic of the constipation of British governance. Modern European Union governments, except that of Britain, tend to be unicameral (one house of parliament) or have an additional elected upper house. No other European democracy favours an unelected upper house at least partly based on heredity and the rest on appointments rather than elections. There are currently around ninety hereditary peers still sitting in the House of Lords. As a report from Democratic Audit put it:

> The House of Lords remains completely unelected. All peers can hold their seats until they die (if they want to) and thus are not accountable to or removable by citizens in any way. However, peers can now 'retire' if they wish to from the Lords (but still use its facilities as a London 'club') and some members have taken this course.[24]

Labour and the Liberal Democrats have committed to creating an elected upper chamber but this has been blocked by the Conservative Party. At times, when the Lords have failed to bow to the wishes of a Conservative government, anonymous government spokesmen have threatened to pack it with newly appointed peers, in what undoubtedly would be a manifestation of Britain as an elective dictatorship bowing to the whims of the prime minister of the day. Of course, many noble Lords work extremely hard and are experts in various fields outside government. Nevertheless, the House of Lords, and the way in which it could be packed by a prime minister's caprice, is merely the most obviously rotten part of the British system of 'democracy'. There are others.

Pure Gold vs. Paper Money

The second big difference between the British 'unwritten' constitution and the documents the Founding Fathers of the American constitution so painstakingly drafted is that Americans accepted the need for some kind of rule book. They met in Philadelphia to agree what they did not want – the British system that Tindal thought the epitome of perfection – and then to debate what might work – to separate the instruments of power and to prevent the kind of abuses they believed they experienced at the hands of George III. The US constitution has its own problems. It institutionalizes gridlock. Getting things done can be difficult where powers are separated. That means that any bold change – as President Obama found when he tried to reform health care – can be painfully slow. Worse, the US has its own very specific 'democratic deficit'. The Electoral College system means that Americans do not directly elect the president, by popular vote. Instead each state has a number of electoral college votes which can mean, as it did for Hillary Clinton, winning a majority of the popular votes yet failing to win enough electoral college votes in key states to secure the presidency.

The constitution does specify roles and limited powers for the executive (the presidency), the legislative branch (Congress) and the judiciary (the Supreme Court). Most important of all, the Founding Fathers recognized their own fallibility. They made it possible, though in practice somewhat difficult, to amend the constitution, to modernize it, especially during and immediately after the worst crisis ever faced by the United States, the prospect of the end of the union as a result of the Civil War. In that period the Thirteenth, Fourteenth and Fifteenth Amendments to the constitution were passed, abolishing slavery and prohibiting the denial of the right to vote on racial grounds. Despite the recent fetishization of parts of the constitution, in particular the Second Amendment on gun ownership, the Founding Fathers recognized that it was not some kind of biblical truth. They knew their constitution would not get all things right for all time, even though some on the American judicial right nowadays do try to second guess what the Founding Fathers really 'meant' back in 1776 in order to justify their own ultra-conservative positions in the twenty-first century, a doctrine sometimes called 'originalism'. The US constitution is therefore both capable of change in changing times and also a significant constraint on a president with Trump's authoritarian instincts, in a way that the uncodified British constitution cannot be on the powers of a prime minister.

The simple fact of creating a clearly written political users' manual for government was the most obvious rejection (by what were His Majesty's subjects in North America) not only of the monarchy of George III but also of that great bowl of constitutional fudge that Reverend Nicolas Tindal devoured so avidly. Tindal is not alone. Worship of the Unwritten Constitution is a peculiarly English disease. The fuzzier and less clear the constitution is, the better some folk appear to like it.

The Whig politician and thinker Edmund Burke was a contemporary of Tindal and shared some of his reverence for the British system of government. Burke, for example, suggested that there was no need to translate Magna Carta from the original Latin because the people of the United Kingdom 'instinctively understood it. It was in their hearts'.[25] Since by Burke's time in the mid-eighteenth century the King James translation of the Bible was the most popular and most read book in Protestant Britain, Burke was actually suggesting that in some mysterious way Magna Carta had entered the English soul without actually being understood while the Word of God required an English version in the vernacular.

Thomas Babington Macaulay, Lord Macaulay, the Victorian historian, was equally enamoured of the British way of doing government. He thought written constitutions were like paper money, a trashy substitute for the real thing, pure gold. There is an obvious counter-argument. Even in Macaulay's day advanced countries used paper money. Perhaps in the twenty-first century only countries in which people actually do pay for things only in gold, if any exist, should retain an unwritten constitution. In a time of one-touch payments, Bitcoin and Apple Pay, the idea of pure gold is simply more comforting nostalgia; and nostalgia is always comforting, even when it is dangerous and pointless. Nevertheless, constitution-worship from the era of horses and carts still permeates British public life.

In his famous work *The English Constitution* (1867), a series of observations made at the height of British power and with Queen Victoria on the throne, Lord Macaulay's contemporary Walter Bagehot famously asserted that the monarch represented the 'dignified' part of the unwritten British constitution while governments represent the 'efficient' part. The role of the monarch was to 'excite and preserve the reverence of the population'. Most British people would agree that in 2020 the Queen has been very highly regarded in that role, although whether her successor will be as widely admired is a matter of some debate. As to the 'efficient' part, Bagehot asserted that governments were responsible for those institutions through which the country 'works and rules'. Contemporary views of more recent British governments as 'efficient' and even 'competent' are less in evidence. At any rate, Bagehot was no fan of written constitutions nor of American-style 'checks and balances', nor of universal suffrage. As he put it:

a country of respectful poor, though far less happy than where there are no poor to be respectful, is nevertheless far more fitted for the best government. You can use the best classes of the respectful country; you can only use the worst where every man thinks he is as good as every other.[26]

Every man (and woman) thinking he is 'as good as every other' is our modern vice. It is interesting that Bagehot's views of the constitution are still treated with great reverence in England when his view of democracy itself is more obviously a historical curiosity. Perhaps we can conclude that an unwritten constitution is entirely suited for a country where gold coins are in circulation and a nation in which the 'respectful poor' are happy to be ruled by 'the best classes', and constitutional theorists are proponents of ancestor worship in the deification of Burke, Macaulay and Bagehot on these matters. If such a society exists, it is not one that is obvious in twenty-first-century England, Scotland, Northern Ireland or Wales, outside the nostalgic imagination of some Members of Parliament.

In more recent times, the distinguished judge Lord Scarman pointed out that the British constitution is not strictly unwritten, merely – I am paraphrasing – incomprehensibly hidden in any number of written judgements, legal precedents and political conventions that few can understand and those who do understand disagree about what it all means. For an ordinary citizen this is rather like being told we are allowed to read commentaries about the Ten Commandments without actually being able to read that Thou Shalt Not Kill. We just have to take the word of a special group of scholars for it. The parallel with religious belief surfaces in these discussions time and time again. From Tindal to Burke to Bagehot to David Frost negotiating in Brussels or government spokesmen discussing Dominic Raab's role as prime ministerial substitute, if one asks too many questions, the response is always a variation on Bagehot's famous phrase about the monarchy – that we should not let daylight into magic. That may be true about the nature of God. It may arguably be true of the monarchy itself, but it cannot be true of the pseudo-efficient parts of the constitution, which have proved themselves so inefficient, or rather ineffectual. British citizens in the twenty-first century are kept as much in the dark about what our system of government truly entails as European Christians were in the time before Martin Luther and the Reformation ensured that the Bible was available for all to read.

The trouble with all this constitutional hocus pocus is that it depends upon trusting authorities to let us peek a little into what they say the constitution entails. As the pope found out in the early 1500s, when people lose trust in authority, big changes are inevitable. In the twenty-first century trust in governance in the United Kingdom has been diluted so far that a political reformation is now required. That reformation will take years. Real reformations always do. Germany, for example, has just finished celebrating the 500-year anniversary of the Protestant Reformation, but they call it in Germany the 'Luther Decade'. The decade is the ten years from 1508, beginning when Martin Luther arrived in (Lutherstadt) Wittenberg. Then he was a loyal but sceptical Catholic monk, but he ended up nailing on a church door his ninety-five theses questioning church teaching. By 1518, he was accused of heresy, and the real struggles of the Reformation began. They lasted a century and a half in Germany, longer in other places in Europe and interminably on the island of Ireland. The Reformation was itself a process, not an event. Britain's constitutional and institutional struggles will be a long process too, although it is obvious that this process has already begun. Scepticism about how we order our political life is also widespread. Whether this scepticism develops into some kind of political rebellion is not yet certain. Either way, a secular reformation is already upon us. In Chapter 10 there will be suggestions how it might proceed. But I want to conclude this chapter on Muddle England by asserting why our traditional complacency about the constitutional status quo is neither acceptable nor sustainable.

Our Democratic Recession

The historian of Britishness Linda Colley wrote a powerful twenty-first-century rebuttal to the ideas of Macaulay, Burke, Tindal and Bagehot: 'With only one major exception no polity has achieved what passes for full democracy without generating some kind of written constitution. That exception is of course the United Kingdom.'

Then Colley goes on to say: 'The flattering notion that the British were masters of good government helps to account for an apparent paradox. Although Britain has no written Constitution, British lawyers, civil servants and diplomats have been conspicuously active in writing constitutions for other countries.'[27] We have the skills and the arrogance to redesign systems of governance for others. We have not had the inclination, or perhaps the humility and the need, to do so for ourselves. This example of British or English exceptionalism would not matter if all were well in our politics and society and the British people trusted the system under which we are governed. It isn't, and we don't.

In January every year the New York PR company Edelman publishes its Trust Barometer. It is an extensive series of surveys in twenty-eight OECD countries. The idea is to measure how far the general public in those countries trusts the four types of institutions that are most important in our lives – government, business, NGOs and the media. In the 2020 survey the UK came second to bottom, twenty-seventh out of twenty-eight countries. The only country to score worse for trust was Vladimir Putin's Russia, a country under the rule of the most powerful Russian leader since Stalin, a man who had been in power since 2000 and was manoeuvring to stay in the Kremlin until 2036. In an interview for a podcast series on Putin I presented in 2020, Gary Kasparov, the Russian chess grandmaster and former world champion, said that 'every state has its mafia. In Russia, the mafia has its own state'.[28] It is therefore worth repeating that by January 2020, even before the coronavirus crisis hit and before predictions of the worst economic downturn for 300 years, the United Kingdom was already just slightly ahead of Putin's Kremlin kleptocracy for trust in government.

In a similar vein that month, Cambridge University's Centre for the Future of Democracy produced a dispiriting but not entirely surprising report suggesting that more than half of British people say they are dissatisfied with democracy itself. In September 2019 an ITN/Channel 5 poll found that fewer than one in ten adults (9 per cent) trusted politicians, while seven in ten (71 per cent) felt MPs were untrustworthy. The Ipsos Mori 'Veracity Index' survey of November 2019 showed that trust in British politicians had fallen by five percentage points in a year to a new low. MPs displaced advertising executives as the least-trusted profession in the survey. That meant that at the start of the 2019 General Election campaign, just 14 per cent of the British public said they trusted politicians in general to tell the truth. Trust in politicians has always been in short supply, but this figure matches previous lows recorded in 2016 (15 per cent), 2011 (14 per cent) and 2009 (13 per cent) – the 2009 figure coming after some MPs faced criminal charges amid allegations of expenses fiddling. Interestingly, trust in professional civil servants continues to rise. In 2019, two-thirds of respondents – 65 per cent – trusted civil servants to tell the truth, up from 62 per cent in 2018. Ipsos Mori reported that 'trust in civil servants has increased by nine percentage points since 2016, and 40 percentage points since the start of this poll in 1983'.[29]

British politics this century has been blighted by one global, and two Britain-specific, trust-busting experiences. The global problem came with the 2008 financial crisis, and loss of trust in banks and financial institutions compounded by the British government's policy of austerity. The first of the two specifically British experiences that eroded trust in the same period was the MPs expenses scandal. Some MPs demanded ludicrous sums as 'allowances', including attempts to claim public money for a duck house, heating horses' stables and cleaning a moat. The second trust-destroying, self-inflicted wound was Brexit itself, which brought about gridlock in parliament and the slow dawning of the reality that the consequences of David Cameron's badly conceived referendum will continue to blight our lives for years to come. The thirtieth edition of the British Social Attitudes Survey had a slightly different set of figures from the surveys quoted above but reached the same broad conclusions:

In truth, Britain has never had that much trust in politicians and the political process, but trust has fallen further over the last 30 years. Back in 1986, only 38 per cent said that they trusted governments to place the needs of the nation above the interests of their own political party. By 2000, this had more than halved to just 16 per cent.[30]

Again, Britain is not entirely exceptional in this democratic recession, and politicians are not the only group of people in whom a degree of confidence has been lost. Other institutions worldwide have also seen a decline in trust, noted by Edelman and other researchers, and often connected with various scandals. As we noted, two US presidents have been impeached since 1997, the only other impeachment being in the nineteenth century; we have seen the first resignation of a speaker of the House of Commons in 300 years, Michael Martin; and the first resignation of a pope in 600 years, Pope Benedict. Enormous reputational damage has been inflicted on well-known business brands from BP to Volkswagen, media conglomerates, banks and financial institutions and even charities like Oxfam. If you are a sports fan and I mention the words 'FIFA Ethics Committee' or Olympic drugs cheats or paedophile scandals within the Roman Catholic Church and sexual abuse allegations within charities, you may immediately understand the diminution of trust in institutions worldwide extends to organizations previously considered above suspicion.

For those of us living in the nations and under-served English regions of the United Kingdom the key question, most obviously, is whether reform of our political system can begin to reverse the decline in trust of democracy itself, because the situation of the UK is acute. In 'The UK A Parable of Distrust' (2020) Edelman's Ed Williams noted 'the cradle of parliamentary government, the defender of free speech, bastion of the rule of law, appears to be losing faith in the idea of democracy itself.' He concluded: 'While Brexit did prove to be the spark that lit the gunpowder, the conditions were set by years of institutional failures – the financial crash; the MPs expenses scandal; phone hacking and the advent of fake news on social platforms; and the Oxfam scandal in Haiti – that had already rocked trust in business, government, media and NGOs. British institutions failed to recognise what happened and how to respond to it. They were too slow. Too bureaucratic. Not agile enough. Then, the failure to deliver Brexit – which had been an argument narrowly won by a British desire to "Take Back Control" – demonstrated how little control voters actually had.'

To return, then, to the question posed at the very start of this book, can Britain reinvent itself for the next century, or will we see the trend of competing nationalisms and democratic malaise come to an inevitable conclusion – the end of Britain? And whatever solutions we arrive at, what – at last – is our answer to Dean Acheson's question? The empire has gone. A role in Europe has gone. Being best friends with the United States is fraught with difficulty in the era of Trumpism and America First. Singapore-on-Thames is a bizarre fiction. So what is the United Kingdom's future role in the world, if it has one? Let's begin with some good news.

It Could Be Worse

When British people talk about being 'deeply divided' over Brexit or Scottish independence, mercifully we really haven't a clue. Most of us do not know what deep political divisions look like. It's true that during the Scottish independence campaign there was a bit of heckling, and in at least one incident a few pro-independence supporters threw eggs at the Labour MP Jim Murphy in Kirkcaldy. He claimed a campaign of intimidation was organized by Yes Scotland, although the independence campaign including First Minister Alex Salmond publicly condemned 'all forms' of abusive behaviour. For my BBC reports I was targeted online by a number of anonymous trolls, and nutty conspiracy theorists. For them the Deep State apparently included the BBC. It was nasty but relatively anodyne stuff. I've reported on elections involving truly deadly violence in Northern Ireland, Latin America and elsewhere, and the abuse from a tiny minority in Scotland was by these standards quite civilized.

A year after the 2014 Scottish independence campaign, during the 2015 General Election, I happened to be filming with the former first minister, Alex Salmond, in his constituency near Aberdeen. Mr Salmond went out of his way to tell those attending that it was possible for any SNP members, including himself, to have arguments with the BBC, but he expected all journalists and film crews to be treated with respect. I was, and we were. To my astonishment, at one meeting two men whom I had never met before came up and introduced themselves as two of those who had been rather viciously trolling me anonymously on Twitter. They offered their apologies. We parted on good terms after agreeing that on social media people act out the less fortunate sides of their characters.

The Brexit 'divisions' include some horrific events. The Labour MP Jo Cox was murdered by a far-right Nazi obsessive. Other MPs, particularly women who took a strong anti-Brexit stance, received death threats and were warned on police advice to look after their security. The MP Anna Soubry was publicly harassed as she walked to the House of Commons. Many MPs receive hate mail and have been trolled online. Several black and minority-ethnic MPs also had to harden themselves to racist abuse. I am not minimizing any of these events, and we all know from friends and relatives that many of us – whether Leave or Remain – will have someone close to us with whom it is not advisable to discuss Brexit at Christmas dinner, the office party or a family wedding. But – to keep a bit of perspective on this unpleasantness and occasional violence – neither in England or Scotland or Wales does any of this amount to the kind of violence that scars a truly divided community. Another part of the United Kingdom, Northern Ireland, was very different.

My first report as a totally inexperienced journalist in Northern Ireland came when ten Protestant workers were murdered on their way home from work in South Armagh. All the real journalists were sent out to report on that atrocity. I was fresh from university and barely allowed out from the *Belfast Telegraph* office. Then a bomb went off a few hundred metres away in North Street. The news editor had no one else to send, so I went. My first glimpse of the political disorder known as the Northern Ireland Troubles was therefore a severed leg in a car park and half a dozen women with faces cut by flying glass. At work my own car was parked in an area on the north end of Belfast where I was hesitant of walking around at night as a result of the activities of a loyalist gang known as the Shankill Butchers. It was suggested that drivers should check under their cars for suspect devices before starting the engine. The *Belfast Telegraph* offices were bombed by the IRA. A teenager I knew from where I lived in County Antrim was kneecapped by a loyalist paramilitary organization, the UVF, for not being enthusiastic enough about his membership. Gerry Fitt, the MP for West Belfast, whom I knew and whose family I liked very much, had to draw his personal protection weapon (a 9 mm pistol) to drive off a gang of Irish republican invaders who broke into his house. A member of a loyalist paramilitary organization warned me that in his area (east Belfast) petty criminals faced a local 'rough justice' system. For a first offence they were kneecapped. I asked what happened for a second offence.

'We kneecap your fucking head.'

That loyalist leader, whom I had come to know well, was himself assassinated with a car bomb.

Those are just a few glimpses of politics as they once were in part of our United Kingdom. And so, however divided the people of Britain may now at times feel – and we are very divided over Brexit, Scottish independence and other matters – a bit of trolling from a few Scottish rude boys and an uncomfortable Sunday lunch where Brexit, like Lord Voldemort, must not be named, is hardly what in other places would be taken for signs of nascent civil war. Nevertheless, if the United Kingdom is to be reinvigorated we need to move beyond our historic vice of self-congratulation and answer a series of questions about how to operate a constitutional monarchy involving an increasingly federalized system of complex moving parts and competing nationalisms without a written constitution. My simple answer is: we can't. It doesn't work.

Like most questions of governance and constitutional issues, this sounds famously dull. One for the wonks. That is why politicians have recognized in the past that their attempts to make the supposedly 'efficient' parts of the constitution more, well, efficient, do not usually lead to great expressions of public joy or voter interest.

When Labour came to power under Tony Blair in 1997, as part of its manifesto the party promised widespread constitutional changes. These included reform of the House of Lords, a Freedom of Information Act, incorporating the European Convention on Human Rights into British law, devolution for Scotland and Wales and new regional bodies in England. These Labour manifesto pledges were opposed by the Conservatives. But with Labour in power from 1997 until 2010, progress was made on fulfilling most of these promises at least in part, although Tony Blair revealed in his memoirs that he had come to regret the Freedom of Information Act, and he was notably lukewarm about devolution. In 1997, he suggested that Scotland's new powers might be equivalent to those of a parish council, remarks which did not endear him to Scottish nationalist voters. Other pledges were half-hearted in their execution.

Reform of the House of Lords, for example, ended up cutting the number of hereditary peers but did not embrace the more radical suggestion of a democratically elected upper chamber based on the nations and regions of the United Kingdom. Nor did Labour move ahead by reforming FPTP – the 'first past the post' system by which United Kingdom governments can secure a significant majority of seats in the House of Commons without winning a majority of the votes. One of the problems with ending that system is like Catch-22. Any government which has the power to end FPTP owes its majority in parliament to precisely the unfair system that they wish to bring to an end. And yet the distortions FPTP introduces, as we noted, are obvious: strong governments are produced with enormous majorities even if they win only a minority of votes. Tony Blair won three landslide victories in this fashion The biggest was in 1997, when Labour won by a 179-seat margin with only 43.2 per cent of the votes. In 2005, he won a 66-seat majority with 40 per cent of the vote. The system remained unchanged.

When the Liberal Democrats joined in coalition with David

Cameron in 2010, they insisted on constitutional reform. A referendum on proportional representation was held in May 2011 on the same day as local government elections. Even so, the turnout was just over 40 per cent, and the overwhelming majority of those who did take part (68 per cent) voted for no change. The Conservatives campaigned vigorously against reform, and apathy won. The problem, however, remains. Britain's antiquated system of governance has been rejected almost everywhere, including the countries of the former British empire, in places where British experts helped draw up written constitutions, and in the democratic systems in Northern Ireland, Wales and Scotland too. Jill Rutter of the UK in a Changing Europe project noted the decline in how Britain was viewed across the world in an op-ed for *The Guardian*: 'The world has traditionally looked enviously at the solidity of UK institutions: a politically impartial civil service, an effective parliament, an independent judiciary, a pragmatic constitutional settlement and ultimately the United Kingdom itself. But for how much longer?'[31]

Writing in *Britons* (1992), Linda Colley discussed what she called the 'patriotic icons' of Britishness, everything from the royal family to fox-hunting, Protestantism, parliament and empire. She concluded that they were being 'anxiously and incessantly debated as never before'.[32] Since then, that debate has intensified to include debates about the institutions of Britishness as well – from the NHS to the civil service and judiciary as well as the complexities of devolution and Brexit. The royal family has also had to endure several significant scandals or ruptures – over Diana, the role of Harry and Meghan and the very serious sex allegations raised about Prince Andrew. Colley noted, however, that fears about Britain's continuing existence were nothing new. They stretched back to the beginning of the British project in the eighteenth century in ways that had nothing to do with our closeness to the European Union or otherwise. British identity had in the past been too dependent on recurrent wars against a foreign threat, money making through trade and imperial conquest. Colley concluded her study by saying that it was not a resurgent Britishness that made becoming part of a united Europe problematic, but quite the opposite. It was insecurity about British identity, which meant that English people feared the establishment of a real bond with a united Europe. The French and Germans, much more secure in who they are, saw European integration not as a threat but as an opportunity. Colley concluded with a lengthy quote from Sir John Macpherson, a Scottish pro-consul from the 1790s, who thought that Britain, an invented nation, needed to reinvent itself through considering what we have in common as citizens. Macpherson wrote: 'If we have not turned our commercial and Asiatic sovereignty to the real improvement of our own island and to the domestic union of the three kingdoms… we have abused the inheritance which the spirit and minds of our forefathers have acquired for our enjoyment and improvement.'[33]

Macpherson in his day was seen as an eccentric, so no one paid him much attention, but Brexit is not an assertion of national confidence. It is an admission of English insecurity. It is the most striking example of England's inability to find a positive answer to Dean Acheson's question about a world role in the twenty-first century, and a tacit admission that England does not have one. The British failure to turn to Macpherson's 'real improvement of our own island and to the domestic union of the three kingdoms' is at least two centuries overdue. The unresolved question is whether 'real improvement' is still possible. We have missed numerous opportunities. Muddle England may even now continue to wallow in complacency, and the destructive idea that England is exceptional expressed through the constitutional equivalent of ancestor worship. In that case England will end up still muddling through, but alone, and the United Kingdom will accurately be described as a failed state.

10

How to Fix It: Independence and Interdependence

'At the very heart of the independence debate lies a deep disenchantment with the anti-democratic, over-centralised British state, and with the Oxbridge-public school elitism of its ruling London establishment.'

George Kerevan in George Kerevan and Alan Cochrane, Scottish Independence: Yes or No

'Our mission is to deliver Brexit on the 31st of October for the purpose of uniting and re-energizing our great United Kingdom and making this country the greatest place on earth.'

Boris Johnson, in his first House of Commons Speech as prime minister of the United Kingdom, 24 July 2019. (Brexit was not delivered on 31 October 2019.)

'It is certainly true that the English need to rediscover who and what they are, to reinvent an identity of some sort better than the battered cliché-ridden hulk which the retreating tide of imperialism has left them.'

Tom Nairn, The Break-up of Britain

After the failure of the Scottish National Party to win the September 2014 independence referendum, Alex Salmond stood down as first minister. The following May, in the 2015 General Election, he was running for office again, this time for the Westminster seat of Gordon, a stunningly beautiful constituency of small towns and villages in north-east Scotland. One sunny evening during the campaign we met for a drink and a chat in a country pub. Salmond signed for me a copy of a book that he had just published about the independence campaign called *The Dream Shall Never Die*. The title sums up what I have tried to describe as the thrawn characteristics of many of my fellow Scots. After his life's work ended in apparent failure, here was the irrepressible former SNP leader running for office again, combative and, in a way infuriating to unionists, asserting in print that the independence question was never going to go away.

Salmond begins the book with his account of the conversation he had early on the morning of 19 September 2014, when the result of the independence referendum was announced. Salmond called the prime minister, David Cameron, to congratulate him on seeing off independence for the foreseeable future:

> With dawn approaching the Prime Minister goes and makes his speech outside number Ten, which I watch on TV. As he struts out to say that Scottish reform must take place 'in tandem with' and 'at the same pace as' changes in England, I immediately realise the significance... I think, 'you silly, arrogant man...'[1]

In saying he realized the significance of Cameron's words, Salmond means he understood immediately that 'The Vow' would prove worthless. He sensed betrayal, but then felt a degree of optimism that the forces about to be unleashed by David Cameron would reinvigorate the independence campaign: 'The real guardians of progress are no longer at Westminster, or even at Holyrood, but the energised activism of tens of thousands of people who I predict will refuse meekly to go back into the shadows.'[2]

He was correct in these predictions. On the copy of his book Salmond handed me he also added a handwritten inscription based, I'm guessing, on Aristotle: 'The truth is a virtue that the ruling classes fear.' And whether you are a British unionist or one of the several versions of Scottish, English, Welsh or Irish nationalists, the truth I have attempted to describe in this book, is that the United Kingdom is now united in name only. The choice before us is either to come together and make profound changes to the way we are governed or to accept that the UK is ultimately a failed state and come apart. Scotland, as Salmond says in the final lines of his book, will seek its independence because 'everyone deserves a second chance. Every person, and every nation'.[3]

And that brings us back to the questions with which this book began, and which will return again and again until they are resolved. We – that is, the people of these islands – have to decide whether what we call the United Kingdom is worth saving, giving an ancient political settlement a second, third or even fourth chance. If so, we then have to ask whether it can be reinvigorated and reshaped in the twenty-first century as it has been reformed every hundred years since it was first created in 1603. Another British reformation is overdue. However, if competing nationalisms mean that the union cannot be saved, then we have a different set of questions. How can the four nations of England, Scotland, Northern Ireland and Wales, plus the Irish Republic, to which we remain conjoined, reach an agreement to resolve our widening differences through some kind of 'independence' but also recognizing our inevitable interdependence? And finally, there is the Dean Acheson question: do these islands which have played such a significant role in the world in the past, have a future role through which we can fully express the talents of our people? If so, what is it?

What follows, then, is not a series of prescriptive answers to these questions, but rather an outline of some principles which I hope will help shape a reasoned discussion.

*

Never Let a Serious Crisis Go to Waste

Rahm Emanuel, a former mayor of Chicago and White House chief of staff, was famous for advising never to 'let a serious crisis go to waste... it's an opportunity to do things you think you could not do before'. The United Kingdom in the second decade of the twenty-first century is enjoying a concatenation of crises – an economic crisis, a health-care crisis, a political crisis, a crisis of trust and loss of confidence in institutions. Things look bleak. But some eighty years ago, in January 1941, the outlook for the United Kingdom and the British empire looked very much worse. That winter was one of the darkest times of the war. The daily lives of British people were taken up with surviving the Blitz, finding food and coping with the system of rationing. But people were also thinking and planning ahead for a better life after the war. As the writer and YouGov pollster Peter Kellner put it:

> the editors of *Picture Post*, a popular weekly magazine, did something bold, risky and, with hindsight, brilliant. They decided that the bleakness of the present made it all the more important to reimagine the future. They devoted a whole issue not to the war but to what kind of society we should have once the war was over.[4]

The *Picture Post* cover showed a bunch of happy children enjoying a slide, and also trumpeted 'A Plan for Britain' that laid out more or less all the promises of reform that ended up in the 1945 Labour manifesto. It drove the creation of the new Britain after the war – a National Health Service, the widening of opportunity in schools, raising the school leaving age, better old-age pensions, the building of new towns and eventually new universities. The foreword explained why the editors felt it necessary to speculate about the kind of Britain that those making such sacrifices in wartime were fighting for:

> Our plan for a new Britain is not something outside the war, or something after the war. It is an essential part of our war

aims. It is, indeed, our most positive war aim. The new Britain is the country we are fighting for… What we have done in this number is simply to rough out a plan. We have tried to outline a fairer, pleasanter, happier, more beautiful Britain than our own – but one based fairly and squarely on the Britain we have now.[5]

'A Plan for Britain' reconfigured the relationship between the citizen and the British state, giving the state a wider role. By the 1970s, when Britain saw itself and was seen by others as 'the Sick Man of Europe', the relationship between the British state and its citizens was to change once more. Margaret Thatcher promised 'A New Beginning'. In the 1979 Conservative Party manifesto she wrote:

No one who has lived in this country during the last five years can fail to be aware of how the balance of our society has been increasingly tilted in favour of the State at the expense of individual freedom. This election may be the last chance we have to reverse that process, to restore the balance of power in favour of the people. It is therefore the most crucial election since the war.[6]

Mrs Thatcher used the economic crises of the 1970s to redefine the relationship between citizen and state just as Clement Attlee had done in a different way in the 1940s. Now our current malaise means we have a chance to do it again. This time we must do so by reforming the way in which we elect our leaders to 'restore the balance of power' in favour of the institutions which can be closest to the people they serve.

In this final chapter, therefore, we will offer some basic principles on what a British political and national reformation could entail. The principles could be styled the three Rs – Recognize, Repair and Reform. The dissatisfaction and unfairness in our current system coupled with the incompetence with which the UK government has dealt with some of the most challenging issues of our times means that we have to remain hopeful that a national reformation of Britain is still possible. Hope, however, is not the same as optimism.

Recognize

We need first to recognize – and that means to cease ignoring – the various problems outlined above. This requires coming to terms with the profound complacency of those in leadership positions in Britain. In particular we need to recognize that the idea of English exceptionalism is dead. Across the world no one mistakes England for the New Jerusalem or this other Eden; no one outside England talks of English institutions as 'the envy of the world'. No one outside England cares who won the World Cup in 1966 or, indeed, the victories at Crécy and Agincourt. The world does not look to Westminster as a model of governance, nor to the NHS for a way to organize health care. We should also recognize many good things about our strong identification with our towns, our cities and our counties. We have hugely inventive people, caring communities, extraordinary schools and universities, strong pride in our shared history and a creative, inventive and generally tolerant culture. In crises, we tend not to turn to violence for solutions. When coronavirus first struck, British people rushed to stockpile toilet rolls. Americans stockpiled guns and ammunition.

We also have something even more positive which we should recognize. We have created in our institutions the federal system by stealth I have in part described. This system can be built upon, improved and codified. The man credited with being the father of modern Conservatism, Edmund Burke, memorably wrote in *Reflections*, 'To be attached to the subdivision, to love the little platoon we belong to in society, is the first principle (the germ as it were) of public affections. It is the first link in the series by which we proceed towards a love to our country and to mankind.' We also need to recognize that the 'little platoons' of our affections are all too often squashed by the failures and carelessness of central government, notably the failure to devolve powers and resources to areas congruent with the places with which people most identify. One final area of recognition is necessary – to recognize that there is no such thing as complete independence in an interdependent world. The future, like the past, is likely to belong to the biggest players. The more we devolve power, the more we also need to connect with others.

Repair

Repair means fixing those institutions which we admire and depend upon while ridding ourselves of those which are clapped out and beyond reinvention. The NHS – the institution that most British people most admire – needs to be repaired. Its core values are excellent but in implementing those values the NHS requires not just more nurses. The institution itself needs nursing to better organizational health, to live up to its values and the extraordinary dedication and skills of its staff. In June 2020 the health-care think tank the Nuffield Trust produced a report on some of the challenges for the NHS, beyond coronavirus. The trust's chief executive, Nigel Edwards, was blunt:

> Even before the pandemic the NHS already had many outdated hospital buildings, extremely high bed occupancy, serious workforce problems, overcrowded A&Es and rising waiting lists. These problems coupled with the challenge of containing infection and tackling the ongoing coronavirus crisis will mean a profound change in the way we deliver services.[7]

The NHS delivers superb health care extremely efficiently, while requiring an investment per capita which is lower than that of similar countries – France and Germany for example – and much lower than the percentage of GDP devoted to health care in the USA. Put another way, Britain gets health care on the cheap.

We are – and should be – proud of the NHS, but we need to recognize it is a symbol of British institutions which we believed were 'the envy of the world', while no other nation has copied them. German doctors with whom I have discussed this, for example, are astounded that the United Kingdom has an annual and predictable beds crisis every winter. The answer to a hospital beds crisis, as one German doctor put it to me, is not a secret. It is to have more beds. Germany has approximately 8.0 hospital beds per 1,000 people. The UK has approximately 2.5 per 1,000. Germany does not have a 'winter beds crisis'. The UK has one every year. It is a systemic failure, rooted in the fact that the NHS institutional structure in England is unwieldy and underfunded and needs to be devolved to local English regions. Social care needs to be rethought and integrated with the NHS. We need more investment in modern hospitals, and more local accountability. Local government, especially in England, is another potentially great institution which also needs to be repaired. In the years of austerity since 2010, local councils have been starved of cash by an increasingly remote central government, and the Westminster government has, at the same time, asked councils to do more. Repeatedly demanding more for less has proved, unsurprisingly, to be unsustainable.

Reform

A British Reformation is already upon us as a result of the series of crises we are facing. Evidence of the UK pulling apart is all around us. There is obvious political discontent in Scotland, Northern Ireland, Wales and many areas of England about Brexit, about the handling of coronavirus, and about the arrogance of an out-of-touch Westminster system. Discontent in England about the narrowness of English political culture, reflecting London and its economic priorities but ignoring vast swathes of England, is also an enduring part of our public life. The case for bringing the Westminster voting system and English politics into the twenty-first century is unanswerable, but governments do not advocate reform because the two-party system benefits from elections that produce parliamentary majorities for parties which almost never win a majority of the votes. Democracy should be based on the principle that the numbers of elected Members of Parliament should roughly reflect voting patterns across the country through a fairer voting system. There are many better systems on offer, including those used in the devolved administrations across the UK. My personal preference is for the system of multiple-member constituencies and the single transferable vote, but almost any system is better than the one we have.

Home Rule for All Nations

What ties these three imperatives of recognize, repair and reform together is one further principle – the idea of Home Rule for All Nations. The three devolved parliaments in Belfast, Cardiff and Edinburgh have come a long way in a short time. They have their imperfections but they are close to the people they serve and should enjoy more powers. England has been left out. A voice for England-outside-London is notably lacking. There are various ways to fill this gap, including an English parliament or a much stronger system of devolved powers for local government in areas English people identify with – Greater Manchester, the West Midlands, and so on. Home Rule for All Nations means that we must finally recognize that the vague Pollyanna-ish pretence involved in accepting the Good Chap theory of government doesn't help us any more. If the United Kingdom is not to break apart, we need to offer a clear set of basic rules governing the relationship between the nations, regions and parliaments of the UK, and create a more clearly defined role for local government in England.

The prize of a successful British Reformation is obvious. We can avoid significant political dislocation, reinventing a different idea of Britain for the next hundred years as a federal United Kingdom. Surprisingly to people in England, this could look remarkably like the plan proposed by the Scottish National Party in 2014 and rejected in the referendum of that year. Indeed, that plan has broad similarities to the idea first floated in England in the 1860s, the idea of Home Rule for All Nations. Such plans implicitly recognize that 'complete' or 'total' independence on these islands is neither possible nor desirable in an interconnected world. Rather than bandying around value-loaded words like 'separatism' and 'divorce' and 'union', we need to consider what 'independence' and 'Home Rule' might mean in reality. A good starting point is to note that the arguments for Scottish independence were made in language strikingly similar to Nigel Farage's arguments for the UK Independence Party and Brexit Party policy demanding British 'independence' from Brussels. Admittedly neither the SNP nor Mr Farage will wholeheartedly enjoy the comparison which follows.

The Language of Discontent

George Kerevan is a Scottish writer and former Scottish National Party MP with whom I worked for some years at the *Scotsman* newspaper. In a book he co-authored in 2014, *Scottish Independence*, Kerevan made the case in favour of an independent Scotland, broadly in line with official SNP policy. The language Kerevan uses has strong echoes of the words and phrases used by Nigel Farage and other Leave campaigners in 2016 during the Brexit debate. Kerevan writes: 'At the very heart of the... debate lies a deep disenchantment with the anti-democratic, over-centralised British state, and with the Oxbridge-public school elitism of its ruling London establishment.'[8] Kerevan actually wrote: 'at the very heart of the *independence* debate', but his critique of the status quo is often very similar to Nigel Farage speaking of the Brexit debate instead.

Mr Farage argued for years against what he described as a remote political structure in Brussels dictating rules that affected people who felt disconnected from that structure. He even called his English nationalist party the UK 'Independence' Party and used language already familiar to Scottish independence campaigners. Both railed against elites, the London establishment and the anti-democratic and remote nature of Westminster, and, in Mr Farage's case, of Brussels too. For both Kerevan and Farage the failure of Westminster politics-as-usual was a matter of broad consensus.

Two other voices from different aspects of our culture in their own robust ways make the same point in expressions of working-class anger and loathing of 'the system'. Here, again, is Johnny 'Rooster' Byron from Jez Butterworth's play *Jerusalem*, proud, disgusted and ready to fight the Power: 'Bang your gavels. Issue your warrants… take your leaflets and your meetings and your Borstal and your beatings and your Health and Fucking safety and pack your whole poxy, sham-faced plot and get…'

And here is Mark Renton in the Danny Boyle film of Irvine Welsh's novel *Trainspotting*, again speaking of those remote from people in power: 'It's shite being Scottish! We're the lowest of the low. The scum of the fucking Earth! The most wretched, miserable, servile, pathetic trash that was ever shat into civilization. Some hate the English. I don't. They're just wankers. We, on the other hand, are colonized by wankers. Can't even find a decent culture to be colonized by. We're ruled by effete assholes.'

Or Rooster again: 'I, Rooster Byron, and my band of educationally subnormal outcasts shall swoop and raze your poxy village to dust. In a thousand years Englanders will awake this day and bow their heads and wonder at the genius, guts and guile of the Flintlock Rebellion…'

There is an apparent consensus that the idea of Britain and Britishness is broken or weakened and less important than the idea of English, Scottish, Welsh, Northern Irish and Irish identities. The anthropologist Kate Fox writes that 'Britishness seems to me a rather meaningless term; when people use it they nearly always really mean "Englishness".'[9] It was not always so. In 1895 at one of the most striking addresses in Scotland, Number 1 Princes Street, at the end of the central thoroughfare of Edinburgh, the North British Railway Company began construction of the North British Station Hotel. By North British they meant Scottish. A century later, by 1991, after a major refurbishment, the hotel was renamed the Balmoral. The idea of Scots being 'North Britons' had passed into history. In Ireland after the Act of Union some in England referred to Ireland as 'West Britain'. Even the 'Liberator' Daniel O'Connell used the phrase in a speech in 1836, but O'Connell added an important qualification:

'The people of Ireland are ready to become a portion of the Empire provided they be made so in reality and not in name alone; they are ready to become a kind of West Britons, if made so in benefits and justice; but if not, we are Irishmen again.'[10]

O'Connell's 'provided that' and 'if not' are the key phrases in a reluctant acceptance of Britishness. The 'benefits and justice' of being 'West Britons' never arrived for most Irish people. The Famine arrived instead. In Ireland today the words 'West Briton' can only be used pejoratively of an Irishman or woman who in some ways seems subserviently pro-British. To describe a Scot as a 'North Briton' would not even be an insult now, merely meaningless or a bit of a strange joke. The 'benefits and justice' of Westminster-directed Britishness are not evident to today's Rentons and the Byrons and many others. There are few credible cheerleaders for the idea of Britishness in British politics. There are, of course, Union Jack flag-wavers on the English political right, the Johnsons, Farages and Rees-Moggs, but to many Scots (and many English and Welsh people too) they represent precisely the posturing Englishness pretending to be Britishness of the kind that Renton so eloquently defines as the equivalent of being colonized by self-pleasuring incompetents. One serious voice, the journalist John Lloyd, does attempt to make the case for the endurance of Britishness, in *Should Auld Acquaintance Be Forgot – the Great Mistake of Scottish Independence*. Lloyd writes of his own Scottish and English background as a 'mongrel identity' and says a 'forced choice is uncomfortable. Should we, on the model of American blacks, claim "blackness" – or in this case Scottishness – as our dominant identity?' This is an awkward comparison, although Lloyd is on stronger ground when he speaks of 'the almost incredible lightness of being able to be Scots while also being British'.

The trouble is that this idea is now out of date. Brexit means Lloyd and the rest of those of us who are Scots are forced to miss out our third level of identity, as Europeans within the European Union. And Scots have clearly and overwhelmingly chosen to retain that European identity. The implication therefore is that Scots may be willing to sacrifice their British identity instead.

Cultural Change and Political Change

Gordon Brown is perhaps the last serious frontline politician who has tried to reinvent the idea of Britishness. When he was chancellor of the exchequer, he and I talked at length about our British 'shared values' for a BBC Radio 4 series. He spoke of creativity, adaptability, a belief in freedom, individual rights, duty and fair play. His sense of Britishness was genuine, passionate and eloquent but it had obvious flaws. People from most other nations round the world could credibly be described in similar terms – creative, adaptable, freedom-loving and so on. These are signifiers of common humanity not of British identity. New Labour and Blair and Brown's attempts to reinvent Britishness through promoting Britpop and Cool Britannia were also, for a time, a sign of a young administration promising profound changes to rebrand the United Kingdom amid a new mood of optimism. But in terms of British identity, as we have seen from so many of the surveys about identity quoted throughout this book, it was to prove the flickering of a dying candle.

In 2013, *The Sunday Times* conducted a survey in Scotland asking people to imagine they were meeting a stranger for the first time. How would you feel more proud in introducing yourself? Two-thirds (63 per cent) said Scottish. Only one in five (19 per cent) said British. The way in which Scots feel about their identity has changed significantly since the war. The same is true for English nationalism. As George Kerevan noted: 'British togetherness is already dead. The 2011 census included an intra-British identity question for the first time. Some 60% of people in England gave their national identity as English "only" compared with 19% who gave it as British only.'[11] The Scottish literary critic Cairns Craig argues that when Scotland voted for political devolution in 1997, 'it had much earlier declared cultural devolution... politics was following cultural activity rather than leading it'.[12] What was true of cultural change in Scotland from the deindustrialization during the Thatcher years of the 1980s and 1990s leading to political change and devolution from 1997 is true once more in the twenty-first century. Cultural changes – repeated surveys about identity, the rantings of Rentons and Roosters – are always ahead of political change, but political change is certain to follow.

The erosion of Britishness does not however mean that the most important relationships between the people of these islands will cease. A shared language, history, geography and culture cannot disappear. 'Auld Acquaintance', to rework John Lloyd's book title, 'cannot be forgot', but acquaintances and friendships are always subject to being re-evaluated and reformed. As we saw earlier, a sense of civic nationalism does not cut off anyone on these islands from European culture or international interconnectedness. Rhetoric about 'building a wall', erecting protectionist barriers on trade or refusing to cooperate on climate change and migration is in the long term empty. Whatever our political arrangements, we will still require economic and financial links, the just-in-time importation of everything from car parts to fresh food, to stop coronavirus, to promote tourism and trade. We depend on cooperation rather than conflict, international supply chains rather than autarky. People in Britain may listen to Korean pop on a Chinese-made phone marketed by an American company, sold through Amazon, and do so while eating a variety of foods from all across Europe and sipping a Chilean merlot or a New Zealand chardonnay. Whatever the political realignments which lie ahead, the populations of the current United Kingdom of Great Britain and Northern Ireland and the Irish Republic will remain attached to each other by self-interest and an unquantifiable but hugely important social union. We will continue to share a common language, an integrated popular culture, the free movement of people, marriages and friendships. We also share a sense of humour. We even laugh at many of the same politicians. But when the laughing stops, we need to decide how to fix things.

Can the United Kingdom Be Saved?

Not everyone agrees with the principle of devolution across the UK even now, although this tends to be a reactionary sentiment confined to a strand of English nationalism. The Bruges Group, an informal grouping on the right wing of the Conservative Party with pronounced anti-EU views, appears to think devolution can be reversed and the United Kingdom can become a unitary rather than a devolved state. As the Bruges Group put it in a Tweet: 'There is a strong argument to be made that too much devolution has only emboldened the separatists in Holyrood who have mistaken governing (badly) under the umbrella of the UK for an ability to stand alone. Time to start treating Scotland as part of the United Kingdom.'[13]

The Bruges Group was founded in 1989 to push the Conservative Party and the country towards hardline Euroscepticism. These English political activists are not all on the Conservative right, but most are. They take their name from a speech their hero Margaret Thatcher gave in Bruges in 1988, setting out the limits of European Union integration she believed Britain could accept. The more prominent members of the Bruges Group are all English and include Iain Duncan Smith, Daniel Hannan, John Redwood, Mark Francois, Lord Tebbit and Norman Lamont, with a sprinkling of Brexit supporters from other parties. They speak of creating an 'independent Britain' – meaning Britain out of the EU – although they are, once more, really speaking about English independence, as the Tweet advocating 'treating Scotland as part of the United Kingdom' suggests. The implication is that Scotland is a fitting object of 'treatment,' a sickly colony to be managed rather than a partner in a union. Imagine if you heard a man saying it was 'time to start treating' his wife as a woman and you get some idea of how inappropriate, patronizing and backward this sounds.

The Bruges Group are literally reactionaries. They want the clock turned back to end devolution and bring Scotland more firmly under the centralized control of a Westminster system which – as we have seen – no longer commands the trust of the majority of people in any part of the United Kingdom. Such a reversal of recent history would be the very definition of the 'democratic deficit' which already causes such disaffection not just in Scotland, Wales and Northern Ireland but also in England-outside-London. For millions of British people who find the political status quo unacceptable, an offer of the status quo ante is ludicrous. And yet the Bruges Group may help us in one respect. In her 1988 speech that gave the group its name and which is venerated as Holy Writ within sections of the Conservative Party, Mrs Thatcher's aim was to ensure that the European Union did not become more powerful through centralizing power in Brussels, but she claimed to be very keen to cooperate:

> I want to see us work more closely on the things we can do better together than alone. Europe is stronger when we do so, whether it be in trade, in defence or in our relations with the rest of the world. But working more closely together does not require power to be centralised in Brussels or decisions to be taken by an appointed bureaucracy.

By again altering a couple of words but not the logical argument of these sentences, Mrs Thatcher could easily be making an eloquent case for less centralization in the British state and greater devolution. Reread her words again, with two changes in italics:

> I want to see us work more closely on the things we can do better together than alone. *Britain* is stronger when we do so, whether it be in trade, in defence or in our relations with the rest of the world. But working more closely together does not require power to be centralised in *Westminster* or decisions to be taken by an appointed bureaucracy.

Most advocates of Scottish independence, admittedly, tend not to be great admirers of Mrs Thatcher. But if her logic about the European Union is correct – stay within it but keep power devolved – then it is difficult to see how even these most reactionary forces in British politics can fail to consider applying the same logic to their own country, even if logic has not always been their most striking attribute.

*

Independence Is a Relative not Absolute Term

Back in 2014, the case for Scottish independence was indeed based on the idea of still working 'closely' with England on many matters, a point missed repeatedly by the London-based media. Hostile British newspaper coverage of the Scottish independence campaign tended to use emotive words like 'divorce', the 'break-up' of the UK, and some TV coverage followed suit, including silly programmes discussing border controls and customs posts, as if explaining a new Cold War rather than the genuine vision of the independence movement. In any case, independence is a relative, and not an absolute term. Scottish, Welsh and Irish nationalists have for generations considered what 'independence' might mean in an interdependent world.

English Brexit advocates have only been united on what they *do not* want – membership of the European Union. They have never been able to agree with any degree of clarity on what they *do* want, which is one of the reasons why from 2016 until 2020 British politics entered the dark ages of disarray. Pro-Brexit luminaries have spent a great deal of time trying to figure out what getting their heart's desire actually means. David Cameron had no plan for what do to in the event he lost the 2016 referendum and so he resigned. Theresa May had no plan either, but she tried to cobble one together. Most importantly, the UK Independence Party and the leading Brexit supporters among the Conservatives, including Boris Johnson, also did not have a plan. The best they have come up with is a blizzard of empty phrases and slogans which tend to disintegrate under even the most gentle scrutiny.

We were told that all kinds of deals were possible. These included arrangements that were called Canada Plus, Norway Plus (and Norway Plus Plus), WTO terms and other supposedly 'bespoke solutions'. When none of these had much appeal, we were then offered something which had never even been mentioned during the 2016 campaign, the prospect of a No Deal Brexit, an outcome serious economists suggested would blight the British economy for a generation. We must all, we are told, climb to the mountain top without first agreeing which peak we are actually going to climb: it is hardly surprising that for years we have been lost in the fog.

For a series of radio programmes I presented in late 2019 I managed to speak with John Bruton, the former Irish prime minister and former EU ambassador to Washington and then separately with Tony Blair. Bruton and Blair, with years of experience in complex negotiations, both pointed out the British dilemma. If the UK manages to negotiate a deal with the European Union, this will inevitably tie the UK's hands in negotiating other deals with other countries, including the United States. But if the UK does not negotiate a deal with the European Union it will be disastrous for the UK economy. Talk of trading solely on World Trade Organization terms was nonsensical, and the idea of a customs barrier with the EU would lead to increased prices for food, wine, cars and many other goods.

Bruton and Blair both agreed that there is no truly 'independent' country in the modern world economy. Trump can claim to put 'America First', but his voters still expect their Chinese-made laptops and smartphones to work. No developed country (or indeed any developing country anyone could think of – although Mauretania was sometimes suggested) 'traded on WTO terms' alone. To obtain a deal with the EU on reasonably favourable terms Britain was faced with accepting agreed standards – on food production, antibiotics, growth hormones in beef, pesticides and so on – or if we didn't, there would be no deal. And if we did accept some EU standards that would by definition bind us in to at least some rules and regulations which could foreclose the option of completely 'free' trade deals with all other countries round the world. This is the Catch-22 of Brexit, and it has always been obvious. It was explained very patiently by Chancellor Angela Merkel in 2016 when she pointed out that Britain could only receive the benefits of the EU free market if Britain was part of the EU free market.

'So,' I suggested to Tony Blair, 'is Nigel Farage right – if we negotiate a deal with the EU we cannot be truly independent. There is no "independence day"?'

Blair laughed. Then he conceded that on this point at least Mr

Farage may be correct. John Bruton similarly pointed out the fallacy of 'independence'. Ireland is an independent country, but in accepting membership of the EU, Ireland is cooperating with twenty-six other nations in ways which – to use a loaded term – dilute national sovereignty, while giving Ireland economic and other benefits including considerable clout in the world when backed by the combined weight and influence of the governments of 450 million people.

The wisdom of Edmund Burke's 'little platoons' becoming more powerful by joining up with international big battalions was put to me even more forcibly during the Scottish independence referendum campaign. In the summer of 2014, a couple of months before the vote, I travelled to the northernmost part of the United Kingdom, Shetland. Shetland is, as you might expect, magnificent, bleak, wild and beautiful. I encountered an old islander with a finely tuned grasp of British and Scottish politics, and asked if I could interview him about his views on Scottish independence. I began by asking him whether he would prefer to be governed by Westminster or by an independent Scottish parliament in Edinburgh. The old man was non-committal on the politics, although he pointed out that where we stood was nearer the Norwegian capital, Oslo, than Edinburgh or London. Not getting a straight answer, I rephrased the question in what I thought was a clever way to assess his sense of national or local identity.

'The oil that has made Shetland so rich,' I began. 'Do you consider it Britain's oil, or Scotland's oil or Shetland's oil?'

At this the old boy smiled and with the soft accent of the islands replied, 'No. 'Tis the oil companies' oil...' He then paused for a few seconds before adding, 'the bastards'.

He then patiently explained to me that the oil companies were more powerful than any single European government, and so were big tech companies like Apple, Google and Microsoft. In his view, the people in Shetland could only stand up to the biggest global economic actors through membership of something large and powerful, such as the EU.

The old man clearly understood how far independence really is a relative not an absolute term. This is the key to understanding why Scottish 'independence' is a significant change in political structures but that is not necessarily the same as 'the break-up of the United Kingdom'. Indeed, those in favour of Scottish independence in 2014 never presented their ideas in that way. But nor did they speak openly of the 'independence' they were fighting for being, in reality, a kind of Scottish Home Rule within the framework of retaining by negotiation some of the most important and successful institutions of the United Kingdom. It's worth looking more calmly at the main principles of what was on offer – and rejected – in 2014.

Re-framing Scottish Independence and English Independence as Home Rule

Scottish independence, in the version publicly advocated by leading figures in the SNP in 2014, does not mean that Scotland must reject all British connections or institutions. Mainstream Scottish nationalism has for years been pursuing a definition of independence that actually recognizes the reality of a strong degree of interdependence. Their vision presented in 2014 would have involved a much closer relationship with rUK (the Rest of the UK) than that which Ireland currently enjoys. Irish citizens can travel freely to the UK, can work and live without requiring work permits or visas and can vote in British elections, while Ireland is also an independent republic which has had membership of international institutions in its own right since the 1930s. George Kerevan wrote of the guiding principle of Scottish independence being to create 'a new and more harmonious partnership between the constituent nations and peoples of these British islands'. (The echoes of Mrs Thatcher talking in Bruges about Britain's harmonious partnership with the EU are here very strong, as we have noted.)

The devilish question is what that new and harmonious Scotland–England partnership would look like. Kerevan begins by observing that keeping the status quo would mean 'letting the ramshackle UK state meander from crisis to crisis'.[14] More positively, Kerevan suggested – again in words which could easily appeal to many Brexit voters – that Scottish independence would:

> de-centralise the British state, democratise British society politically and culturally, free up social mobility after a generation of stasis, and break the hold of the London city-state over the culture and economy of the rest of the British isles... creating the foundations of a twenty-first century society that looks outward to a globalised world rather than... nostalgia for a lost imperial past.[15]

As to the future, he argued against 'the traditional nineteenth-century model of state autonomy' and instead for 'the rebalancing of political and economic relationships within the British Isles in order to meet the challenges of the twenty-first century.'

It's worth pausing to recall what is on offer here. This was not one Scottish political writer flying a kite. Kerevan's case was based on the outline for independence made public by the then SNP leader and first minister, Alex Salmond. It was labelled as 'independence', but Scottish independence was being defined as the codification and expansion of the evolving federal system already existing within the British state. The offer (although it was not publicly described as such) was based on some kind of federal (Kerevan uses the term 'confederal') future for Scotland, to an extent interdependent with the other nations and regions of the UK, internationalist in outlook and building on existing structures that do appear to work.

Very significantly the structures to be retained by the 2014 Scottish independence offer included the monarchy, the currency, the deepest economic ties through the Bank of England, defence policy within NATO and – by extension – the NHS and other institutions that we have in common but which already have a tartan gloss. Kerevan was essentially quoting Alex Salmond's manifesto when he said that following Scotland's independence all current constituent parts of the United Kingdom:

will share a common Head of State, a common currency, free trade, and a common security strategy through NATO... a new confederation in everything but name. In this de facto confederation the individual nations of the British Isles would have their own parliaments and domestic tax arrangements meaning (crucially) that the people of England regain their direct political voice. An English parliament would assuage English populism and let traditional English liberal values shine.[16]

It's interesting to note that Scottish nationalists in 2014 were more alert to the demands and potency of English nationalism than the hapless government of David Cameron. You may care to consider the nature of something called 'Scottish independence' that involves the retention of a common head of state, a common currency, a common defence and security policy and free trade. This was to have been an extremely neighbourly kind of independence, in some ways like an American state – California, for example – ceding significant powers to the US federal government in Washington, including the stability of a common currency and a common head of state, while retaining its own 'independent' state administration. Kerevan insists that this is a confederal structure. Respectfully I disagree. This is the recognition, codification and amplification of an existing federal structure of much of the United Kingdom, with extra tax-and-spend powers for Scotland and potentially for regions of England. There are similarities, say, with the Federal Republic of Germany and the relationship between the state governments in the Länder and the federal administration in Berlin.

Here's *Encyclopedia Britannica*'s version of the difference between federal and confederal:

Confederations usually fail to provide for an effective executive authority and lack viable central governments; their member states typically retain their separate military establishments and separate diplomatic representation; and members are generally accorded equal status with an acknowledged right of secession from the confederation. The term federation is used to refer to groupings of states, often on a regional basis, that establish central executive machinery to implement policies or to supervise joint activities. In some cases such groupings are motivated primarily by political or economic concerns; in others, military objectives are paramount.

The terms confederal or confederacy have unfortunate connotations. The secession of southern states from the United States in 1860–5 demonstrates what happens when a neighbour obsessively demands the right to secede from a union without coordinating any kind of a divorce settlement or recognizing a shared history and geography. The controversial historian of the Confederacy Frank Lawrence Owsley argued in his dissertation *State Rights and the Confederacy* (1925) that the Confederacy 'died of states' rights' when fragmentation meant that during the Civil War some southern governors even resisted the appeals of the Confederate government in Richmond, Virginia to contribute more soldiers.

For Scotland, England, Wales and (perhaps problematically) Northern Ireland to have in future the same head of state, the same currency, free trade and a common security strategy while all other matters are devolved would be the recognition of a federal rather than confederal structure – although being hung up on definitions is rather beside the point. Switzerland, as we will see in a moment, describes itself as both a federal and a confederal state, without any difficulty. In many ways Scotland's independence referendum in 2014 was a missed opportunity not just for Scotland but for England too. What is evident even now is that the beneficiaries of moving to a formalized federal structure would not merely be the people of Scotland, but also the people of England.

Retaining the monarchy would mean a twenty-first century equivalent of the 1603 Union of the Crowns while returning to the idea of strong separate legislatures. You could even still call it the 'United Kingdom' since it would have a single monarch despite having separate parliaments.

However it is labelled, this version of independence is not far away from Keir Starmer's intervention on the subject. In April 2020, in one of his first acts as he was confirmed as Labour leader, Starmer wrote an op-ed piece for the popular Scottish newspaper the *Daily Record*, the newspaper which printed 'The Vow' in 2014. In it he echoed his namesake and the founder of the Labour Party, the Scotsman Keir Hardie:

> Labour's pioneering leader, Keir Hardie, was not a supporter of nationalism but of home rule for Scotland within the UK. I said during Labour's leadership election that I want to build a future on the principle of federalism. We will establish a constitutional convention in opposition *that applies that principle of federalism* and a new settlement for the UK. I want to see Scotland use the powers it has got. I also want it to have more powers itself.[17]

In Scotland some nationalists immediately rejected Starmer's overture, especially since he himself rejected SNP demands for another independence referendum. Scottish voters who had accepted at face value 'The Vow' promising more devolution felt – with good reason – that they had been fooled by David Cameron in 2014 and were not about to be fooled again. The respected Scottish writer Ruth Wishart Tweeted in response to the Starmer proposal: 'We have been down this road many times… but the F word is yesterday's news.' Others concluded that Starmer was merely panicking, recognizing that an independent Scotland sending no political representatives to Westminster would likely doom Labour's chances of ever forming a government in London for at least a generation.

A more optimistic view suggests that with appropriate negotiations the words 'Home Rule', 'federalism', 'confederalism' and even 'independence' are sufficiently elastic to be able to bring about for Scots the kind of settlement that the SNP had in mind in 2014, while maintaining cordial relations between all four nations of the UK, and bringing a reinvigorated democracy to England, Wales and potentially even Northern Ireland. In each case building upon the

UK's existing quasi-federal structure is the obvious way to proceed. Freed of the last illusions of empire and English exceptionalism, Westminster would be forced to reform itself. It would have the chance to become the cornerstone of a modern federal democracy. One possibility would be for the House of Commons to accept electoral reform and reconstitute itself as an England-only parliament. The House of Lords could be stripped of a constitutional role, preserved in the formaldehyde of history and replaced by an elected Senate drawn from all four nations, which would have powers only on those issues that most urgently demand a united approach – trade, the economy, the currency, defence and security. Systems like this work in other, similarly complex modern countries, even if among English nationalist politicians such systems traditionally have been treated with derision. One example is Switzerland.

The Cuckoo Clock

Switzerland has the second-highest GDP per capita in the world. It also has four official languages, and remains one of the world's most stable and peaceful countries. In Carol Reed's 1949 version of Graham Greene's novel The Third Man, the Orson Welles character points out that Italy under the Borgias had warfare, terror, murder and bloodshed, while producing Michelangelo, Leonardo da Vinci and the Renaissance. As for Switzerland, 'they had brotherly love, they had five hundred years of democracy and peace – and what did that produce? The cuckoo clock.' The anglophone contempt of prosperous Switzerland in the 1940s was in part a reflection of irritation that the Swiss avoided the worst of the Second World War by staying firmly neutral while leaving others to do the fighting to defeat Hitler. But it's worth thinking how Swiss democracy works now – not as a cuckoo clock but rather as a cleverly constructed luxury chronometer.

The Swiss written constitution dates from 1848. It was produced in just fifty-eight days, and a central feature is that the founding fathers

– and they were all men – recognized the constitution was imperfect and should be open to future changes. Rather like the United Kingdom of four nations, Switzerland has four main language groups, each dominant in a specific area, with a population whose first language is German (63 per cent), French (23 per cent), Italian (8 per cent) and Romansh (0.5 per cent). The country is also split on religious lines between Protestants and Catholics. To hold all this together within what the Swiss call the Swiss Confederation, they have one federal chancellor, a Federal Council (or parliament), twenty-six cantonal (or regional) governments and more than 2,000 communes (or local administrations). The federal government is responsible for external affairs, defence, the national road network and nuclear energy. The cantons have their own parliaments, governments, courts and constitutions and are responsible for education, health, culture and police. The communes look after local government, planning, local schools and the fire service. The parliament is horseshoe-shaped, and parties have to cooperate to form a government because no one party is ever likely to win power.

There are many parts of the Swiss system that I find unattractive. Referendums are frequent but they may offer a binary solution to complex problems. Public opinion tends to be very conservative, so conservative that until February 1971 women did not have the vote. Moreover, the Swiss system cannot simply be taken off the shelf to create a future federal UK. Nevertheless, what Switzerland does demonstrate is that an ancient state with a history of bitter cultural and religious differences can overcome its past through constructing a constitution which delineates powers, responsibilities and their limits, while devolving as much power as possible as closely to the people involved. It is a useful example, rather than a model.

What Next? – A Modest Proposal

In the case of the United Kingdom, a constitutional convention could consider how far English regions and cities could be given greater powers over their own affairs based on existing local government structures; how far Scotland and Wales wish to have more powers; what role and structures would be required to make a future federal administration work; and how to deal with the contentious issue of Northern Ireland in accordance with the Good Friday Agreement and the views of people on the whole island of Ireland.

In any future scenario it is impossible to envisage the continuation of the House of Lords as an upper chamber of any legislative branch. If it really is necessary to retain ancient honours and titles, then rather than Lords and Ladies being rewarded by the taxpayer with attendance allowances to turn up in an upper chamber of government, perhaps peers of the realm could retain their titles, be stripped of any legislative duties and actually pay annual subscriptions to enjoy what would be one of the best-connected social clubs in London's clubland.

Wales would undoubtedly benefit from more powers and responsibilities. The people of Wales could then decide how closely they wish to shadow developments in England or perhaps – as they have done with coronavirus – adopt policies that are much closer to those of Scotland and Northern Ireland.

Questions about a United Ireland will continue to be raised and will remain contentious for many years. But given the Johnson concession of an all-Ireland customs union, relationships between Dublin and Belfast may improve without provoking the necessity for a referendum on Irish unity. If Northern Ireland Protestants cannot rely on Mr Johnson's Conservative and 'Unionist' Party, they are clearly not alone, and they are hard-headed enough to understand that in many ways the Irish Republic of the twenty-first century is not the dreary, repressive and illiberal Roman Catholic state they have always feared.

These various ideas are thrown out for consideration in an attempt to address some of our difficulties in a positive spirit. But whatever the precise nature of the reformation of our political system, we require a road map for the way ahead. That means a written, codified and broadly agreed constitution to keep the lines of responsibility clear between and within the constituent nations of these islands.

The English genius in matters of political flexibility is often considerable. Scholars and constitutional experts from all over the United Kingdom are up to the task of devising a simple-to-understand constitutional settlement that is capable of satisfying all but the most irrational nationalist impulses on these islands while at the same time codifying how we may continue to work together on the things which we have in common. The English language, which so beautifully rendered the Bible into the vernacular after the Union of Crowns, is more than up to the task of explaining the principles of how our politics should proceed in language we can all understand.

But there is one major sticking point in all this. How can a federal United Kingdom function if parts of that federation wish to remain within the European Union, and yet the biggest part – England – does not? My answer would be that with Home Rule for All Nations within the UK, we would all best benefit from remaining within the European Union. But if the people of England wish permanently to 'secede', 'divorce' or 'break up' from the European Union, then Scotland and Wales do have potentially another answer. Surprisingly, it is Boris Johnson who may have found a solution.

The Conservative Party apparently believes – if one can say with any assuredness that it believes anything beyond its own survival in power – that Northern Ireland can somehow remain within the EU for customs purposes while remaining part of the United Kingdom in terms of citizenship. Very well. If that is true then somehow that same Schrödinger's cat-like miracle may be possible also for Scotland and, should they wish it, for the people of Wales.

We have therefore three main options if we wish to reform a clearly broken Britain.

Option One is the pretence that we can stay as we are, and in some way reinvent Britishness. For all the reasons we have discussed I can see no possibility of this working for any part of the UK. The Monty Python dead parrot sketch has become political reality. Britishness is dead. It has ceased to be. With Brexit the idea of Britain as an 'imagined community' of four nations all pulling together cannot be rebuilt, and no one is energetically trying to rebuild it. The idea that we can go even further back by ending devolution, as the Bruges Group wishes, can best be answered by the Prince of Salina in Giuseppe Tomasi di Lampedusa's novel *The Leopard* (*Il Gattopardo*) about the decaying Sicilian aristocracy and the birth of a united Italian state: 'If we want things to stay as they are, things will have to change.'

Option Two requires the formalizing of federalism. This appears to me the most rational and least disruptive of the possible options. Federalism within the United Kingdom has one huge advantage. It is a recognition of current realities. Federalized or nearly federalized institutions could be supported, expanded and formalized in a new constitution settlement, learning from models elsewhere including Switzerland and Germany.

Under the 2014 Salmond Scottish independence plan all the things that seem to work best in a UK-wide structure would be retained. All the bits of political life which do not work and cause friction (Westminster, the Trident base at Faslane) will have to be rethought. The downside of this idea is that it could entail years of wrangling about who retains what, who is liable for what and whether and how far Scotland would or should have a say at Westminster. This is sometimes called the 'West Lothian question'.

My answer is that England should have no right to vote on devolved Scottish, Welsh or Northern Ireland matters and vice versa. But representatives from all four nations should have the right to vote and help decide future federal matters. This would inevitably give England the greatest decision-making powers on, for example, trade, macroeconomic and currency matters, Bank of England policy and defence requirements within NATO. Disagreements would be unavoidable, but a reformation of the political system with governments truly reflecting the divergence of opinion in each of the four nations will tend to lead to consensus rather than conflict. To put it bluntly, the West Lothian question is history. It is yesterday's problem, and today's opportunity. Forget for once the dreary politics of British exceptionalism and look around the world. In Germany, federalism means that Bavaria decides for Bavaria but has a voice in Berlin.

In Switzerland, Geneva decides for Geneva but has a voice in Bern, and in the United States, California decides for itself, while exerting huge influence in Washington. Are those hung up on the West Lothian question really telling the world that British exceptionalism means we cannot solve a problem which others dealt with long ago?

Inevitably some Scots and English nationalists will never be satisfied. They would prefer a bigger schism, but Keir Starmer's idea of a constitutional convention is a reasonable first step. For England the big advantage of a federal (or confederal) solution would be a secure border to the north, a border that in trade and population movement terms would be no different from the existing administrative boundary. England would also have the opportunity to revitalize big cities and local English governments and choose what kind of England-only Home Rule parliament suits the country best.

Scotland and Northern Ireland would have the advantage of currency stability, greater devolved powers, and the benefits of a common military and security structure. Wales could demand as much or as little of Home Rule as Welsh people themselves felt appropriate. Northern Ireland could look forward to a new and fruitful relationship with the Irish Republic, without a divisive and forced imposition of Irish unity.

The presence of Scotland in this new arrangement would help calm the age-old fears of Protestants about being an endangered minority on the island of Ireland.

Option Three, unfortunately, may in the end be the most likely, given the incompetence of British governments over the past few years. In this scenario, Brexit turns out to be a disappointment even for those who voted in favour of it. Brexit does not, because it cannot, solve the problems of English nationalism and England's democratic deficit, which is really a resentment of Westminster. Scots, under this gloomy scenario, become increasingly discontented by a Westminster government that refuses to permit a second independence referendum, becoming even more scunnered, thrawn and determined to seek a more extreme form of independence than that on offer in the Salmond plan. The continuing refusal of Westminster to allow the democratic expression of the will of the Scottish people in a referendum becomes the most perfect definition of the phrase 'democratic deficit'. Northern Irish unionists wonder that if they are treated as part of the Irish Republic for customs purposes, perhaps they might be more welcome in a united Ireland as full citizens, with full rights inside the European Union. In the meantime, our much-loved British monarch passes away and the monarchy as a unifying force loses its lustre as the residual core of Britishness. If this third and gloomy scenario seems familiar that's because it is like an echo of the years after the death of Queen Victoria and before the First World War, when vicious disagreements over Irish Home Rule were tearing the country apart. We could not avoid the terrible consequences then. We can now.

Why 'Home Rule All Round' Failed Before – But May Now Succeed

In 1886 the Liberal politician Joseph Chamberlain was among the first to propose a version of devolution known as 'Home Rule All Round'. Chamberlain, as a former mayor of Birmingham, understood how local democracy and strong city or regional governments can be closest to the people they serve, and most effective in delivering vital services, in Birmingham's case, the provision of clean water. By 1895 the prime minister, the Earl of Rosebery, said that he, too, favoured Home Rule for all the nations of the UK. In that same year the future prime minister David Lloyd George won a House of Commons motion supporting the principle.

Ireland finally achieved its part of that grand-sounding scheme when after decades of discussions the Home Rule Bill finally passed through parliament in September 1914. By that time the British empire was otherwise engaged, more concerned with defeating Germany than internal structural changes to the way Ireland was governed. The Easter Rising, the bloodshed that followed, and the Anglo-Irish war should remind us of the terrible price reasonable people pay for failing to settle differences amicably. Unreasonable people took more extreme measures which, a century later, are still not forgotten.

The tragedy of Ireland – and the opportunity for us all now – is that we can learn from what went wrong in the past, and use it to steer a different course.

In 1912, the moderate Irish leader John Redmond made an impassioned plea to the House of Commons during the Third Home Rule Bill debate. He said he wanted to initiate Home Rule reforms not only because they were just, but also to prevent more extreme elements in Ireland creating a situation which in the end might poison relationships for years to come. Given our political divisions, it is worth reconsidering this prophetic argument for our own times. Redmond told the House:

> Unionist orators… have constantly been saying that the Irish people want separation, and that the Irish leaders are separatists. I will be perfectly frank on this matter. There always have been, and there is to-day, a certain section of Irishmen who would like to see separation from this country. They are a small, a very small section. They were once a large section. They are a very small section, but these men who hold these views at this moment only desire separation as an alternative to the present system, and if you change the present system and give into the hands of Irishmen the management of purely Irish affairs even that small feeling in favour of separation will disappear, and, if it survive at all, I would like to know how under those circumstances it would be stronger or more powerful for mischief than at the present moment.[18]

In our own time, the people of Britain have been remarkably calm and slow to anger. But some politicians have begun to conclude that civil strife may be part of our future, even if it does not recur with the intensity of the past. Lord Wallace of Saltaire is a Liberal Democrat peer based in Yorkshire. In 2019 he considered the future of England:

> For the first time, people at Westminster have started to talk about the adverse effects of 'English nationalism'… Our nuclear

deterrent base in Scotland, and other military assets, would go; it's possible that such a smaller country might find other states questioning its privileged role at the UN and other international organisations. If an independent Scotland then joined the EU, the English would become like the Swiss: surrounded on all sides by EU neighbours, dependent on them for access and cooperation, struggling to negotiate bilateral agreements. Switzerland has 140 such agreements with the EU so far, with further difficult negotiations now under way. Life might not be easy for England's poorer post-industrial North, either. England is the most centralised country in the democratic world, with the central government controlling the flow of tax revenue and expenditure. Public investment, in transport, infrastructure, university research and innovation, has favoured the South through successive governments since the 1980s: reinforcing success, rather than working to reduce the sharp regional imbalances which industrial decline left behind. Neither the Conservatives nor Labour have champions of the North among its leaders: national politics revolves around London and the marginal seats of the home counties. Outside the EU, London's financial and associated services may flourish; but prosperity is unlikely to trickle down to neglected towns and cities elsewhere. And voters in the South will resist paying to regenerate the North. The break-up of Britain may well prove one of the many unintended consequences of Brexit. The easy promises of three years ago are turning into hard choices. English nationalism harks back to the glories of imperial Great Britain, without taking into account the contributions that Britain's other nations made to that imperial past. It thrives on distrust of foreigners. And if Britain breaks up, I might join my son in Edinburgh.[19]

*

In 1912, my relatives signed the Ulster Covenant against Irish Home Rule because they were fearful of the break-up of Britain. They were proud to be British, and saw no reason to leave the presumed certainties of the greatest empire the world had ever seen for the uncertainties of an Ireland they saw as economically and culturally backward, dominated by peasants, Catholic priests and the Church of Rome. In 2014, apparent certainty versus uncertainty also played a part in the Scottish independence referendum result. I was unable to vote in that referendum because I have lived out of Scotland – in England, Northern Ireland, Wales and the United States – for years.

One afternoon outside the Scottish parliament in Edinburgh, I complained in a television interview to the then first minister of Scotland Alex Salmond that there were many Scots, like me, who wanted a say in Scotland's future but who, under the electoral rules, were not allowed to vote in such an important referendum. He responded reasonably that the only way to decide Scotland's future was to allow the voters actually living in Scotland to take part. He, his security detail and advisers then left to go back to his office in the Holyrood parliament. About half an hour later, on his way back to his official residence, and this time alone, he walked towards me. He had clearly been thinking about our on-air conversation.

'You want to vote on our future?' he asked.

'Of course.'

He put an arm around me and whispered in my ear, 'Then buy a house.' He meant: come home.

Nations are indeed imagined communities. Despite living outside Scotland for longer than I have ever lived in it, and despite the fact that my Ulster roots are in the past, I imagine I am strongly attached to Scotland, but also to Ireland north and south, England and Wales. I am also attached to an idea of Britain, but not to the reality of the failing state the United Kingdom has become. That imagination is real, but so is the disappointment and the fear that, unless we change course, the entropy of failure will win in the end.

In the 2014 Scottish independence referendum, the modest version of Home Rule on offer to voters would have been good for Scotland and good for England too. A Yes vote would have shocked English politics out of generations of complacency. But there was one issue which would have stopped me for voting for Scottish independence in 2014. That was the enormous uncertainty caused by the threat that an independent Scotland would not be part of the European Union. The safer thing to do in 1912 for my family was to stay in the United Kingdom and reject Irish independence; the safer thing for Scotland to do in 2014, the Scottish electorate decided, was to stay in the European Union by staying in the United Kingdom. The parties of 'The Vow' promised them as much. They insisted that only by staying in the United Kingdom could Scotland stay in the European Union. This proved to be false and the opposite is true: staying in the UK meant Scotland being forced out of the EU.

Three prime ministers – two of them old Etonians and all three Oxford graduates from the narrow ground of English life – have brought us to this. Breaking 'The Vow' by failing to act on the promise of much greater Home Rule for Scotland was part of David Cameron's contribution to breaking up the United Kingdom. He compounded his error by holding a badly thought out 'advisory' referendum on membership of the European Union without recognizing the possibility that the different nations and regions of the United Kingdom might vote differently. Theresa May and Boris Johnson through incompetence and carelessness have completed the work of making it likely that it is the Conservative and Unionist Party that will take the credit for destroying the union they claim to defend. Boris Johnson in particular has indeed done more in a few months to bring about a united Ireland than the IRA managed in three decades of bombings and shootings. His record is not conservative. It is radical and incompetent. Nor is it unionist, except in name only.

English nationalism and the Brexit vote mean that those of us in these islands who believe that democracy is best served by devolving power as far as possible locally while cooperating with our closest neighbours feel betrayed. The biggest leap in the dark we have contemplated since the Second World War is being orchestrated by the most meretricious and distrusted English nationalist government of our lifetimes.

Home Rule for All Nations will not be easy. But it is probably the last chance of saving the many good things about our United Kingdom. Perhaps it is now too.late. Our continuing rule by a narrow, nationalist elite means that we are following incompetent leaders to an unexplained future based on impossible promises to choruses marking the end of another old song. Through such carelessness is How Britain Ends.

Epilogue

An End and A Beginning

Every ending contains within it seeds of a new beginning. The end of the Scottish parliament in 1707 provided the opportunity for the British empire to expand beyond all imagination and for the United Kingdom to become the richest country in the world. The end of Britain as it is currently constituted also contains new hopes and possibilities. Throughout this book I have argued that while the fundamentals of our lives – geography, history, language and interdependence – are immutable, political arrangements are not, and that they do not 'just evolve'. We have a hard core of functioning institutions. These can be deliberately modified and improved to cope with whatever structures the nations of the United Kingdom finally settle upon, whether we call that future relationship federalism, confederalism or independence.

As I was completing this book for publication, the prime minister Boris Johnson announced he was to travel to Scotland to save what he called 'the sheer might of the Union'. He flew to Orkney (not Glasgow, the biggest city, or Edinburgh the capital), posed in a photo-opportunity with some crabs, visited a factory and after a few hours of saving the union, returned to London. The visit was announced as First Minister Nicola Sturgeon was celebrating her 50th birthday. Scottish Nationalists sarcastically rejoiced that merely by his presence Mr Johnson was offering their fight for independence a birthday present for Ms Sturgeon. The veteran SNP politician Angus Robertson commented:

> Boris Johnson's day trip reminds voters in Scotland he is a prime minister they didn't vote for, heading a party that hasn't won an election in Scotland since 1955, delivering Brexit which they oppose. No wonder a majority now supports independence.[1]

An Irishman, George Bernard Shaw, once quipped that 'England and America are two countries separated by a common language.' The same appears true nowadays for England and Scotland. On one side of the border, Mr Johnson speaks of his 'fantastic' successes, 'world leading' tracing systems for coronavirus and 'world beating' policies. He compares himself to Churchill and Franklin Roosevelt and claims he is 'as fit as a butcher's dog'. To increasing numbers of Scots the union he claims to save is as outdated as his vocabulary. For them, Mr Johnson personally is a symbol not of Britishness or the union but of a living fossil, the out-of-touch English nationalism which they reject.

All four nations of the United Kingdom are divided by that most potent political expression of English nationalism – Brexit – which of course is still not 'done'. It will rankle for years. To take just one example, the Scottish government asserted its right to set food standards for Scots after Brexit begins to take effect in 2021. Similar impulses in Northern Ireland and Wales have deepened the gulf with Westminster. Scotland's Cabinet Secretary for Constitution, Europe and External Affairs, Michael Russell, wrote to Michael Gove, the UK government minister in charge of Brexit planning, setting the tone for the struggles ahead:

> I am writing following reports that it is the UK Government's intention to consult on proposals that would dramatically undermine devolution and the democratic choices made by the Scottish Parliament. I do so prior to their publication because I want to make it crystal clear at the earliest possible moment,

that the Scottish Government could not, and would not, accept any such plans. Nor would we co-operate with them.[2]

Boris Johnson was equally contentious. He claimed the SNP wanted to take control of seventy different legislative powers over various issues transferred from the European Union. He said giving these powers to Scotland rather than Westminster would be 'the biggest single act of devolution in modern memory'.

Around the same time[3] a new poll by Panelbase for *The Sunday Times* showed a record 54 per cent of Scots backing Scottish independence. The poll forecast that Nicola Sturgeon and the SNP could be heading for a landslide victory in the 2021 Holyrood elections. Boris Johnson's phrase about the union as 'sheer might' began to sound like a Spoonerism.

Meanwhile, the Conservative former health secretary Andrew Lansley offered a boost to a possible future federal Britain by asserting in a newspaper article that there had been a 'chronic failure to give autonomy and cash to (English) local governments' and that the 'pandemic response failed to take account of different local circumstances'. He called for more decentralized decision-making in England.

In Wales, First Minister Mark Drakeford expressed his frustration over travel arrangements and other restrictions caused by Westminster's cack-handed response to coronavirus. He said that 'dealing with the UK government over the last few days has been an utterly shambolic experience... I just have to say it's been an impossible experience to follow.' The Welsh nationalist party Plaid Cymru renewed its call for a Welsh independence referendum.

In Northern Ireland preparations continued for operating a customs border between the province and the rest of the UK. No one appeared sure how the new bureaucracy would work, amid continuing speculation about another poll on Northern Ireland's future. Boris Johnson achieved the near-miracle of uniting Ulster unionists and Irish nationalists who both had reasons to distrust him. First Minister Arlene Foster, the leader of Ulster unionism, spoke of Northern Ireland's 'betrayal' by 'the person who broke their word'.

And, finally, back in England, a You Gov/YesCymru poll[4] noted the ways in which the Conservative Party had become the English nationalist party rather than the party of union. The pollsters concluded that 'half of the Conservative supporters in England do not want the United Kingdom to continue'. When 'don't knows' and 'won't say' were ruled out, among Tory voters 49 per cent in England favoured what was described as 'English independence'.

One of my favourite Scottish legends is that of the kelpies. A kelpie is a magical shape-shifting water spirit, often imagined as a beautiful horse. Kelpies are celebrated in two enormous metal horse-head sculptures on a plain in Scotland's central belt, just outside Falkirk. Kelpies appear docile and attractive but any traveller who thinks they can tame a kelpie finds that they are immediately stuck on the shape-shifter's back. The kelpie turns into a monster, jumps into a loch or river and the unfortunate traveller is drowned and eaten. Nationalisms are shape-shifters. They are benignly rooted in the pride of belonging, but once stirred they can be destructive and impossible to tame. Scottish, Welsh and mainstream Irish nationalists have gone to great lengths to persuade followers that their brands of nationalism are not wild rides on a monster. They have been sober about tempering their modern civic nationalisms with internationalism. English nationalism has roots as strong and benign as the others, but Brexit is the English nationalist kelpie. It started as the pleasing promise of 'sunlit uplands' and the 'easiest trade deal in history' with a gentle ride to a wonderful and prosperous future. But now that the United Kingdom is firmly attached, Brexit is drowning the union. They say that kelpies can be tamed, but only if you grab their bridle and take back control. Of course, that's only a legend.

GAVIN ESLER
Deal, Kent, October 2020

Select Bibliography

Among those books and publications that I have found most useful are the following:

Black, J., *English Nationalism* (Hurst & Co, 2018).

Butterworth, J., *Jerusalem* (Nick Hern Books, 2009).

Colley, L., *Acts of Union & Disunion* (Profile, 2014).

Colley, L., *Britons* (Vintage, 1992).

Defoe, D., *A Tour Through the Whole Island of Great Britain* (Penguin, 1986).

Edgerton, D., *The Rise and Fall of the British Nation* (Penguin, 2018).

Fox, K., *Watching the English* (Hodder, 2004).

Goldin, I., *Divided Nations* (Oxford University Press, 2003).

Grayling, A. C., *The Good State* (One World, 2020).

Heaney, S., *North* (Faber, 1975).

Hobsbawm, E. and Ranger, T. (eds.), *The Invention of Tradition* (Cambridge University Press, 1983).

Hobsbawm, E., *Fractured Times* (Abacus, 2014).

Hutton, W. and Adonis, A., *Saving Britain* (Abacus, 2018).

Hutton, W., *The State We're In* (Vintage, 1996).

Jones, O., *Chavs* (Verso, 2012).

Kennedy, L., *In Bed with an Elephant* (Bantam Press, 1995).

Kerevan, G. and Cochrane, A., *Scottish Independence: Yes or No* (The History Press, 2014).

King, A. and Crewe, I., *The Blunders of Governments* (One World, 2013).

Macwhirter, I., *Disunited Kingdom* (Cargo Publishing, 2014).

Mikes, G., *How to Be a Brit* (Penguin, reissued 2015).

O'Toole, F., *Heroic Failure* (Head of Zeus, 2019).

Paxman, J., *The English* (Michael Joseph, 1998).

Salmond, A., *The Dream Shall Never Die* (William Collins, 2015).

Sampson, A., *Who Runs This Place?* (John Murray, 2004).

Shaw, G. B., *John Bull's Other Island* (Amazon ed., first published 1904).

Snyder, T., *The Road to Unfreedom* (Bodley Head, 2018).

Notes

Part One: Nations and Irritations

Chapter 1: The English Question

1 Kate Fox, *Watching the English* (London, 2004), p. 90.
2 David Edgerton, *The Rise and Fall of the British Nation* (London, 2019), p. 7.
3 David Edgerton, pp. 7 and 29.
4 Jeremy Black, *English Nationalism* (London, 2018), p. 12.
5 David Edgerton, 'Boris Johnson Might Break Up the U.K. That's a Good Thing', *New York Times*, 10 January 2020.

Chapter 2: British or English?

1 *Die Zeit*, 29 August 2017.
2 *Private Eye*, no. 1463, 9 February 2018.
3 Neil McGregor, 'Germans Are "Bewildered" by British Obsession with the Second World War, British Museum Director Says', *Daily Telegraph*, 23 September 2014.
4 Pauline Schnapper, 'The Elephant in the Room: Europe in the 2015 General Election', *French Journal of British Studies*, XX 3(2015), available at: https://doi.org/10.4000/rfcb.613
5 Iain Macwhirter, *Disunited Kingdom: How Westminster Won a Referendum but Lost Scotland* (Glasgow, 2014), p. 118.
6 Fintan O'Toole, *Heroic Failure* (London, 2018), p. 218.
7 Anthony Barnett, *The Lure of Greatness* (London, 2017), p. 123.

8   Peter Kellner, *The Article*, December 2019.
9   Peter Kellner, *The Article*, 2 January 2020.

Chapter 3: Us and Them

1   *Times*, 13 January 2020.
2   Daniel Defoe, *A Tour Through the Whole Island of Great Britain* (London, 1978), p. 671.
3   Ludovic Kennedy, *In Bed With An Elephant* (London, 1995), p. 313.
4   Interview with *The House* magazine, September 2018.
5   BBC News website, 25 January 2019.
6   Andy Pike et al., *Uneven Growth: Tackling City Decline*, Joseph Rowntree Foundation, available at https://www.jrf.org.uk/sites/default/files/jrf/files-research/tackling_declining_cities_report.pdf

Chapter 4: Another English Question: England, Which England?

1   *Independent*, 25 April 1993.
2   Benedict Anderson, *Imagined Communities* (London, 1983).
3   Roger Scruton, *England: An Elegy* (London, 2006), p. 1.
4   Ibid., p. 4.
5   https://englishlabournetwork.org.uk/2020/02/28/general-election-2019-how-labour-lost-england-new-report/
6   https://www.opendemocracy.net/en/opendemocracyuk/england-nation-that-is-not-to-be-named/ 29.10.2018
7   Seumas Milne, 'The Battle for History', *Guardian*, 12 September 2002.
8   'General Election 2019: How Labour Lost England – new report', *English Labour Network*, February 2020. See also https://www.ons.gov.uk/peoplepopulationandcommunity/culturalidentity/ethnicity/articles/ethnicityandnationalidentityinenglandandwales/2012-12-11
9   David Rickard, 'If you're English, you're white – that's according to the "National" Census', *OpenDemocracy*. See also https://www.opendemocracy.net/en/opendemocracyuk/if-youre-english-youre-white-thats-according-to-national-census/
10 Afua Hirsch, *BRIT(ish)* (London, 2018), p. 17ff.
11 Ibid., p. 33.
12 Afua Hirsch, 'Why Britishness, as an Identity, Is in Crisis', *National Geographic*, 19 April 2018.
13 Black, op. cit., p. 194.

14 Owen Jones, *Chavs* (London, 2016), p. 75.

15 Simon Winlow, Steve Hall, and James Treadwell, *The Rise of the Right* (Bristol, 2016).

16 Ibid., p. 125.

17 Ibid., p. 132.

18 Ibid., p. 135.

19 Ibid., p. 164.

20 Ibid., p. 176.

21 Black, op. cit.

22 Interview with Sam Tarry in Owen Jones, *Chavs* (London, 2016), p. 232.

23 'Health Equity in England: The Marmot Review 10 Years On', *Health Foundation*, February 2020.

24 Matthew Parris, 'We're Talking Ourselves into a Brexit Bust-up', *Times*, 29 February 2020.

Chapter 5: God's Chosen People

1 Black, op. cit., pp. 92–3.

2 'Leadsom's rally speech: full text', Conservative Home, 7 July 2016.

3 'Boris Johnson's first speech to parliament as UK Prime Minister', Reuters, 26 July 2019.

4 www.memri.org, 12.3.2019.

5 George Mikes, *How to Be a Brit* (London, 2015).

6 *King John* II, i.

7 Quoted Dominic Sandbrook, *The Way We Were – Britain 1970–1974*, 2011.

8 Linda Colley, *Acts of Union and Disunion* (London, 2014), p. 25.

9 *Daily Telegraph*, 15 October 2018.

10 Linda Colley, op. cit., p. 125.

11 Edgerton, *The Rise and Fall of the British Nation*, pp. 23–20.

12 Quoted Jeremy Paxman, *The English* (London, 1998), pp. 80–81.

13 Jeremy Paxman, *The English*, pp. 78–81.

14 Steven Fielding, 'The Spirit of the Blitz Isn't Back, It's Bunk', *Financial Times*, 21 March 2020.

15 Louis De Bernières, 'Louis de Bernières: Why I Believe In Brexit', *Financial Times*, 23 January 2020.

16 George Bernard Shaw, *John Bull's Other Island* (London, 1994), p. 16.

17 Black, op. cit., p. 12.

18 David Edgerton, *New York Times*, 10 January 2020.

Chapter 6: Othered and Scunnered

1   *Daily Record*, 8 June 2019.

2   Tim Lott, 'What Caused Britain's National Nervous Breakdown', *Guardian*, 16 July 2019.

3   *UK Press Gazette*, 25 June 2019.

4   Hugh Trevor-Roper, *The Invention of Tradition* (Cambridge, 1983), pp. 21 and 28.

5   Foa et al., *Global Satisfaction With Democracy*, University of Cambridge Centre for the Future of Democracy (Cambridge, 2020).

6   Macwhirter, op. cit., p. 108.

7   26 June 2020. See also https://twitter.com/nigel_farage/status/12765350534 68741632?lang=en

8   'The Food Standards Agency's Response to the Migration Advisory Committee Call for Evidence on EEA and Non-EEA Migrant Workers', Food. gov.uk, 27 October 2017.

9   ONS, *Migration Statistics Quarterly Report*, May 2020.

10 Scottish Government website, https://www.gov.scot/policies/europe/eu-citizens/

11 'Migrants Welcome', https://news.gov.scot/news/migrants-welcome

12 'Nicola Sturgeon tells EU citizens: "This is your home, you are welcome here"', *Belfast Telegraph*, 5 April 2019.

13 'Moment MPs "snub" the SNP as they walk out of Commons', *The Sun*. See also https://www.youtube.com/watch?v=TLcJsuRandw

14 'Minister defends exclusion of Scottish press from Westminster briefing on Brexit', *Press and Journal*, 4 February 2020.

15 'Standoff between Downing Street comms chief and Westminster lobby', *PR Week*, 4 February 2020.

16 Nicholas Kristof, 'Will Great Britain Become Little England?', *New York Times*, 2 November 2019.

Chapter 7: Ireland's English Question

1   *Britons*, op. cit., p. 21.

2   Tim Hazelwood, 'Ireland Faces Potential Shortage of Catholic Priests Within the Next 10 Years', *Irish Post*, 29 October 2019.

3   David Green, 'Northern Ireland Is a Burden on the Rest of the UK. We Can't Let It Get in the Way of Brexit', *Daily Telegraph*, 10 October 2019.

4   Quoted Alan O'Day, *New Frontiers in History* (Manchester University Press, 1998).

5   17 January 2020. See also https://twitter.com/johncleese/status/1218274404
     070776833?lang=en

6   Fintan O'Toole, 'Britain's Irish Question Becomes Ireland's English Ques-
     tion', *Irish Times*, 21 October 2016.

7   Mary Lou McDonald, 'Brexit Is A Game Changer', *Times*, 15 February 2020.

8   '"What ish my nation?" Shakespeare's Irish connections', *Irish Times*, 23
     April 2016.

9   Matthew Parris, 'A United Ireland Would Be Good for Everyone', *Times*,
     18 January 2020.

10   https://www.askcymru.com

11   *Newsnight*, BBC2, 5 November 2019, available at https://www.youtube.
     com/watch?v=OtoO5uoX6LA

Part Two: Institutions and Solutions

Chapter 8: Do 'British' Institutions Exist?

1   Televised address to the nation, 31 January 2020.

2   *PM*, BBC Radio 4, 27 May 2020.

3   *PM*, BBC Radio 4, 27 May 2020.

4   *Observer*, 17 May 2020.

5   *iNews*, 11 May 2020.

6   *Observer*, 17 May 2020.

7   'Are we all in this together? It doesn't look like it from the regions', *Obser-
     ver*, 17 May 2020.

8   'Nicola Sturgeon warns Scotland won't be "dragged" into decisions amid
     air bridges row', *Herald*, 29 June 2020.

9   'As lockdown consensus unravels, Boris Johnson divides nation and party',
     Observer, 17 May 2020.

10   26 March 2020. See also https://twitter.com/AndrewWilson/status/
     1242953999478919170

11   Linda Colley, *Britons*, p. xvi.

12   *Today*, BBC Radio 4, 27 December 2019.

13   *Today*, 28 December 2019.

14   Macwhirter, op. cit., p. 65.

15   Speech to Parliament, 4 May 1977. See also https://www.royal.uk/silver-
     jubilee-address-parliament-4-may-1977?page=4

16   Anthony Sampson, *Who Runs This Place?* (London, 2005), p. 33.

17   Sampson, op. cit., p. 32.

Chapter 9: Muddle England

1   Quoted in Black, op. cit., pp. 93–4.
2   A. V. Dicey, *The Introduction to the Study of the Law of the Constitution* (Indianapolis, 1855).
3   *Today*, BBC Radio 4, 7 April 2020.
4   'Britain's good-chap model of government is coming apart', *The Economist*, 18 December 2018.
5   British Sociological Association, *Work, Employment and Society*, June 2019.
6   Andrew Blick and Peter Hennessy, *Good Chaps No More? Safeguarding the Constitution in Stressful Times*, The Constitution Society, 18 November 2019.
7   Andrew Blick et al., *Populism and the UK Constitution* (London, 2019).
8   Quoted *The Invention of Tradition*, edited by Eric Hobsbawm and Terence Ranger. Cambridge University Press, 1983. This edition 2012. David Cannadine essay 'The Context, Performance and Meaning of Ritual', p. 101.
9   David Cannadine, *The British Monarchy 1820–1977*, quoted in Trevor Roper, op. cit., p. 152.
10   Harold Nicolson, *King George V* (London: Constable, 1952).
11   Ibid., p. 103.
12   Cannadine, The Invention of Tradition, op. cit., p. 102, p. 158.
13   The British Library, https://www.bl.uk/victorian-britain/articles/the-great-exhibition
14   *Financial Times*, 9.11.17.
15   Jonathan Powell, 'Britain Once Punched Above Its Weight. Now We Are Irrelevant', *Guardian*, 13 November 2017.
16   *Financial Times*, 3.4.19.
17   Steven Erlanger, 'No One Knows What Britain Is Anymore', *New York Times*, 4 November 2017.
18   Quoted *New Civil Engineer*, January 2014.
19   Fox, op. cit.
20   https://www.newstatesman.com/politics/uk/2016/07/boris-johnson-peddled-absurd-eu-myths-and-our-disgraceful-press-followed-his
21   Fox, op. cit., p. 90.
22   Quoted in Jeremy Black, *English Nationalism – A Short History* (London: Hurst and Co., 2018), p. 94.
23   op. cit., p. 94.

24 'How Undemocratic Is the House of Lords?', *Democratic Audit*, 2 October 2018, https://www.democraticaudit.com/2018/10/02/audit2018-how-undemocratic-is-the-house-of-lords/

25 Linda Colley, *Acts of Union and Disunion*, op. cit., p. 141.

26 Walter Bagehot, *The English Constitution* (London: Chapman & Hall, 1867), p. 54.

27 Linda Colley, *Acts of Disunion*, p. 143.

28 https://www.thebigstealpodcast.com/

29 Ipsos Mori, *Veracity Index*, 26 November 2019.

30 https://www.bsa.natcen.ac.uk/

31 Jill Rutter, 'How Brexit Has Battered Britain's Reputation for Good Government', *Guardian*, 27 December 2019.

32 Linda Colley, *Britons*, p. 396.

33 *Britons*, op. cit., pp. 396–7.

Chapter 10: How to Fix It: Independence and Interdependence

1   Alex Salmond, *The Dream Shall Never Die* (William Collins, 2015), pp. 1–2.

2   Salmond, op. cit., p. 4.

3   op. cit., p. 256.

4   Peter Kellner, 'What kind of Britain will emerge from the crisis?', *The Article*, 9 April 2020.

5   Quoted Kellner, *The Article*, op. cit.

6   1979 Conservative Party manifesto, http://www.conservativemanifesto.com/1979/1979-conservative-manifesto.shtml

7   'Here to stay? How the NHS will have to learn to live with coronavirus', *Nuffield Trust Report*, June 2020.

8   Kerevan, *Scottish Independence: Yes or No* (London, 2014), p. 9.

9   Fox, *Watching the English* (London, 2004), p. 88.

10 William Fagan MP, *The Life and Times of Daniel O'Connell*, Volume II, 1848, p. 496.

11 Kerevan, op. cit., pp. 16 and 92.

12 Cairns Craig, *Scotland: Culture After Devolution* (Ulster, 2003).

13 14 February 2020.

14 op. cit., p. 9.

15 op. cit., p. 10.

16 Kerevan, op. cit., p. 11.

17 Sir Keir Starmer, 'Sir Keir Starmer Plans Devolution Revolution for UK and More Powers for Scotland', *Daily Record*, 6 April 2020.

18   Hansard, 11 April 1912, Volume 36.
19   William Wallace, 'Brexit and the Rise of English Nationalism May Break Up the UK and Force Me to Move to Scotland', *Yorkshire Post*, 28 October 2019.

Epilogue: An End and A Beginning

1   23 July 2020. See also https://twitter.com/angusrobertson/status/1286197130504351747
2   3 July 2020. See also https://www.parliament.scot/S5_Finance/General%20Documents/2020.07.14_Binder_1.pdf
3   5 July 2020. See also https://www.drg.global/our-work/political-polls/wings-over-scotland-poll-3rd-july-2020/
4   30 June 2020. See also https://www.yes.cymru/english_independence_poll

Acknowledgements

I'd like to thank friends from all four corners of our (formerly) United Kingdom from vastly different political views who spared the time to share their insights and thoughts about the perilous state of the union. These friends include Brexiters and Remainers, nationalists of various nations, Conservatives and Unionists, as well as former Conservatives and Unionists, and members and supporters of parties across the political spectrum, including the Scottish National Party, Sinn Fein, the Liberal Democrats and Labour. In particular I'd like to thank my agent Andrew Gordon at David Higham Ltd. Andrew was behind this project from the outset, and so was Neil Belton, at Head of Zeus. Throughout the coronavirus lockdown and beyond, Neil offered guidance, knowledge, wit, historical parallels and cultural insights that I had either forgotten or simply did not know about. This is a far better book thanks to Neil, Clare Gordon and the team at Head of Zeus. Any errors are of course mine. The driving force behind this book has been my wider family, my wife Anna and my children. They have many layers of identity – Scottish, Irish, Ulster, English, British, German, Greek, American, Protestant and Catholic – and they also recognize, in E. M. Forster's famous phrase, that the future belongs to those who 'only connect'. I should also thank British governments over the past few years, in particular that of Boris Johnson. They have inspired me to think how it came to pass that such a creative, competent and diverse group of people inhabiting these islands has ended up with a generation of leaders of astonishing complacency and incompetence. We can do better.

Index